To Connie
Best wishes & May –
Loretta
2008

Thank you for your support
Deppus Crane
2008

These Kaleidoscope Hills

These Kaleidoscope Hills

A Collection of Short Stories

L. L. Bartell
Contributions by D. Crane

Copyright © 2008 by L. L. Bartell.

Library of Congress Control Number: 2008903762
ISBN: Hardcover   978-1-4363-3854-7
               Softcover   978-1-4363-3853-0

All rights reserved. No part of this book may be reproduced or transmitted in any form or by any means, electronic or mechanical, including photocopying, recording, or by any information storage and retrieval system, without permission in writing from the copyright owner.

This book was printed in the United States of America.

To order additional copies of this book, contact:
Xlibris Corporation
1-888-795-4274
www.Xlibris.com
Orders@Xlibris.com
47517

Contents

Foreword 11
Acknowledgements 13

Part One ♥ The River

1	The Beginning of the End	17
2	Our Heritage	22
3	Linn Creek Grows	29
4	The Marriage	34
5	The Ha'nt	39
6	Crossing the River	45
7	The Family Mules	48
8	Bountiful Harvest	51
9	Stolen Treats	57
10	Vacation	60
11	The Circus	67
12	Life on the River	76
13	Molasses	80
14	Winter Comes to the Holler	84
15	It Can't Be Done	88
16	Florence's Dream Comes True	90
17	Crane Holler	95
18	Treed Possum	100
19	Fishing	105
20	Christmas Program	109
21	Christmas	114
22	Beryl's Whipping	120
23	Unexplained Happenings	123
24	The Flood	128
25	Thomas and the Ash Hop	132
26	Changes Are Coming	135

27	Florence Teaches School	137
28	Gravediggers	142
29	The Move	147
30	Goodbye	151

Part Two ♥ Dry Ridge

31	New Beginnings	175
32	Starting Over	177
33	Moving to Dry Ridge	179
34	Growing Children	182
35	Florence Gets Married	186
36	Disobedience Comes to the Moulder Home	191
37	The Tobacco Patch	197
38	Listen to the Corn Grow	200
39	Making Hay	204
40	A Night to Remember	209
41	School on the Ridge	211
42	The Field Trip	218
43	Ruby	225
44	Harvest of the Grains	230
45	Hauling Water	236
46	Everything but the Oink	238
47	Entertainment	248
48	First Date	252
49	Easter Tradition	259
50	Legs	262
51	California	264
52	1943	270
53	June Helps Out	277
54	The War Ends	285
55	There's a Stranger in Town	292
56	June Marries the Marine	303
57	Thomas	310
58	Time to Retire	314

Epilogue 317

I have dedicated my book,
These Kaleidoscope Hills to my mom,
June Slusser.

Mom died in 2001 after suffering several years with Type II diabetes. Therefore, I would like to donate part of the proceeds from the sale of the book to the American Diabetes Assoc.

Martha June Moulder Slusser

June 22, 1928-August 5, 2001

It was Mom's wish to leave to her grandchildren an insight as to what life was like for her family during the early 1900s. We, her children, spent countless hours listening, laughing, and crying while she shared with us these colorful stories about the hardships her family encountered, the fun they had, and the abundance of love they shared, while living in the woodlands of the Missouri Ozark Hills.

I personally owe Mom a huge debt of gratitude for having the insight to videotape the thoughts and stories of her seven sisters, all in their seventies and eighties at the time. Through this videotape, I have cherished memories that could have been lost forever.

I love you, Mom!

Foreword ♥

We are blessed with a rich and bountiful heritage, and it is with pride we present a brief sketch of the lives of some of our family members. The Moulders and the Gerhardts are part of that old German stock that caught the dream of a new and rewarding independent life in America. Each generation that followed was determined to contribute something to their society that would enhance the surroundings for the next generation. Strong, independent loyal men and brave, sturdy women pushed through the wilderness into Tennessee, Kentucky, and portions of Missouri to wrestle out a scant but independent subsistence from the hills. The events that transpired in their lifetime are worthy of being recorded and remembered.

We also present a brief record of the present generation, which so quickly will be history. The strength of our heritage lies in our people—those who have gone before, those who are living now, and those yet to come. Dates, names, and circumstances contained in this historical documentation are from memory and may or may not be exactly as recorded. For any errors, your author sincerely apologizes.

D. Boone Osborn, editor of the *Camden County Rustic* newspaper published in Old Linn Creek, Missouri, moved his newspaper business to Macks Creek, Missouri, in 1902 and started publishing the *Central Missouri Leader*. The slogan that graced every edition was "I know not how the truth may be, I tell it as 'twas told to me". This slogan effectively captures my sentiment about these stories.

D.Crane

Acknowledgements

To my family and friends, I can't thank you enough for the encouragement you have given me during the writing of this book.

Keith, after reading my first writings, you patiently pointed out all the things I needed to learn. I hope I have been a good student.

My dear friend Pat, when my life took a drastic turn and I was ready to quit, you were there encouraging me to continue. You offered me a shoulder to cry on when I became discouraged. You allowed me to use you as a sounding board when putting my thoughts together. And most important, you helped me to remember the main purpose of this book. I thank you from the bottom of my heart.

To my sister Donnis, for spending many hours with me, talking, laughing, and crying as we remembered the stories Mom has shared with us. Without your help, we would not have been able to fulfill Mom's wish.

To my dear aunts, Nera, Florence, Zilpha (Dick), Mayme, Ruby, Fern, and Beryl. Thank you for taking time to document your lives on paper and for the wonderful times we were able to spend together while you shared the experiences of your life. Without your efforts, this collection of homespun stories would not have been possible.

May God bless you all!

Part One

The River

1

The Beginning of the End ♥

A shrill ring of the telephone woke me from a sound sleep. I stumbled out of bed. My breath caught in my throat when I saw the numbers on the clock glowing 3:00 a.m. With a shaking hand, I reached for the phone. Was this the call I had been expecting for months?

"Hello?" I whispered.

My sister, Donnis, who is the emotionally strong one in the family, gasped into my ear, "Mom's quit breathing."

I could tell by the tone of her voice that she was close to panicking.

"Calm down. What's going on?" I asked, even though the knot deep in the pit of my stomach was a forewarning that I already knew.

"I'm at the emergency room with Mom," she cried. "She doesn't have an updated *do-not-resuscitate* order. I don't know what to do!"

Trying to remain calm, I told her to call Dad and that I was on my way. It had been my parent's decision that in case of an emergency, the hospital would notify Donnis, since she lived only fifteen minutes away. Then Dad and the rest of us would be contacted. Hurriedly I dressed, grabbed my keys and purse, and raced out to the car. The hospital, which was located in Wichita, Kansas, was thirty miles away. As I drove, my mind started to replay the events that had transpired over the last six months.

Martha June Moulder Slusser, my mom, had been fighting a battle with diabetes for over twenty years. The disease had destroyed her kidneys and was now taking a devastating toll on her body. During the last six months, the rest of her organs started to shut down. I stood by her side, watching her slowly die. I had never felt such a total feeling of helplessness. Mom pleaded with Dad, my sisters, and brothers to get prepared for the inevitable. She somehow knew her time on earth was coming to an end. Of course, none of us believed her.

As I continued to drive toward the hospital, I subconsciously noticed the headlights on my car, glaring down the highway, reaching far into the unknown of what lay ahead. I tried to shake away the cold lonely feeling that had seeped into my heart. I had made this trip many times before, so

I wasn't paying much attention to my driving as I let my mind focus on my wonderful childhood memories.

Mom had been born and raised in the Ozark Hills in south central Missouri. During her senior year of high school, she met and married my dad, Max Slusser, a young good-looking ex-marine from Kansas. She was the only one of eleven children to leave Missouri. Over the years, the Ozarks kept calling her back, to green meadows and forest-covered hills. However, Mom stayed in Kansas with Dad. Together, they raised six children. I am their fourth child and was the youngest for five years until my little sister Marla was born. During that time, Mom and I became buddies. As I grew into a woman, we became best friends. We spent every weekend we could in Missouri, visiting her folks, traveling on vacations together, shopping, and socializing with each other.

During the past six months, Mom had been admitted to the hospital numerous times. Days would pass as she laid in the intensive care unit, just staring into space.

"What are you looking at, Mom?" I would ask.

"Nothing, dear, just nothing," was always her reply.

Her doctors would manage to get her condition stabilized then release her to a local care facility. "Maybe this is just one more time," I prayed. As I entered the city limits of Wichita, the streetlights glowed eerily, guiding me toward the hospital and my mom.

When I arrived, Mom had already been admitted to the intensive care unit. I found my way to the elevator and walked inside. I was so lost in my thoughts I didn't notice when the elevator started its ascent to the fifth floor or the soft bounce as it came to a stop. When the door slid open, I almost stumbled into Donnis's waiting arms.

"The doctors did CPR and got her heart beating," she cried. "I called Phyllis. She has sent someone for Dad. They should be here soon." Donnis was once again in control. Phyllis is our oldest sister.

Holding each other's hand, we started walking down the long hallway toward Mom's room. A small group of nurses looked up from behind the nurse's station and nodded their acknowledgement of us. A soft ticking and whirring noise came from the direction of several machines and television monitors that were lined up around the wall. I glanced at them, wondering which one was monitoring Mom's life signs. As soon as we passed the nurses, they turned back to their duties. It was still the middle of the night. Everything was so quiet. The hall lights had been turned down low so as not to disturb the patients asleep. I tried to walk softly, but the rubber on the soles of my shoes made squeaky noises so loud, I was sure I would awaken everyone. Finally, we were standing outside of a small room. A white curtain was covering the partly opened glass door.

I hesitated to go in. I was frightened as to what I might find. I felt my sister's hand slide around my waist, nudging me forward. Holding my breath, I stepped over the threshold. It took a minute for my eyes to become accustom to the dim light. Looking through tears that were now swimming in my eyes threatening to overflow, I tried to see the small, helpless body lying on the bed across the room. Donnis gently pushed me closer. Stopping in the middle of the room, I turned my focus away from the bed, to the blood pressure cuff attached to Mom's arm. It was expanding with air, and then slowly deflating. I was vaguely aware of a constant low whirring sound coming from a respirator machine that stood close to the bed.

Finally, with tears streaming down my cheeks, I continued the next few feet, coming to a stop beside the bed. Looking down, I saw Mom, so still, lying there. She was wearing a white hospital gown that was too big for her small body. There was very little contrast between her beautiful white hair, framing her soft pale face, and the stark white pillowcase she lay on. I saw her brow was furrowed as she frowned in her sleep. Even though she wasn't moving a muscle, Mom seemed to be fighting the tube protruding from her mouth.

"Is she aware of what's happening?" I whispered.

"The doctors don't think so. It took them several minutes of CPR to get her this far." There was a pause in her voice. Then she continued, "Even though Mom is using the respirator to help her breath and her heart is beating, it is just a matter of time."

I looked around the intensive care room trying to come to terms with what was happening. I guess Mom was right after all. Her time on earth was coming to an end. She had fought a valiant fight. She was exhausted and was now ready to let go. *Would I have the strength to let her go?* I wondered. Donnis and I left the room when Mom's nurse came in to check on her. We found the waiting area, sat down to wait for the rest of our family.

Before long, Phyllis came walking into the waiting room, followed by her three grown children Lonnie, Chandi, and Torrie. Her son-in-law Jeff had gone to get Dad and would be there soon. After exchanging a quick hug with each other, my sister and her children went in to see Mom. While they were gone, Jeff and Dad arrived at the hospital. Dad's shoulders were sagging, and he looked so tired.

He had struggled right along with Mom for many years. He had helped her come to terms with all of her medical issues, taking her to doctor's appointments, staying with her day in and day out, while she lay in bed, unable to even lift her head. In all that time, he never wavered one bit. He was Mom's strength, the support she needed to lean on and to cry with. Dad had even offered Mom one of his kidneys when he found out that hers had ceased to function. Now his toughest job was looming in front of him, allowing her to die with dignity.

The doctor must have been watching because he immediately followed Dad into the little waiting room. Dad lowered his eyes to the floor and, in a whisper, asked for Mom's prognosis.

"Your wife's heart is beating, and she is breathing on her own," the doctor said. "But her body is shutting down."

Still looking at the floor, Dad asked, "How long does she have?"

"She could remain alive for another day but probably not much longer. Max, what do you want me to do?"

Pulling back his shoulders, Dad looked directly into the doctor's eyes. In a strong voice I hadn't heard in months, he said, "Over the last few years, Mommy's body has been invaded time and time again. If you can bring her back so she can get out of that bed and walk out of here, then do so. If not, do only what you have to, in order to keep her alive, until our two youngest children get here." Dad then left the room to go stand once again by Mom's side.

Phyllis, Donnis, and I spent the next few hours making phone calls to the rest of our children, nieces, nephews, and friends. My oldest brother Tom and his family were going to remain at their home in Illinois. We were to keep him informed of any changes. Marla, my younger sister, and her husband, Steve, had left a couple of days earlier to go on vacation. We located them in Seattle. After being notified of Mom's critical condition, they made arrangements to fly back to Wichita. However, they wouldn't be back in town until early evening. My youngest brother, Rusty, soon arrived at the hospital with his wife, Donna, and their three small children.

By the time the morning sun began streaming through the window, the little waiting room was overflowing with Mom's children, grandchildren, and great-grandchildren. There was now enough family at the hospital; we could take turns staying with Mom, while the others gathered around Dad, making sure he was holding up. During those predawn hours, we sat together in one small room, lost in our own thoughts and prayers. Looking up into the faces of my wonderful family, I thought to myself, *What a legacy Mom is leaving. All this love, in one room, coming from just one small backwoods little girl who left her beloved family and home in Missouri in order to start a life with a man she had known for only a few months.*

In a voice, just above a whisper, I asked, "Do any of you remember the stories Mom and her sisters used to tell us? Stories about what it was like for her family living in the rural areas of the Ozarks?"

Several pairs of eyes turned to look at me. "Yes, I remember," nodded Donnis. "But I'm sure these little ones don't. They probably haven't even heard most of them."

Rusty's oldest daughter, Emily, looked at me and pleaded, "Please tell us."

"Yes, do," the rest of my family, replied.

While Mom lay in a hospital bed holding on to the last threads of life, her children started telling the stories of her precious memories as they held on to each other.

2

Our Heritage ♥

After I made the statement that Mom's maternal and also her paternal grandfather five generations back was the same man, I had a very captive audience consisting of about thirty family members.

"How can that be?" asked Emily, joining me on the couch.

"Well," I said, putting my arm around her shoulders, "this is what I was told . . ."

Before the United States had become independent from England, John Mohllar Sr. (1733-1810), Mom's great-great-great-great-great-grandfather came to American from Germany. The year was 1742, and this country was still mostly wilderness. John, only nine years old, set sail with his two brothers and a young girl named Susannah Swingle.

"That's my age," Emily said, looking up at me with a surprised look on her face.

"It sure is," I replied giving her shoulder a gentle squeeze. I continued, "Landing on American soil, the three young men and one young girl continued on to Pennsylvania, where they decided to settle. A few years later, John and Susannah were married. After the Revolutionary War ended, John heard, from returning explorers, that land located just west of the Mississippi River and south of the Missouri River in the southern part of what would someday be the state of Missouri was wooded and full of wild game. Rivers and streams, in abundance, crisscrossed throughout the land. The wild area could provide plenty of food and an ample way to make a living.

Making the decision to join the stream of pioneers heading west, John, Susannah, and their children packed their meager belongings in a sturdy covered wagon. When the tools, a few articles of clothing, dishes, food, ammunition, and a rifle were safely secured, John hitched up his team of horses. They headed south to North Carolina, then west to Tennessee, crossing the Appalachian Mountains. Using only the tracks left by wagon trains that had passed this way before to guide him, John traveled over the Blue Ridge Mountains, down hills and into valleys, through grasses as high as his horses belly, as they crossed open prairies. The trails disappeared at each river crossing, only to appear again on the far side. Mile after mile, day after endless day, John followed the tracks. While traveling across the country, John couldn't help but notice small wooden crosses placed at grave sights dotting the countryside. These crosses joined the wagon trails, marking the way of hundreds of families moving west. John's dream of settling in the new unsettled territory was not to be fulfilled. Due to his untimely death in 1810, a small cross marking his final resting place is located just outside of Traswell, Tennessee. Susannah and her children remained in Traswell, close to the grave of her beloved husband.

In 1821, Missouri became the twenty-fourth state. In 1837, twenty-seven years after John Mohllar's death, his grandchildren, children born to Felta Valentine Mohllar, headed toward the Ozarks in the Missouri hills to fulfill their grandfather's dream. George W. (1799-1885) and Rufus (1770-1816), Mom's grandfathers, four generations removed, along with their brothers Felta Jr. (1815-1863), Silas (b. 1819), John (b. 1804), and one sister, Betty Moulder Evans (1810-1895), packed all their worldly goods into covered wagons. Traveling on horseback, they left Tennessee. While traveling through Kentucky, John's horse became lame, and he wasn't able to continue with his family. Promising to join them, John bid his family goodbye and watched them ride off toward the western horizon.

I paused for just a moment to explain. It was about this time the spelling of the family name "M-o-h-l-l-a-r" was changed to "M-o-u-l-d-e-r."

George W. and Rufus, along with two other brothers and one sister, made their way to south central Missouri, settling along the banks of the Osage River. This wild territory proved to be all that was told to them by their grandfather. The land was made up of hills, valleys, and forests, filled with wild life. Fish in abundance, swam in the Osage, the Big Niangua and the Little Niangua rivers. Their only security was blue smoke curling up from the chimney on top of their log cabin and a worn split-rail fence surrounding a cleared piece of land.

In 1841, the state of Missouri established an area bounded on the north by the Osage River. The Big Niangua River, entering from the south, running diagonally to the northeast and the Little Niangua River, entering from the west, merging with the Big Niangua before flowing into the Osage River, just south of the town, Linn Creek, Missouri. This area was named Kinderhook County. That same year, the first grocery and mercantile store opened its doors for business, and Linn Creek was established, becoming the county seat. A couple of years later in 1843, the General Assembly of Missouri changed the county's name of Kinderhook to Camden. By 1850, Linn Creek was fairly established with government officials, bankers, merchants, preachers, and farmers.

"That's cool," remarked Anetta. "Our family, the Moulders, helped to build that area."

Then my youngest daughter, Suzanne, asked, "But what about Grandma Myrtle's family? Where'd they come from?"

"Well, here's the Gerhardt's story," I said.

In the year 1834, before John Mohllar's grandchildren headed west to Missouri, a little boy was born at Brueckenstrasse, Germany, in the western part of the town Koelleda. His name was James August Gerhardt. In old Germany, when the country was divided into almost countless kingdoms, there were very rigid personal restrictions. An individual couldn't just leave his village to pursue his livelihood wherever he wanted. So as the little boy grew into manhood, he dreamed of pursuing his own destiny. In the year 1851, at the age of seventeen, James evaded the Prussia Army by stowing away on a merchant ship bound for America.

In the new country, August, as James was now called, married Eliza Jane Wallace of Cole Township in Benton County, Missouri. Together, they homesteaded a small farm on a piece of land near Warsaw, in central Missouri. August served in the Union Army during the Civil War from 1861 to 1865 in Company F., Eighth Missouri Calvary. He fought valiantly at the Battle of Wilson, near Springfield, Missouri. After his service in the war, August returned to Warsaw and his family. He and Eliza Jane established a store at Duroc, Missouri, located directly on the Osage River. Their son, Fredrick James, Mom's grandfather, was born on January 7, 1863, followed by ten more children.

August dreamed of expanding his holdings. He found and bought a one-hundred-sixty acre spot near the mouth of Prairie Holler nestled between the Big and Little Niangua rivers, about five miles from Linn Creek in Camden County. He named the settlement Coelleda, fashioning his dream town after his native village in Germany. However, before the town became a reality, August died in 1884 leaving his widow and a young family. He was buried in Brushy Chapel Cemetery, about three miles north of Duroc on county road AB in Benton County.

When John Mohller and August Gerhardt left Germany, they left family and home, everything that was familiar. They had the foresight to overcome the obstacles that faced them: a treacherous journey across a dangerous ocean, coming to a place whose language they didn't understand. And yet they made the choice to come. How did they do it? How did they overcome all the fears they must have felt? It's simple. Mohllar and Gerhardt, along with millions of others, were guided by an ideal. It was an idealized vision, undoubtedly romanticized. But by coming here, they gave something back to America. Making it even more special, they worked hard making this country better, fairer, and to build a more prosperous life for themselves and their children. Our ancestors were pioneers who made life a little better for their neighbors. They represented the unwavering spirit of the early American dream. Continuing their heritage and setting a strong example for the rest of their family, they believed that any work worth doing was worth doing well.

After his father's death, Frederick James moved with his mother, brothers, and sisters to Coelleda, fulfilling his father's dream. Eliza Jane helped her oldest son establish the new settlement until her death in 1916. She is buried in the Roach, Missouri Cemetery.

On January 7, 1883, Fred J. married Minnie Mary Martha Melinda, daughter of Rufus Moulder (1816-1876), John Mohllar's grandson. Mat, as she was lovingly called, was born on January 31, 1867. On October 11, 1885, at their home in Coelleda, Missouri, the first of fourteen children was born. They called their daughter Myrtle.

In order to support his large family, Fred engaged in farming with oxen in addition to operating the local mercantile. In 1888, when Myrtle was very young, Fred asked his brother Herman to take over running the small store while Fred took his family to points in southern Missouri, Arkansas, and Oklahoma. As they traveled, Fred invented and constructed bedsprings. Not aware of the importance of his invention, Fred didn't have the notion to apply for a patent. His only intent was to help supplement the family's meager income. During the next few years, Fred and Mat operated stores in Pumpkin Center and Banister, Missouri. When times were hard, patrons of his general store would buy items, promising to pay for their goods in due time. Fred didn't press his friends for their money; so therefore, he went bankrupt and had to relocate to another town, trying his hand at yet another store.

During one trip across the southeastern part of Missouri, the family came to a river crossing that was filled with quicksand. A wagon train was already there, the travelers helping each other across. A woman, traveling in one of the wagons, looked like Mat. Upon inquiry, they discovered that she was the granddaughter of John Mohller, who had stayed back in Kentucky. The woman was in fact a cousin to Mat. In 1900, the Gerhardts returned to Coelleda.

There was a natural spring waterway on Fred's land. The water ran along the base of a fifty-foot thick bluff, separated from plush grassland on the other side. Realizing he needed to get water through the bluff to his oxen, Fred had no choice but to resort to his own bare hands. Using small charges of dynamite, a pickax, and a shovel, Fred dug a hole through the bluff, just large enough for him to crawl through. A never-ending supply of water began to flow freely under the bluff to the other side, pooling on the land.

"And children," I explained. "To this very day, that hole can be seen and is referred to as 'the hole in the wall'."

Fred bought Wolf Pen Griss Mill from Os Pearl, an ex-slave. He installed a water mill at the "hole in the wall." He milled grain for the local farmers and once again entered into the family mercantile business. Meat and produce were brought in from the outlying hills—geese, chickens, cream, eggs, butter, and feathers. Fred had to be ever alert to the possibility of fraud when dealing with some of the farmers coming into town to trade their goods. A small potato could be hidden in the center of a mold of butter in order to add to the desired weight. Produce was bartered for supplies at Fred's store. In exchange, Fred might give a local farmer a coin called a Due Bill. This flat piece of metal, usually a six-sided coin bearing Fred's name and the amount of credit due, was good toward purchases in the store at any future date.

Fred could not remarket all of these traded goods to the local people, so on Monday mornings, before daylight, freight wagons were loaded for the trip to market. Pulled by two mules, a wagon could carry about fifteen hundred pounds. In unusually bad weather, freighters double-teamed. Adding another team also enabled them to carry heavier loads, sometimes up to two thousand pounds in good weather. Securing boxes, barrels, cream cans, and chicken coops, they pulled out for market. It took three days to make the trip to Lebanon, Missouri, and back. Creeks were forded at dangerous levels, water sometimes running through the wagon beds. But no matter what time they reached Lebanon, midnight or after, someone was always there to help unload.

Teams were fed and stabled before the drivers rested. Early the next morning, they bought flour, salt and crackers in wooden barrels, peanut butter in wooden buckets, yard goods, and hardware. The thirteen thousand people in Camden County in the 1800s created a remarkable consumer market.

As Myrtle grew into a young lady, she enjoyed helping her father with the store, post office, and mill. Children liked to come to Fred's store because there was always a free piece of candy available for good boys and girls. Myrtle admired the ladies riding up to the side porch of the store before dismounting from their sidesaddles. She secretly hoped someday she too would have a fancy sidesaddle of her own. Men of the neighborhood would gather at the general store and mill to visit, talk about the weather, and discuss farming and livestock prices in the surrounding areas.

After returning to Coelleda, Fred served as judge for Camden County. He was known to many of his friends as the *Father of Good Roads*, for it was during his term that the *Good Road Plan* of Camden County got under way. Fred was instrumental in supporting schoolteacher Tom Hart in successfully bidding for the county contract to build the suspension bridge, later to be called *Hart Bridge* across the Big Niangua River.

Fred would take his family to attend worship and community gatherings at Lower Prairie Hollow Church and school. The church, located near Coelleda, was the first Baptist church established in Camden County. It was served by traveling preachers as well as a place for more than thirty children to attend school.

Both the Moulder family and the Gerhardt family had come to settle in and around the little town of Linn Creek, Missouri.

By the mid-1800s, Linn Creek was not only the central government location for Camden County, it was the chief shipping, wholesale and distributing point of southwest Missouri and beyond. The Osage River catered to the many fur traders coming through the area as well as settlers moving west. The trade volume of one of its businesses *Jones, McClurg and Co.* amounted to three-quarters of a million dollars annually

As the town continued to grow, many a drifter also found his way to the banks of the Niangua River. Green Long was among those immigrants, who migrated to the Ozarks. During his stay, he met and courted a young local woman named Martha Jane Cyrus. Martha soon found herself smitten by this young newcomer. The courtship grew strong, and the young couple fell in love. Martha became pregnant and was faced with the task of telling Long she had conceived his child. The strict code of the hills frowned severely upon men who got an unmarried woman in the family way. Sometimes the punishment was death. Listening to the local gossip about what could happen to him, being a drifter and all, Long became frightened and left town. He packed up what little belongings he had and moved, leaving his love to fend for her self and their unborn child. While living in Texas, Long never proved up on his claim and was referred to as being a squatter.

Continuing to pine for his sweetheart, he never married. Over the years, Long kept in touch with Sarah Jane Richardson, a cousin from Richland, Missouri, who was living with Long's brother and his wife, Aunt Sis. Sarah Jane knew Long still pined for young Martha and might try to contact her. She also knew Aunt Sis would destroy any mail that arrived from him, since she was the *biggest duck in the puddle* causing Green Long to leave Missouri in the first place. So just in case there happened to be a letter, Sarah Jane made certain it was she who retrieved the post from the mailbox each day.

On March 15, 1884, Martha Jane Cryus gave birth to a son, naming him Alonzo Belford (Lonnie). Martha Jane soon married a widower by the name of Thomas Hart Benton Moulder (T.H.), grandson of George W. It was a marriage of convenience. Martha needed someone to help raise her son, and T.H. needed a mother for his young motherless children. T.H. adopted Lonnie, giving him the Moulder name.

While still a small child, Lonnie received a letter from Green Long. In the letter, Green explained he was sorry for the way he had left. He told Lonnie that he had always loved Martha but was afraid to stay in fear for his life. Several years passed. Then Martha received a letter, postmarked Mart, Texas. It was from a man named John Patter, informing her and Lonnie that Green Long had shot and killed himself. In later years, Lonnie found out what Aunt Sis had done. He could never forgive her selfishness.

"That's so sad," remarked Emily.

Standing up to stretch, I asked Donnis if she would like to continue the story.

"Sure I will," she said.

My family's attention turned toward my sister, as I slipped out of the room to go check on Mom.

3

Linn Creek Grows ♥

While Donnis continued telling our family story, I walked down the hall to be with Mom and Dad. I hesitated at the door of the intensive care room, until my eyes became accustomed to the dim light inside. I saw Dad had moved the recliner close to Mom's bed. He was fast asleep. I thought to myself, *during the past fifty-five years, these two people had slept together in the same bed. That is, until Mom got sick.* Dad's face was void of any stress or worry, as he slept soundly.

There were prickly little whiskers just starting to show around his jaw line. In my memory, I heard Mom say, "Max, don't you think it's about time you shaved?" Was it really an irritant for her, or did she just like mothering him? And did he mind? I think he just liked hearing her complain. Fearing that he was going to need all the strength he could muster in the days to come, I let him sleep.

Gently, I took Mom's hand in mine. As I stood there beside the bed, watching fleeting movements behind her eyelids, I noticed, ever so slightly, her lips moved. *Why does it seem as though she is fighting that tube in her mouth? Does she know what's going on? Does she know I am here and how much I love her?* I wondered. Time seemed to stand still as I stood in that dim room holding Mom's hand while the rest of my family was just down the hall. Donnis had the family's undivided attention as she continued talking in her storytelling voice.

During the second half of the 1800s, railroads were becoming the primary trading supply routes throughout the entire mid and Southwestern United States. The river trade that had once centered in Linn Creek drastically diminished. Wholesale merchandising came to an abrupt end for Linn Creek and was now being done at locations with rail service. In addition, the Civil War had left its destruction throughout the land, and Camden County did not escape the war's devastation. Most of the stores in Linn Creek had been looted of all goods that could be used by troops, and some of the buildings had been completely demolished. Boats had been burned at the wharves, and the wharves succumbed to destruction. The town was practically destroyed.

After the war ended, railroad companies were faced with rebuilding railroads destroyed by the war and building even more railroads to supply goods to the growing Western states. When railroads were built through the Ozark region, their path did not include Camden County, largely because of its rocky and wooded terrain. But the county had timber, and lots of it!

By the thousands, men migrated into the county to cut timbers and to hew out railroad ties. A man and his wife often worked together. They brought their crosscut saws and their broadaxes. With a worker handling each end of the crosscut saw, they felled the trees. Eight-foot tie lengths were sawed from the trunk and then squared or hewn with the broadax. A skilled woodsman could make twenty to thirty ties per day for which he was paid about ten cents each. The whirring of the saws and the chopping of the axes could be heard echoing through the woods. It was a sound of prosperity and growth.

With such a rapid influx of people coming to the area, shelter and supplies were scarce. The workers often had to house themselves by confiscating a deserted shanty, pitching a tent or even throwing a canvas tarp over some underbrush. Cooking was done over an open fire, mainly in a dutch oven set upon a bed of coals and covered with more coals.

Some Ozark landowners sold the right to harvest the trees to contractors, who made ties, while other landowners made their own. Many ties were hewn far from the river, a road or even a trail. These were snaked out of the woods by hitching a horse to a singletree yoke and attaching the yoke to the ties. Sometimes the ties were pushed over a high bluff to slide down to the riverbank. Scars resulting from these tie slides, as they were called, could be seen along the countryside above the Osage and the Niangua rivers. Wagons loaded with ties also traveled toward the river. Wharves became the site, where thousands of ties were piled to await the brander who would, for a fee, burn the owner's brand into the side of the tie for identification and payment. Next the buyer came and negotiated terms with the timber owners. He would log the numbers into journals, issuing the owner a receipt.

Returning to its glory days, the Osage and Niangua rivers came back into its own. After ties were branded and dollar amounts recorded, a new force took over—the rafter. When enough ties arrived at any tie banking, they were placed into long row sections of thirty to thirty-five ties. Working in water waist deep, the rafter would bind the ties together with binders of white oak saplings to make a raft. Two men usually manned a raft on the smaller streams, one at each end guiding, snubbing, and maneuvering around river bends, paddling through placid eddies and slowing the progress through swift shoals by dragging the snub pole along the bed of the stream. When night overtook them, the raft was tied along the bank, near enough to a farmhouse for the men to find food and shelter.

Where the Osage and the Big Niangua rivers joined, single rafts were bound to other rafts, until there were sometimes as many as two thousand ties. More men were needed on these rafts, and an oar on the bow aided in control. Meals were cooked upon the raft by building a fireplace of mud and stones. The men slept in shifts. For such strenuous effort, they were paid one dollar and fifty cents per day with meals. The ties were floated down the Osage River to Osage City where they were unbound, taken from the water, loaded upon flat cars, and taken wherever they were needed for construction of roadbeds.

Linn Creek was at the heart of the tie-cutting activity. Almost destroyed when the river traffic made way for the railroad, the town soon became known as a "tie town." With so many families moving in, many new stores were built. Hardware stores kept a large supply of tools needed in making rafting ties, repairing wagons and harnesses for horses and mules. Groceries, dry goods, and clothes were available to the men and their families in the local mercantile. Doctor's offices, cafés, hotels, blacksmiths, fur-buying office, branders' offices, newspapers and business agents including Bennett & Haunstein, Moulder & Watson, F. Hooker and Thomas Ezard were among the establishments that hung out their shingles to serve the woodsmen and the rafters.

In truth, the Ozarks during the exciting decade at the turn of the century was still very much a part of the United States, and the interest and aspirations of its citizens were no different, except perhaps in degree and opportunity of fulfillment.

From the days immediately following the Civil War, and throughout the early 1900s, Linn Creek, with its busy wharf, remained a bustling growing town in the heart of the Ozarks. The residents had free public schools, places of worship, opera houses, newspapers and a strong sense of patriotism, community pride, and railroads. Through mail-order catalogs, the wonders of the urban department stores were known to the Ozark farmers and, if he could afford them, were readily available. The old isolation was breaking down.

"How's Mom?" Phyllis asked, looking up at me, as I entered the room.

"There's no change. Dad's sleeping though," I shared with my family.

"Good, he needs to rest."

As soon as I took my place back on the couch, beside Emily, Donnis continued.

Alonzo Belfred Moulder (Lonnie, adopted son of Thomas Hart Benton Moulder and great-great-great-grandson of John Mohllar Sr.) and Myrtle

Gerhardt, daughter of Fred, descendant of James August and Martha Moulder, who was the great-great-great-granddaughter of the same John Mohllar, met in the town of Linn Creek, Missouri. They married, raised their family, and lived their whole life within fifteen miles of their birthplace.

Prosperous times existed throughout the nation in the early 1900s, and people were beginning to take advantage of the conveniences of newly invented products that made their daily lives less tedious and more enjoyable. The United States had celebrated the centennial of its founding. The war seemed a distant memory, and its wounds had all been healed. It was a time of discovery, of self-improvement, and of rapid change. The telephone was in its infancy, and people were starting to realize its potential. Automobiles were replacing horse-drawn buggies and wagons, and the first airplane flight had been made in North Carolina. People of the nation struggled to absorb the wonders of the ten-story skyscraper, electric street railcars, fantastic industrial growth, and many mechanical marvels of the age. Thanks to modern, faster means of traveling from place to place and acquiring information from the newspapers that abounded throughout the nation, people became aware that life had a lot to offer, more than just the daily grind of heavy labor and familiarity within their small communities.

The populations surrounding Linn Creek, Missouri, were exploding due to the vast numbers of people coming from many states throughout the nation to the wooded terrain seeking employment in the tie-making industry. Log houses gave way to frame structures, and sawmills became a thriving business. At one time, it was estimated that the population of Camden County topped ten thousand people.

Life was hard for most rural families and demanded continuous, unrelenting labor. The workweek kept the outsiders busy cutting trees, hauling them to the water's edge, and rafting timber down the rivers, while the local hill folks tended to their regular duties of planting and harvesting and the general activities of day-to-day life. Still time remained, at least at certain times of the year, for even the most remote farm family to participate in special leisure events. Most Ozark communities were still relatively isolated from the outside world and from each other, so everyone looked forward to time away from their work, when the locals invited the newcomers to share their traditional get-togethers, including Saturday night socials and dances, box suppers, end-of-school programs, Sunday go-to-meetin' morning worship, and afternoon baseball games. An area farmer would clean out his barn, or the community schoolhouse or the local church would open its doors where everyone could gather to have fun and share good times with their friends and neighbors. For the Ozark Mountain residents, it was exciting to include the outsiders in their socials, to hear the latest news of places apart from their little communities. In return, the outsiders were grateful for the down-home hospitality offered by the hill people.

The Saturday night socials became an important time, of fun and relaxing, after a long week of backbreaking work in the woods and on the farms. Everyone wanted to have a good time, especially the young people. But the men folk were just a little wary of anyone who wasn't born and bred in the hills. Knowing the men would far outnumber the women, dads and brothers planned on escorting their ladies, young and old, to every event. Ozark men understood their unspoken duty—to keep a close watch over their sisters and daughters.

4

The Marriage ♥

The morning slowly passed as I sat with my family in that little room. None of us wanted this day to end, for we knew that before a new day dawned, we would have to say our final goodbye to our mother. But for now, it was comforting to hear about those days past. Somehow, it made us feel a little closer to her. And perhaps to some, helped to know her a little better.

Phyllis was just returning to the room when she met three family friends in the hall. They were carrying a tray loaded down with donuts and cookies and a jug full of orange juice. They had been in to see Mom and were now looking for us.

"We thought you might be needing something to eat," Lois remarked.

"Thank you so much. Would you like to join us?" Phyllis asked, taking the tray full of food. "We are telling our kids and grandkids what it was like for Mom and her family growing up in Missouri at the beginning of the 1900s."

"Sure, we can stay for a while," Lois said, pulling the chairs, that had been out in the hall, into the already-crowded room

Once again, I looked around the room into the faces of my loved ones. Dad, now awake from his nap, looking somewhat rested, was sharing a small couch with Donnis. They were sitting in front of a big window. I couldn't help but notice how the sun, streaming in through the glass, turned Donnis's red hair into a beautiful copper color. Phyllis, Mom's big helper when all of us children were small, was sitting in a big overstuffed easy chair. Her oldest son, Lonnie, was standing behind her, ready to protect his mom if needed, while Chandi sat on the floor, her elbow resting in a protective sort of way on her mom's knee. Torrie was leaning against the doorframe, blocking the opening. Rusty, my youngest brother was sitting at a small table where the food had been placed. His beautiful wife sat close by, holding his hand, while their youngest child, Matthew, sat on his lap. My nephew Jessy was talking softly into his cell phone. I caught a flicker of relief cross his face. He had finally been able to locate his sister Mandi who was now on her way to the hospital to join us. I prayed that Marla, their mom, would get here soon. She had called earlier to say they were now in Phoenix waiting on a flight back to Wichita. My younger nieces Emily, Katie, Danielle, and Samantha were lying on the floor, using their folded arms as pillows. My two daughters, Anetta and Suzanne, were sitting on the floor at my feet. Suzanne's husband, Steve, stood close by while Anetta's husband, Jay, was home, caring for their two small children, Chelsea and Aaron. Once again, tears welled up in my eyes. I looked around the room. I remembered how Mom had instilled in each of us the importance of family. "Family is the most important possession you will ever have," she would say. "Love them, lean on them, and comfort them." This must be what she was talking about. Taking a deep breath, I softly patted my daughter's shoulders, as I continued.

"Now that you have heard about our heritage and where we came from, I would like to tell you about Mom's parents, her seven sisters, and three brothers. Mom is the youngest of eleven children, so these stories I am about to tell you have been passed down from her sisters to her, then from her down to me, just like I am now passing them on down to you.

"One Saturday morning, Myrtle Gerhardt, our grandmother, was hurrying through her morning chores, humming with contentment. Myrtle had a good reason to be happy. Her pa had given permission for her to become betrothed to a strong and responsible man named Lonnie Moulder, adopted son of Thomas Hart Benton Moulder.

"Wait a minute," Rusty interrupted. "Doesn't that make Thomas Hart a cousin to Mat, Mom's grandmother?" he asked.

"It sure does," I replied. "Thomas Hart's grandfather was George W., and Mat's grandfather was Rufus, both grandsons of John Mohller." Smiling, I looked at each one of my nieces and nephews while I explained. "That's how it came to be that your great-great-great-great-great-great-grandfather happen to be the same man."

"Wow, that's a lot of greats. Hey, we're part of a really great family!" Danielle boasted, as she gave Emily a high-five hand slap.

I picked up the story where I had left off.

Myrtle's dad, Fred, knew that Lonnie came from good stock, and that he was a hard worker. He had no qualms about his oldest daughter marrying this robust young man. After Myrtle completed her chores, she went to the kitchen to start preparing food she would take to the box-supper event planned for that evening. She wanted to make this meal special because Lonnie would be sharing it with her. However, they could not stay late because tomorrow was their wedding day.

When the bread dough had been thoroughly kneaded, Myrtle placed it into bread pans before putting the pans on a shelf above the cook stove.

The heat from the stove caused the dough to rise, doubling in size. She then slid the pans into the hot oven. When the bread turned a golden brown, Myrtle carefully removed the pans, sending a tantalizing aroma throughout the house. After removing the bread from the pans, Myrtle spread fresh churned butter generously on the loaves, giving it a nice delicate crust. Her mouth watered, as the butter melted, running down the sides making little amber pools on the table. When the bread was cool, she cut it, wrapping the big thick slices in a dishtowel.

While the chicken that had been butchered earlier that morning was frying in a cast iron skillet, Myrtle mixed boiled potatoes, fresh hard-boiled eggs, sweet pickle relish, a little heavy cream, and a pinch of sugar together for a potato salad. Finally, she baked a dried apple cake. Putting the scrumptious meal into a wicker basket, her dinner was now ready.

With just a couple of hours left before time to leave for the evening social, Myrtle made sure her wedding ensemble was in order. With the help of her good friend, May Jackson, whose family lived on a nearby farm, Myrtle had painstakingly sewn her wedding dress. The dress was made from blue cashmere with a nine-gore skirt and a square yoke over laced with trim. She had purchased a pretty hat that matched her outfit perfectly. After Myrtle was assured that her clothes were all neatly packed in her traveling trunk, ready for her honeymoon trip, Myrtle went outside to the barn. Swinging open the big double doors, the smell of sweet hay accosted her nostrils. Walking into the dim interior of the building, Myrtle saw her beautiful brown sidesaddle lying across one of the stall gates. It had been polished and buffed to a soft shine and had the strong odor of new leather. Rubbing the soft saddle with the palm of her hand, Myrtle smiled to herself as she remembered the reaction she had gotten when she sold her new calf to purchase this saddle. It was custom that the bride's grandmother gives her a calf to be used as a dowry. This was a means for a young woman to bring some monetary value to her marriage. Myrtle was a sensible and hard-working young girl. However, remembering the fine ladies riding up to her father's store, sitting on their beautiful sidesaddles, and her dreams of someday owning her own, she had shown her parents and grandparents a side of her that was rarely in evidence.

Sunday, March 5, 1905, dawned bright and clear with just a hint of coolness in the air. Lonnie and Myrtle had plans to be married at Parrack Grove Church immediately following the worship service. Reverend Frank Osborn was to reside over the ceremony. While Myrtle attended the morning service with her parents, Lonnie stayed home in order to get their personal things packed in his wagon and his horses geared up for the wedding trip. He was to meet his bride later at the church. Lonnie expected it to be a private ceremony. However, when he and his best friends, Jess Jackson and

Yomer Yaden, rode up the hill to the little country church and saw a crowd of people lingering in the yard, Lonnie was overcome with jitters.

"Whoa," he called to his team of horses. Taking off his hat, he scratched his head. "What do you make of that?" he asked his friends.

"Ya," stated Yomer, in a thick Swedish accent. "Der's a bunch a people."

Jess reining in his horse asked, "What cha gonna do, Lon? Myrtle's waitin' for ya."

Looking at his friends, Lonnie remarked, "Now just wait a cotton-pickin' minute. Let me think."

When Myrtle realized that Lonnie was not waiting for her outside of the church, a devastated feeling came over her. More than a little embarrassed, Myrtle began making apologies to her family and friends, while back on the hillside, and out of sight, Lonnie came up with a solution. He told Jess and Yomer to go the church and secretly shepherd Myrtle, just up the road, to the reverend's home. Lonnie would join them with the preacher. He hoped they could quietly be married without the hubbub!

The entire crowd at the church had thoughts of their own. They cared a great deal about the well being of this young couple, so they left the church and followed them to the reverend's home to witness the wedding. So much for avoiding a crowd! That morning revealed something new to Myrtle about her groom. Lonnie, forever long on opinions but never wanting to be the center of attention, was painfully shy in a crowd.

A couple of days after returning from their wedding trip, Lonnie and Myrtle were accosted at their home by a group of well-wishing neighbors. It had also been long practiced that the bride's mother would host a shivaree for the newly married couple. So friends and neighbors came across the hills and valleys, banging cooking pots together and firing off shotguns. Their intent was to keep the newlyweds awake all night.

Lonnie was aggravated with their friends' interruption to his quiet evening of relaxing by a fire, reading the *Revielle* (the local newspaper), smoking his pipe, and enjoying the company of his new bride, as she sat in her chair at his side. Lonnie's early frustration turned to fun when he got into the swing of things, jig dancing, laughing, and acting out with the best of them, becoming a fun-loving host. Laughter, loud music, and boisterous, rowdy joking could be heard wafting through the hills, ringing out good cheer for the young married couple until the early morning dawn.

Lonnie and Myrtle began living as husband and wife between Coelleda and Linn Creek in Camden County, Missouri. They traded a cow to Ed Johnson for homestead rights to a small claim approximately five miles north of what would soon be the new Highway 54 and just off Highway 5. For one hundred sixty dollars, they bought a team of mules from Lewis

Capps, a family friend. Jude and Molly, the faithful beasts of burden, served the family well for over thirty-five years. Four children were born at the Ed Johnson homestead. Howard Valentine, April 3, 1906; Nera Pearl, September 14, 1907; Raymond Earl, January 4, 1909; and Florence Irene, September 2, 1910.

The family moved to the Vander Moulder place in 1912. On November 6 that same year, their daughter Zilpha May was born. Five-year-old Nera and her two-year-old sister Florence were unable to pronounce the baby's name. No matter how hard they tried the best they could say was "Dilka."

"Maybe we should call her May," suggested Myrtle.

Lonnie didn't like that idea, so he gave her the nickname of Snook-um Dick. When Zilpha entered grade school, the name was shortened to Dick and remained Zilpha's nickname throughout her life.

In 1914, Lonnie moved his family to the Collins place, which was closer to Linn Creek and located above Bridal Cave. On December 12, 1914, their daughter Ila Mayme was born. The Moulders remained at this home until the summer of 1916 when Lonnie moved his family to a farm on the Big Niangua River just eight miles from Linn Creek. The farm was located on fertile bottomland, near where the Little Niangua River converged with the Big Niangua.

5

The Ha'nt ♥

Donnis took over telling the story.

Bessie Long was the previous owner of the property and advised Myrtle and Lonnie not to move into that house. She said it was haunted or as they say in the backwoods, "ha'nted." Lonnie, being a big brave husband and daddy, tried to act fearless but was a little spooked by the whole idea of moving his family to a place with such a shady reputation. Myrtle simply "did not hanker to such nonsense," or so she said. So they moved to their new home and called it Happy Holler.

The farm was rich, river bottomland bounded on the south by the Big Niangua River and on the north by the Little Niangua River. A small stream of water ran between the house and the barn like a ribbon of liquid life. Its origination point was a cold, clear hillside spring that snaked around the terrain, pooling under a hillside cliff, and then running steadily down to the Big Niangua. Lonnie and Myrtle's family called the small stream the Branch.

Lonnie built a springhouse, a small wood-framed building, over the spring to keep the dogs and wild animals out. The springhouse was used as the family's refrigerator. Then he dug a cavity in the ground, just at the point where the branch ran under the springhouse, and lined the hole with gravel, creating a pool. In the deep cold of winter, Lonnie would have to break away a thin layer of ice that formed over the spring to let the water flow. The rest of the year, the pool was always full and used for the family's cold, clear drinking water. Water was collected from the spring in a galvanized metal bucket and carried to the house. A dipper, shaped like a bowl, attached to the end of a long metal handle, was used to scoop water from the bucket for a delicious and refreshing drink. Everyone drank from the same dipper, and no one thought any better of it.

Overflowing the pool at the spring, the branch made its way on down to the river. When the branch froze over, Lonnie took his crosscut saw, removed one handle, and cut out pieces of ice, about two feet square. He loaded the blocks on the wagon and hauled them to the hills behind the house. He dug caverns into the hillside, wide and deep enough to store about three hundred of these ice blocks, and then he hauled in about four wagonloads of sawdust to cover the ice, about two feet thick. The ice helped to preserve their food for a long time.

The family's home was small, with only three rooms downstairs and an attic room above. The largest of the three rooms was the living room. The room had hardwood floors and tall narrow windows. A potbelly stove stood in one corner and was the only source of heat. One of the smaller rooms was the bedroom. There was a full-size bed and a small trundle bed that stood in opposite corners. A homemade corn shuck and straw mattress lay across ropes that had been tied from one side of the bed frame to the other. Both mattresses were covered with a feather tick mattress made from large pieces of cotton material sewn together and then filled with goose feathers. A pretty homemade quilt finished the beds. A smaller room was attached to the back of the house. A cast iron wood-burning cook stove, a large rectangle table with ladder-back chairs, and a baker's cabinet were the only furniture in the kitchen. Along the back wall and next to the outside door was a sturdy shelf for holding the water bucket, dipper, and a metal wash pan.

One small door separated the family's living area from the attic. A long narrow, steep stairway led up into the dark space above. The attic was used for storing the family's food. Forty-pound sacks of corn meal were neatly stacked along one wall. Jars of canned green beans, tomatoes, and beets were lined up on a wooden shelf. A fifteen-gallon crock of sauerkraut set off in one corner. There was a large pickle barrel and a pile of dry corn for popping. Long strings of onions and turnips were tied together and hung upside down from the rafters next to the bundles of dried herbs. Garlic, rosemary, and thyme made the everyday produce mighty tasty after a long winter season.

It wasn't long before the family forced the warning about ha'nts out of their minds and settled into their new home. For several months, nothing mysterious happened, so the thought of ghosts haunting the home was all but forgotten.

One cool spring evening, Lonnie had built a fire in the potbellied stove and was sitting in his big oak rocker. Under the flickering light of a coal oil lamp, he read the *Reveille* while Myrtle, with her little strong hands, worked on the never-ending task of mending the family's clothes. The children were tucked in their beds. Nera, Florence, and Dick in the small bed while Howard and Ray lay in the trundle bed beside them. Mayme was sleeping soundly in the wooden cradle that was at the foot of Lonnie and Myrtle's bed. The children were getting drowsy as they listened to the soothing crackle of the fire and soon started to doze. A gentle wind was blowing through the hills; a low rumble of thunder sounded in the distance. As the evening wore into night, the wind began to increase its force and started rattling the windowpanes.

"Must be a storm brewing," Lonnie told Myrtle.

Suddenly, and without warning, the door to the attic slowly creaked open. Small flecks of dust and wood ash that had gathered in the corners of the room were airlifted and floated across the room just above the floor. The door stood open for a few minutes. Then just as suddenly, the attic door softly closed. The dust and ash drifted slowly down to lay on the floor once again. Lonnie turned to look at Myrtle, just as Myrtle turned to look at Lonnie.

"My, what was that?" whispered Myrtle, not wanting the sound of her voice to intrude into the quiet atmosphere of the room.

"Must be the ha'nts I guess," replied Lonnie. But even as he teased, he was just a little wary as to the possibility of something foreign coming to reside there in the house with them and their children.

Time quickly passed for the young and growing family. That fall, while Howard stayed home to help his dad, Nera, Ray, Florence, and Dick attended the Arnoldt country school. Lonnie became a master at trapping on the river, and his time was consumed doing bone-hard work to keep the family cared for. Myrtle worked equally hard, canning and putting up food from her gardens to ensure that her family would not go hungry.

The cold months of winter brought heavy snows that drifted high up on the sides of the little house. Tucked away safe and snug in the valley, the family had few worries that hunger would find them before the rivers thawed in the spring. Everything seemed calm in the Happy Holler home. The incident of the spring evening, when the door leading to the attic swung open and then closed again, was all but forgotten. They had even come to wonder if the stories Bessie Long related were only old wives' tales told by a worrisome old woman. Listening to frogs croaking and millions of bugs chirping their way through night into morning, they had all but forgotten the warning about ha'nts.

One night, late into the night, Myrtle woke. Groggy, she thought it had been a dream that had disturbed her. She felt cold. Staring up at the ceiling, she strained to listen. The family was sleeping nearby, and Lonnie was gently snoring in bed next to her. Nevertheless, a feeling of aloneness saturated her being to her very soul. She struggled to shake off the mood and convince herself that her imagination was running away with her. She definitely did not want to wake Lonnie. He would tease her, even though she knew he blustered his way with false bravery whenever the subject of ha'nts came up.

Overhead, a board creaked. Old houses make noises at night, and this one was no exception. Myrtle had learned that quickly about the Happy

Holler house. Restless, she shifted in her bed as she lay watching the light of the waning moon. Firmly, she set her mind on the list of chores for the next day. When the sound came again, she frowned, glancing automatically at the ceiling. The creaks and groans had not disturbed her before. She had slept soundly in this house for many months and had been able to ignore the warnings about ha'nts. She bragged she wasn't afraid and was able to take care of herself. Determinedly, she shut her eyes and tried to turn off her nervous, rambling thoughts.

Was that a footstep on the stairs, or was it all in her imagination? As fear flowed through her, she thought of the warning from Bessie. She bit down on her lip to keep from making a sound. Her heart was lodged in her throat, pounding. She felt alone, even though Lonnie was asleep right next to her. Her fingers curled into the blanket, as she lay stiff, straining to hear. Very slowly, Myrtle turned her head and made out the sleeping form of her husband in the bed, the moonlight coming through the small window, shining softly on his face. Even though she was looking for comfort, she could not bring herself to wake him.

Closing her eyes once again, she tried to even her breathing. She tried to convince herself it was just the boards settling when she heard another movement overhead. Hysteria bubbled and was quickly swallowed. There was nothing now, no creaks, no soft steps on wood, but she was still on guard. Being careful not to make a sound, she climbed out of bed. Tiptoeing through the dark room to the potbellied stove, she found the wood-stove poker. Sitting with her muscles tensed, Myrtle propped herself in the chair, facing the attic door. Gripping the poker in both hands, she prayed for morning.

Morning dawned with no further incidents, and Myrtle felt like a fool. She was awakened, stiff and sore from the night in the chair, by Lonnie playfully tugging at her nose. The wood-stove poker had lain across her lap like a medieval sword. The bright sunlight and the birdsong had convinced her that she had imagined everything and then had magnified every small noise the way a child magnifies shadows in the dark. Perhaps she wasn't quite as brave and acclimated to living in the Happy Holler house as she'd thought. At least, she was grateful she had not awakened Lonnie. If she had, everyone in the valley would know she was a nervous ninny.

Myrtle thought her tense night awake was long forgotten when one night, in the wee hours of the morning, she was awakened again, this time by a rattling noise. *Think,* she ordered herself. *Stay calm and think.* How many times in the past few weeks had she stated she could do just that? She pressed a hand against her mouth so that the sound of her own rapid breathing wouldn't disturb her concentrated listening. She was sure she heard a chain, ever so slowly, clank and rattle, like it was being dragged. She squeezed her eyes shut. If Lonnie heard nothing that disturbed him, then she reasoned there was nothing to worry about. But the sound of a chain being dragged across the floor of the attic had her eyes flying open again. With the clatter of clangs, rattles, and bangs, the chain fell down the opposite side wall and landed with a thump. She wondered how Lonnie could sleep through the racket. Maybe she really was imagining it. All was once again quiet. *Am I going crazy?* she wondered.

A few nights later, it started again. The chain was being dragged up through one wall, across the floor of the attic, only to fall down the opposite wall. Myrtle was tired of being awakened in the night. She'd had it! She threw the covers off the bed and jumped up. She was determined to stop this ha'nt. In her rush of excitement to take care of the problem, she woke Lonnie and the children.

"I'm gettin' it!" she yelled.

"What if the ha'nt gets you?" shouted Lonnie, as Myrtle darted away from the bed.

"So be it!" On this night, not fearing even the devil himself, Myrtle yanked open the attic door and rushed up the stairs to catch the ha'nt in action. She was on a mission, and nothing was going to stop her.

The worried family huddled together in their beds and waited downstairs. They wondered what was going to happen to their little mother. She was brave, but sometimes her daring overtook her common sense. Once Myrtle reached the top of the stairs, everything grew deathly quiet. Then they heard hysterical and out-of-control laughter. The family was concerned about Myrtle's sanity, for they just knew the ha'nts had possessed her for sure. Then the ruckus began. The sounds of an unruly scuffle, crates being moved and overturned, and Myrtle's moaning, groaning, and grunting resounded from the attic. They were too wide-eyed and afraid to move. Finally, she returned to her family downstairs, spent and disheveled. Laughing, tears streaming down her face, she made quite a picture standing there in her nightgown, barefoot and her hair standing straight out, looking like a mad woman. Stretching out her arm, she held a four-foot length of chain. Attach to the end of the chain was a ten-pound river rat, squirming to get loose. The rat had managed to get the chain loose from a trap, but the chain was still attached to its leg. Looking for food, the rat had made its way up through the walls of the little house into the attic, crossing the attic floor to the opposite wall. Tired from the exertion of dragging the chain, the weight overtook the rat on the way down the other wall and ended up clanging to the bottom. To the relief and amusement of the whole family, the mystery of the ha'nt had been solved, and they all slept soundly in their Happy Holler home after that.

From this peaceful corner of the world, set in the shadows of the Ozark Mountains, Lonnie and Myrtle's work consisted of a wide variety of tasks in order to sustain a living. Lonnie hunted, trapped, fished, and farmed. He raised and sold horses, mules, and pigs. He harvested tobacco and a huge molasses patch. Myrtle, an equally hard worker, cooked the family meals, cleaned the house, and sewed her family's clothing. She sowed and harvested a large truck garden in the spring, picked berries in the summer, milked the cows, and raised the chickens. Large families were needed to help in the fields, do daily household chores, and tend the younger children. There was no question or argument. It was simply the way of life.

Five of their children were born at this home place: Ruby Edith on March 31, 1917; Ethel Fern on July 20, 1919; Letha Beryl on July 1, 1922; Thomas Fredrick on April 24, 1926; and Martha June on June 22, 1928.

"That's Mema," cried Katie, when she heard Donnis say "Martha June." Mema is the pet name that Mom's grandchildren called her.

"It sure is," Rusty told his daughter.

6

Crossing the River ♥

Donnis continued.

All the families who lived in the holler were desperately poor but didn't realize it until years later when progress of civilization exposed them to other facets of the world. What they lacked in creature comforts, they were able to improvise. The population, manners, and customs remained fixed in their own little valley, as great torrents of migration and improvements made never-ending changes in other parts of this restless country. Wanting his children to have the opportunity of a good and prosperous life, to be able to cope with changes in the country he felt would come, Lonnie was insistent that they attend the local country school. By the time Howard had completed three years of school, he knew the basics of arithmetic and was able to read and write. Lonnie figured this was plenty enough learnin' for a man to be able to run a farm. So while the other children attended the Arnholdt school Howard stayed home to work beside his dad in the fields and helped with the daily chores.

Early one morning, as the children walked across the lower end of their farm, on the way to school, they heard a roar. The closer they got to the ford in the river, where the normal crossing place was, the louder the sound grew. The neighboring counties to the west had received torrential rains the day before, causing the normally calm river to swell to flood stage. Reaching the bank of the Big Niangua, they watched with amazement as the river rolled and churned its way downstream.

The river was more than one hundred fifty feet wide, and was filled from one bank to the other, with moving obstacles! Beavers and otters, whose dens had been destroyed by rushing waters, could be seen bobbing up and down, as they raced along in the current. Masses of debris bounced and churned in the dirty brown water. Sticks were thrown upward, then splashing down, only to disappear under the fast-moving river.

Myrtle was just stepping outside of her house to throw out a dishpan full of dirty water when she heard the roar. Looking in the general direction of the noise, the riverbank, a shy quarter of a mile away from the house,

Myrtle saw just the tops of big tree limbs racing by. She knew her family would be in great danger when they tried to cross the river. Throwing down the dishpan she was holding, she grabbed her skirt tail and ran to join her children at the ford. Wringing her hands, Myrtle silently prayed to God, "Please, Jesus, see my children safely to the other side."

When she reached her children, Howard was already untying the little flat bottom boat from a sturdy low-hanging tree branch. It was his responsibility to set the kids across the river each morning on their way to school. And this morning was to be no different. However, Howard did realize it was going to be a huge challenge to get his sisters and brother safely across the raging river. Corralling Nera, Florence, Ray, Dick, and Mayme for the ride, he joked, "Everyone in or I'll throw you in." He was trying to make light of the situation to calm his nerves. At the young age of fourteen, he realized this was no laughing matter. Grabbing hold of the bow of the little boat, Howard helped his siblings climbed in before pushing off into the fast-moving river. Jumping into the boat himself, he knelt down, grabbed the wooden ores, and started to row. His young muscles strained against his homespun shirt. The veins in his neck bulged. His knuckles turned ash white as he grasped the oars to keep them from becoming entangled in the brush, being swept down the river. Keeping his eyes on the far bank, and thinking only of reaching safety, Howard also kept a close watch over his sisters and brother. As the boat rose and fell into the swells, the dirty brown water sprayed up and into their frightened little faces. Nera became scared and started to stand up. "Sit down or I'll knock you down!" Howard yelled in a stern voice.

Nera's knees buckled as she dropped back to the bottom of the shallow boat. She respected her older brother and immediately obeyed him, just as if it had been her daddy who had yelled at her. Nera gave credit to Howard. She knew her mom and dad depended on him to help take care of the rest of the children, and he did it very well.

After several minutes, the boatload of small children safely reached the other side. They scrambled out onto the bank, turning to look back across the river for their mom. They spotted her standing on the far bank. Only then did they realize the strong current had carried the boat several hundred yards down river from where Howard had put in. "Thank you God for answering my prayers and landing all of my babies safely on dry ground," Myrtle sent up her silent prayer.

She continued to stand on the bank watching her children roll up their trouser legs and hike up their skirt tails. Wading through the swampy ground, they crossed the lower edge of their uncle Elmore Moulder's farm and trudged up a hill. After her children had disappeared on the other side, and Howard had safely returned the boat, Myrtle turned and slowly walked back to the house to resume her daily chores, knowing her children were once again safely across the river.

Lost in her own thoughts, Donnis stopped talking. I had been watching the facial expressions of my brother and sisters, while Donnis told about the swollen river. I felt as though I could read their minds, which I was certain mirrored mine. I can't imagine the terror Grandma must have felt as she watched her children cross the river. If that boat had turned over, she would have been helpless to save them. We all gave our own children a little hug.

7

The Family Mules ♥

The Ozark Mountain Region, located in southern Missouri, northern Arkansas, and eastern Oklahoma, was a difficult place to get in or out of, and the people were culturally isolated. Goods could not be transported to the area fast enough to supply a large population, so the people wrestled a living from the hills, valleys, and prairies by depending on horse or mule power.

A mule is a crossbreed that results from mating a female horse with a male donkey. Only rarely does a female, or molly mule, give birth. Because they are crossbred, most mules are sterile. An adult work mule usually weighs between nine hundred and thirteen hundred pounds. The mules inherit their size and strength from the mare and their sure-footedness and supreme sense of self-preservation or stubbornness from the male donkey. A good dependable team of mules was an asset and to be respected.

Lonnie bartered the use of his brood mare, Ole Nell, in return for staples needed by the family. Farmers from around the community would bring their jacks to mate with the horse. After she gave birth, Lonnie kept the offspring mules until they were old enough to be harness broke and trained to work in the fields. Unfortunately, many of the mules had one or both of two major problems. Either the mule would balk and not go where you wanted it to go, or it would bolt and go where you did not want it to go.

Lonnie was diligent, though, and as stubborn as the mules he trained. He worked with the mules until he was finally successful. The Moulder family owned scores of mules themselves. Being family pets, as well as work animals, the children named them all. Jack, Jude, Kate, Molly, Beck, Red, Nell, and Raleigh.

These mules were not only beast of burden and family pets they were also a means of transportation. On their broad backs, they would carry the children, sometimes three and four at a time, across the hills and through the woods to school and church. The children were never afraid to enter the dark woods on the backs of their mounts. They knew other children in the valley would come riding up the other side of the hill into the woods to meet them. Sunday evening may find fifteen to twenty young children carrying lanterns, as they walked or rode mules, to Sunday evening worship. The mules would stand patiently, munching sweet clover, waiting for the youngsters to climb back on for the ride home.

Riding mules was a much faster way of transportation than walking when someone needed to get somewhere in a hurry. Other women in the holler often called on Myrtle to be their midwife. Births at home were called granny cases, one farmwoman performing the honor for another and having the honor returned when her time was due.

On occasion, late at night, a knock on the door of the Moulder home would be heard. A neighbor woman's baby was about to be born. Quietly, so as not to wake her family, Myrtle got dressed and most likely wrapped her own nursing baby in a warm blanket. Cradling her small child in one arm, she grabbed a little black satchel, took the coal oil lantern hanging from a peg by the door, and walked to the barn to harness her favorite mule. She would climb up on the bare back of gentle Kate for her trek across the dark hills. The sure-footedness of the mule always guaranteed Myrtles safe passage in the dark, with only a coal oil lantern and the moon to light her way.

One summer day, Lonnie went to the barn to fetch Jude, his field mule. The stall was empty. All the stalls were empty. He looked around the barnyard and down by the river for the mules. They were all gone! Thinking they had wondered out of the barn, crossed the river and into the cool meadow, Lonnie went searching.

"Ready, set, GO!" he heard Ray shout, his voice coming from the direction of the meadow.

The Moulder children had teamed up with the kids who lived up and down the river. They had cut a racetrack in the center of the valley. Round and round the mules ran, full tilt, building up a sweat and getting lathered from the heat of the day. Riding on the mule's backs, the children were yelling and laughing so hard they didn't see Lonnie running down the hill toward them, as fast as his bulk would allow.

"Hold on you, young'uns," he shouted. "What do you think you'ns are doin'?" The sound of his stern voice penetrated their laughter. The children reined in their mounts and turned to look at Lonnie, their eyes wide with surprise. "What's the meaning of this? Are you aim'n to kill those poor animals?" he swore. "Git!" The hills came alive with young children, hurrying to get away from the wrath of Lonnie Moulder. Lonnie had a certain look about him and when his kids saw it, they knew their dad meant business. "Git those mules back up to the barn!" he shouted waving his hat high above his head. His children didn't waste any time, leading the hot sweaty mules toward home. By the time Lonnie arrived back at the barn, all of the mules had been watered and turned out to pasture.

During supper that evening, Ray, Dick, Mayme, and Ruby sat around the table, their hands folded in their laps. With bowed heads, they anticipated what their rightful punishment was going to be. Finally, Lonnie spoke. With a stern look on his face, he shook his finger at each of them, accenting every word as he scolded. "Don't you'ns ever do that stunt again. Is that clear? Now eat your supper 'fore it gets cold."

That night, after the household chores were done, Lonnie and Myrtle went outside to sit on the porch to enjoy the cool evening air. Watching their young children, who were playing in the yard, running and jumping, trying to catch blinking fireflies, Lonnie softly chuckled as he told Myrtle what had happened that afternoon. Shaking his head, he laughed, "Kids will sure be kids."

8

Bountiful Harvest ♥

Life was simple but tough in the rural Missouri hills. Everything used by the family was saved and reused whenever possible. Every container, every scrap of metal, every bit of twine and wire had a purpose. The few material goods the family owned were used over and over again. Nothing went to waste. In order to survive the harsh and bitter cold winters, they had to prepare for it beforehand. The preparation was hard work and took most of the spring and summer months.

Myrtle oversaw the cleaning, cooking, and sewing while making sure her family's essential needs were met. She raised chickens, cultivated large gardens, and supervised the preservation of the family's food. Although Myrtle was less than five feet tall, she was strong as a horse and worked hour by daily hour beside her man. Without complaint, she accomplished these giant tasks while baring and raising eleven children.

Lonnie believed it was "woman's work" to gather wood. So each of his daughters, once she became strong enough, would take her turn, among her sisters, to go out into the woods and drag fallen limbs back to the yard. With an ax, she would chop them into short lengths that would fit into the iron stoves used for cooking and heating.

Each morning, the children were rousted out of bed by daybreak. After wolfing down a hearty breakfast of biscuits, gravy, and side pork, out to the fields Lonnie and the "outside workers," both boys and girls, would go for a long day of plowing, planting, or the harvesting of corn and sorghum. Some of the bigger girls worked as hard as their brothers in the fields. Myrtle and the "inside workers," girls only, busied themselves with their household chores of cleaning, cooking, laundry, and mending clothes. And of course, as with all large families, there were always "young'uns" to watch over.

Lonnie built Myrtle raised garden beds out of native timber close to the back of the house. Stacking the logs three timbers high, Lonnie nailed metal brackets to the corners to form a rectangle box six foot long and four foot wide. He then filled these beds with fertile topsoil.

Myrtle planted an early garden of onions, lettuce, and radishes and a score of different herbs in these beds. It took a pan full of lettuce and all the green onions that the little woman could carry in order to feed her family for one meal.

Later in the spring, Myrtle planted a large truck garden down close to the river. If Lonnie had owned a truck at this time, it would have been less back straining work to get the food out of the ground and up to the house. The family had to cross the winding, twisting branch three times to get down to the large garden. From this garden, Myrtle grew a large crop of corn, green beans, peas and tomatoes for canning, cucumbers and beets for pickling, cabbage to ferment, pumpkins, potatoes, turnips, carrots, and more cabbage to bury. Using the potato eyes, left over from the previous year's crop, Myrtle planted over two hundred pounds of potatoes and six to eight gallons of onion sets deep in the sandy soil. The produce that grew out of this garden kept Myrtle and her daughters busy for days canning, pickling, drying, and burying vegetables in order to preserve them. Bundles of onions, turnips, and carrots were tied around their stems, with a stout jute cord, and hung upside down in the attic.

One summer morning, before the hot sun was a quarter of the way up over the horizon, Myrtle sent Dick and Mayme to the truck garden to plow the cabbage rows. "Take Jude," she instructed the young girls. "That ole mule can pull the plow without much effort from you two. And mind what your doin' so you don't go disturbin' those new plants."

The two young girls headed toward the barn to harness Jude to the plow. Along about noon, Myrtle was fixing her family's dinner when she heard a commotion coming from outside.

"Myrtle, Myrtle. Where's the girls?" Myrtle's sister-in-law Anne, who lived about a half a mile away, was running toward the house. She was yelling and her arms were waving high in the air.

"Calm down. What in the world are you yelling about?" Myrtle questioned the younger woman standing in the yard.

Breathlessly, Anne asked again, "Where's Dick and Mayme?"

Trying to calm her distraught sister-in-law, Myrtle explained, "I sent them to the garden to plow the cabbage rows. Why?"

Anne was pointing her finger in the direction of the Big Niangua. "I was outside, tending the wash, when I heard a terrible ruckus coming from over there. Somebody was screaming and yelling. Are you sure they aren't in the river?"

Not waiting for Anne to finish, Myrtle took off running toward the garden and the river. Splashing through the water at the branch, she left poor Anne far behind. When Myrtle arrived at the garden, Jude was standing at the end of a row of upturned cabbage plants. The mule's sides were heaving in and out. His hide glistened with sweat. The two young girls were lying in the soft plowed dirt behind him.

"What in the world?" Myrtle asked, helping her girls to their feet.

Dusting the dirt off her dress, Dick explained to her mom. "There was a snake curled up under one of the cabbage plants. Jude got spooked and took off running. We pulled and pulled on the reins, but we couldn't stop him. Then we yelled, but he kept on running until he got to the end of the row. It was all me and Mayme could do to hang on."

"Well, as long as you two aren't hurt and only a few of the cabbages have been dug up, I suppose there's been no harm done," Myrtle told her daughters, helping them to their feet. Wiping their dirty faces with the hem of her apron, Myrtle continued, "Go ahead and reset those plants back in the ground then finish the plowing. Dinner's almost ready." Turning to Anne, who was just now arriving, Myrtle asked, "Would you like to stay and have something to eat? There's aplenty."

"No thanks. I have clothes boiling in the pot and need to get back home before they boil down to nothin'."

Waving goodbye to each other, the women left the girls to finish with the plowing, as they headed back to their respective homes.

To ensure her family would not go hungry before the next spring, Myrtle only felt secure when she had reached her goal of preparing a minimum of seventy-five quarts of each kind of vegetable. She would often trade with other women in the area, a jar of this for a jar of that, preparing for the lean winter season with relative abundance. The canned food trades made between these neighbor women made winter meals far more varied, nutritional, and was definitely a welcome change.

When the tomatoes had grown red on the vine, Myrtle and her girls were prepared for long hot days of canning. As boiling pots of water bubbled for scalding the tomatoes, water in a dark blue enamelware canner boiled right along with it. Myrtle only knew one method of canning, the hot-water bath. She claimed it was the only way to get a good seal.

Myrtle and her girls would start the day by bringing in bushel baskets of plump, ripe red tomatoes straight from the vine. Some of the plumpest, juiciest tomatoes never made it to the house for canning. The children would snatch a ripe one or two and bury it deep into the sand, in the cold water at the springhouse, to chill. They couldn't wait for that tomato to get ice cold. It was always the best tomato they ever ate in their whole life.

Taking the ruby fruits that made it to the kitchen, Myrtle would slip them one by one into the scalding water. Like magic, the skins would burst open and shrivel away, sending the succulent aroma of stewing tomatoes throughout the kitchen. Taking a slotted spoon, she would transfer the steaming fruit to a pan of cold water, sitting on a makeshift table nearby.

There, she would peel away the skins, sometimes letting the children help her if they didn't squeeze them too hard. While another batch was being scalded, she would dump the cooled, skinned tomatoes in a pan of cold water to chop them up. Scalding, peeling, chopping, scalding, peeling, chopping—just thinking about the work makes one think Myrtle needed about four more hands. When there was a sufficient quantity of cooled tomatoes, she would transfer them to a big pot on the stove. "Hurry, girls, the tomatoes are done boiling," exclaimed Myrtle. "We have to work fast so they don't turn to mush."

The girls used the wire tongs to dip and rinse the previously washed canning jars and lids in scalding water. Then they set them carefully on a tea towel lying on the kitchen table. Myrtle carried the heavy pot over to the table and, with a great grunt, placed the pot by the jars. Dipping a ladle in the boiling tomatoes, she filled the jar almost to the rim and threw in a pinch of salt. She held fast onto the jar as she mounted the flat to the mouth and screwed on the ring. Grabbing the jar by the cooler ring, and sliding it up through the folds of her apron skirt, she placed it into the canner. All of this had to be done with no dillydallying. Several jars would cook submerged for exactly twenty minutes. Out they came, steamy with the contents boiling like a witch's cauldron. These were set on kitchen towels where no drafts could hit them. Drafts could cool the contents of the jars too rapidly or worse break the seal. The children would listen quietly, waiting for the *pop-pop-pop* of a good seal while Myrtle had just enough time to swipe her sweaty forehead with the back of her forearm and rinse her burning hands in cool water before the next batch came out of the canner. "Now don't forget," Myrtle reminded her young daughters. "A hot water bath for a good seal and keep the jars out of drafts. Oh, and don't forget about the ripe, icy-cold treat waiting for you in the springhouse."

The children especially loved the cabbage. It could be chopped fresh, mixed with sugar, vinegar, and cream to make coleslaw. But the family's favorite was stewed, covered with salt and pepper, and served piping hot. Many mornings, Myrtle would prepare gravy to run over the top of sauerkraut for breakfast. "Now, that's good eatin'," claimed Mayme.

In order to make sauerkraut, the cabbage was shredded, placed in a fifteen-gallon crock, and heavily salted. Myrtle would put a plate on top of the cabbage inside the crock. Then she would place a heavy rock, on top of the plate for weight, to compress the cabbage as it fermented in its own juice. As the cabbage softened and the volume condensed, Myrtle continued to add shredded cabbage, salt it, and place the plate and rock back on top, until the crock was brimful of mouth-puckering, eye-watering sauerkraut.

The core of the cabbage head was not good for stewing and was too pithy to use in the slaw. Not wanting to waist any part of the plant, Myrtle submerged the stalk, down in the center of the stone crock, in the middle of the sauerkraut. After a couple of days, that stalk would be really sour and have a nice crunch. "Don't stir that kraut to try and find the stalk. Best to leave it alone," warned Myrtle.

Unable to resist the idea of a crunchy sour treat, Mayme and Ruby decided they wanted that stalk. So sneaking away from their mother's watchful eyes, they ran to the smokehouse. With dirty little fingers, they plunged their hands deep down in the stone jar full of fermented kraut. Arguments developed between the girls as to who deserved the largest hunk. The sound of the girls fighting soon reached Myrtle. Hearing the uproar, she went outside to investigate. She found her little girls with sour looks on their faces. She immediately knew they had disobeyed her. Marching the girls back into the house, she grabbed a rolled-up newspaper and walloped their butts good.

"Sauerkraut, yuk," commented Danielle, snarling up her cute little nose.

"Maybe you ought to try putting gravy on top of it," laughed her dad, Lonnie.

Rusty broke in, "Hey, don't forget the story about the cucumbers. When I was just a kid, that was one of my favorites."

"What do you mean 'just a kid'? You still are a kid. Okay, little brother, here goes," Donnis said, continuing with the story.

One summer, the weather was very good for gardening, and Myrtle had an extra bountiful garden. When time came to pickle the cucumbers and put them into economy jars, Myrtle realized there were more cucumbers than she could use. But true to her work ethic, for several days she arose early each morning and worked pickling and canning bread-and-butter pickles, lime pickles, kosher pickles, hot pickles, sweet pickles, and dill pickles until there were more than seventy-five quarts of pickles.

Near the end of one long day, she was hot and tired and up to her dill in pickles! She was sick and tired of canning! Thinking she was done, Myrtle sat down to rest. Arching her shoulders and aching back in anticipation of a relaxing moment, she stretched her legs and placed her feet under the kitchen table, only to discover a last bushel basket of bright, green, ripe cucumbers. "Blast it!" Glancing quickly to the left and quickly to the right to see if anyone was about, she grabbed the bushel basket, tucked it securely under her arm, and raced out the back door toward the spring. Making sure no one was around, Myrtle dumped the whole basket of cucumbers into the water. *There*, she said to herself as she brushed her hands together, turned, and walked back to the house.

Lonnie, coming home from town, spied something strange floating in the spring. Unfortunately for Myrtle, the cucumbers floated. He found his wife, standing at the stove fixing dinner, grinning like a Cheshire cat. Wagging his finger in front of her nose, and with a stern tone, he chastised his wife in their waste-not-want-not ways. "Butler, git those cucumbers out of that spring!"

"Butler" was an old man who lived down the river from the Moulders and was as deaf as a rock. When it appeared as though Myrtle was not paying attention, or if Lonnie felt she was being disrespectful, he would admonish her by calling her Butler.

Myrtle immediately spun around, ran out through the back door, and raced down to the spring. Wading into the water, she was able to retrieve every last one of those cucumbers. Wringing the water from her wet dress and brushing back her short brown hair, Myrtle chuckled, as she said to herself, *My, that's the coolest I've been all day.*

Once the canning jars and crocks were full, Myrtle buried the remainder of the root vegetables. A large cavity was dug in the hillside behind the house. Potatoes, cabbage, squash, pumpkins, turnips, and apples were buried in the ground for preservation. With the leaves left on, the plants were buried upside down, root pointing up, so they would not continue to grow and turn pithy. The produce was covered with broom straw and boards.

Myrtle had a certain order in which she wanted the vegetables placed. It never ceased to amaze the family that, after uncovering the hole, she could reach in to exactly the right depth and pull out whatever it was she was after. The remaining produce had to be covered back up very carefully to keep it from freezing.

9

Stolen Treats ♥

    Many berry bushes, grape vines, and fruit trees grew wild just a short distance from the house. Early each summer, the vibrant colors of red, blue, black, green, yellow, and orange beckoned the womenfolk to the blossoming, succulent gems of huckleberry, blueberry, blackberry, mulberry, sand plums, and purple plums, ripe and waiting to be plucked from the vine. Growing among the trees and fanning out over the hillside, the wild berry patches lent their color to the surrounding countryside.

    Myrtle looked forward to a time alone with her girls, enjoying their company, while hunting the fruit. Spotting a bush heavily laden with berries, Myrtle hollered out to her girls, "Let's start here!" Laying baby Fern on a quilt that had been spread out on the soft grass, Myrtle turned her attention to help Ruby and Mayme. They scoured the lower branches looking for berries that had fallen to the ground. Selecting a spot on the bush, where they would begin picking, Myrtle placed a big rock on the ground to pin point the starting place. The older girls Nera, Florence, and Dick had been berry picking with their mom many times before. So with practiced ease, they started going around the bush, reaching as high as their arms would allow. When one of the older girls spotted berries higher than she could reach, Nera, the smallest of the three, would come to the rescue. Florence and Dick turned to face each other, laced her fingers together forming a cradle, and bent toward the ground. Placing her hands on their shoulders for balance, Nera stepped with her left foot into Florence's cupped hands and her right foot into Dick's. One, two, three, up! Florence and Dick gave a mighty boost. Nera was then high enough to pick the cluster of berries. After the girls had made a complete circle around the bush and arrived back at the starting rock, they knew the bush had been picked clean of all berries and were ready to move on.

    Myrtle started up the next hill looking for another bush covered with berries. Dick kept a close eye on her mom. Just as Myrtle walked around a large blackberry bush, Dick popped a sweet juicy plum into her mouth. As she tried to close her gaping mouth around the plump fruit, she was hoping her mom didn't see what she had done. Walking back around the bush, Myrtle raised her apron and pretended to wipe her forehead. She was not surprised when she spotted a trickle of purple juice running down Dick's chin. Choking, she tried to keep a straight face, as she struggled, to swallow the stolen treat she had in her own mouth. Realizing they both had been caught at their playful secrets, they burst out laughing.

Soon the buckets were filled to the brim with ripe berries. While Florence and Dick continued to scour the bushes for any hidden fruit, Myrtle, taking Fern into her arms, joined Nera carrying the overflowing buckets back to the house. No one ever minded the berry-picking chore. It was a pleasant change from their daily household routine.

One day, while Myrtle and her older daughters were attending to household chores, Mayme and Ruby were sent to the garden to get a handful of green onions for supper. But right beside the garden was a mulberry tree. Its branches spread wide, shady, and strong. Lured by the thought of a sweet and yummy treat, Mayme and Ruby climbed that old mulberry tree. After satisfying their hunger, the girls located a sturdy branch to lean into, to daydream on the clouds they saw floating in and out, high above the leaves. Unfortunately that summer, poison ivy vines were growing rampant. There were vines everywhere, especially growing up the mulberry tree. Before long, both girls broke out with the hives. The red watery blisters popped up on their hands, arms, feet, thighs, and even on their stomachs. The girls, scratching and crying climbed back down to the ground and scurried into the house, hoping their mom could provide some relief. Of course, it didn't take much for Myrtle to know they had been playing instead of working. After telling them to strip down, Myrtle grabbed a bottle of calamine lotion. She gave them both a quick scolding as she daubed the pink liquid over their bright red bodies. Once the itch had eased, she sent them back out to the garden to get the onions for supper.

For several days during the early summer months, the Moulders had fresh blueberry, blackberry, and purple plums on their dinner table. Myrtle spent many days canning the fruit whole, in addition to making sweet jams and jellies. After storing away enough of the canned fruits and jellies to sustain her family until the next summer, Myrtle sold the rest to rafters floating down the river, tourist, and the town's people for fifteen cents a gallon. She would save the money she earned, in a jar above the kitchen stove, until she had enough to buy broadcloth material to make new clothes for her growing family.

The family never went without food. Hungry strangers were never turned away from the Moulder farm. Salesmen, tinkers, government agents, rafters, and even beggars were all welcomed. Myrtle would offer them food and a clean bed for the night. She would make an entry in her diary whenever a few extra dollars was made—"2—all night $1.40, 2 dinners—.70 cents."

10

Vacation ♥

"Was the only thing Mema's family did was work?" questioned my young niece Samantha. "Didn't they have any fun?"

"Sure they had lots of fun times," I told her. "I remember a story Aunt Mayme told me about a vacation they took to visit their grandparents, Fred and Mat, in Macks Creek."

"Wait a minute," Samantha interrupted. "I thought Myrtle's mom and dad lived in Coelleda. How did they get to Macks Creek?"

I took a moment to explain to Samantha and the rest of my family. "In the year 1908, just a few years after Myrtle and Lonnie were married, a man by the name of John S. Lea founded a store and post office approximately three-quarters of a mile southwest of Fred and Mat Gerhardt's property in Lower Prairie Holler. He called it New Coelleda. This competition invaded Fred and Mat's livelihood. So Fred sold his property at Coelleda to Lewis and Alice Coffey. They operated the little country store, until the Lake of the Ozarks was built, and the town disappeared beneath the waters.

"Fred and his wife Mat had moved from one small community to another trying to build a successful life for their family. Their last move was from Bannister Springs to Macks Creek, Missouri, where they remained and successfully ran a store and café, until their deaths."

"Okay, that explains it, now tell us about their vacation," Samantha said, stretching back down to lie on the floor.

I continued.

Sitting on the front porch in his big oak rocker, Lonnie was trying to catch a breath of cool air. Placing two of his fingers in front of his puckered lips, he let go with a stream of brown tobacco juice.

"Ma, how would you like to go visit your folks," he asked. "From what I read in the *Reveille*, the circus is coming to Macks Creek. The paper states they are plannin' on bein' set up July 4. Might be a good time to go see your kinfolk. The crops will be in the ground and not much left to do for a spell. Yep, might be a good time to take a little trip."

"That would be nice. I got a letter from Ma last week. She said they could put Nera up at their house. This damp air down here on the river is really aggravating her breathing. She's thirteen years old now and got her eighth grade school certificate this past spring. Maybe she could go on to high school in the fall like she wants," Myrtle remarked softly.

"We don't have money for such nonsense. The only reason a girl needs to go to high school is to get her self a man!" bellowed Lonnie. "She can git one right here on the river."

"But getting away from the river is sure to help her breathing, and she could work at Pa's store and help Ma with the café," coaxed Myrtle.

"Harrumph."

With that, Myrtle knew that this conversation had ended.

The following week was busy with a flurry of activity in and around the Happy Holler home. Myrtle baked cakes, pies, and bread, wrapping them carefully in dishtowels to keep them fresh. Nera remained inside, helping with the household chores and keeping an eye on the younger children while Myrtle and Florence went outside to start the laundry.

Down at the branch, an open fire pit had been dug in the dirt, and hot coals lay in the bottom. Over the bed of coals, an old iron kettle hung from a metal tripod. It didn't take long for the water in the kettle to start boiling. Using a metal dipper, Myrtle transferred some of the hot water into a smaller pot that was sitting off to one side. Then she added walnut hulls to the pot. Once the water turned dark brown, Myrtle immersed the clothes that had faded over time. She gave the clothes a quick stir with a stick and then left them to soak. Returning to the big kettle, she took a long pole and punched the clothes down into the water. When she felt the clothes were thoroughly soaked, she used the pole to raise one article of clothing at a time out of the water. Carefully, she carried each one of them to the edge of the branch where Florence was waiting with the washboard and a bar of lye soap. Up and down, across the ripples of metal that was fastened between two long blocks of wood, Florence scrubbed the clothes clean. After a good rinsing in the fresh clean water of the branch, Florence hung the wet clothes on the clothesline, a wire stretched loosely between to upright wooden poles.

After the majority of clothes had been washed, Myrtle turned her attention to the smaller pot. Retrieving the clothes from the dark brown water, she put them in the big iron kettle of hot water. Several swift punches with the stick, a time or two down the washboard, a quick rinse in the branch and the material was no longer faded, just a nice shade of brown. When the clothes had been washed and dried, Myrtle sorted the clothes that needed a button sewn on, a torn seam mended, or a patch applied to the worn-out elbows and knees and put them in her mending basket.

Florence took the rest of the clothes and sprinkled them down with fresh clean water. Rolling them into a tight ball, she placed them inside a wicker basket. Later that day, she heated up the heavy cast iron on top of the wood burner stove. Shaking the damp clothes from the basket, she pressed them until there were no wrinkles left.

Nera and Dick used the Sears and Roebuck catalog to find the latest fashions in clothing. Using patterns made from old newspapers, they cut broadcloth that had been purchased from the sale of berries into dress pieces. Many late hours were spent hand sewing the pieces of material together. Soon each of the girls had a brand-new outfit to wear to the big 'do'ins'.

Myrtle had finally convinced Lonnie that Nera's health would be much better if she got away from the damp air of the river. Their oldest daughter would remain in Macks Creek with Myrtle's parents. Using material from empty feed sacks, gingham print flour sacks, and the rubber from a discarded tire inner tube as elastic, Nera soon had made for herself two new dresses, a new white petticoat and under drawers. After she finished sewing her new clothes, she carefully pressed and packed them away in a small satchel bag. The week flew by with all the exciting activity of getting ready for the family's much-needed vacation.

Lonnie didn't want to take the chance of losing any of his livestock to a hungry cougar while he was away from the farm, so he bartered with a neighbor to oversee the daily chores of feeding the cows and chickens and slopping the hogs.

After the family had settled down for the night, ten-year-old Florence whispered to her older sister Nera. "I wish I could stay with you in Macks Creek. I just know I am going to grow up to be an old maid. There must be something in life that I'm going to miss by being stuck here on the river. Oh, how I wish I could be you."

"Hush now, Florence," Nera said in her gentle way. "Maybe you can come and stay when you get older, like me. Then you could go to high school too."

"Oh, Nera, you know how Dad feels about girls going to high school. He won't let me. I just know it! I will be stuck here forever!" cried Florence.

"We have a couple of years. I'm sure we can convince him."

"Girls, it's time to settle down," Myrtle called out softly. "We'll be leavin' early tomorrow mornin', and it's goin' be a long day. So stop talkin' and git to sleep."

"Okay. Goodnight," replied Florence and Nera in unison.

Cock-a-doodle-do! The old rooster welcomed the early morning. As the moon sank quickly in the west, the sun was just beginning to creep over the eastern horizon. The bright orange and purple hues, illuminating from the sun's first rays, gave an early warning that it would be a hot and sultry day.

Lonnie, Howard, and Ray were outside in the barn as the cock crowed a second time. They had the wagon packed with a box of clothes, farm tools for emergencies, and feed sacks with fresh oats for the mules. Howard and Ray were seeing to the last-minute adjustments of the load in the wagon box when a man, walking through the barnyard, called out to Lonnie.

"Mornin', neighbor. It's goin' be a scorcher today, ain't it." He had arrived early, so Lonnie could give him instructions necessary to oversee the farm and livestock.

In the house, Myrtle hurried with her morning duties. She woke her girls and went to the kitchen to start preparing a hearty breakfast. Florence helped Fern and Ruby with the buttons on their little dresses. Mayme and Dick scrambled into their everyday clothes and hurried out to the barn to milk the cows and feed the chickens, while Nera neatly made the beds and went to help her mom in the kitchen.

"Breakfast," Myrtle called to the men folk in the yard. "Mornin', neighbor. Care to come in for a bite to eat?" she asked.

"Nope. Thanks anyway but gotta go. Day's awastin'," he called back over his shoulder. With a wave of his hand, he walked out of the yard and down toward the riverbank.

After a quick splash of cold water from the washbasin placed inside the kitchen door, Lonnie and his sons joined the girls as they all sat down to eat. Myrtle put plates loaded with side pork, eggs, hot biscuits, and a huge bowl of cream gravy in the middle of the long table.

Once Myrtle was seated, everyone started speaking at once. Excitement was running rampant through the family. No one had been to a circus before. Would there be clowns and horses and lots of good food to eat at the circus? Would there be pretty girls and handsome young beaus there too?

"Okay, quiet! Eat your breakfast. We need to git movin' before it gits hot," Lonnie told his family. It was a fifteen-mile trip between the Happy Holler home and Macks Creek.

After they had finished with their breakfast, Myrtle packed a box lunch of cheese, soda crackers, leftover cold biscuits, slab pork, and an apple for everyone. Howard helped her lug the carton from the house and carefully placed it under the seat where it would be out of the direct sunlight.

Shortly after the sun had made its climb over the hillside, the entire family, freshly cleaned and pressed, began to climb into the wagon box. As each child got into the wagon, Lonnie inspected the way he or she was dressed and twisted each little ear to check for dirt. Ray tried to climb over the front seat and into the wagon box to avoid Lonnie's once over inspection.

"What's this, sodbuster?" Lonnie exclaimed. "Git back up to the house and wash behind those ears." Ray scurried to do as he was told.

Shortly after Ray returned to join the rest of the family, Howard climbed onto the wagon seat, picked up the reins, and clicked to the mules. "Giddy up."

Sitting on the wooden seat next to her son, Myrtle turned around and looked over her shoulder, double-checking the wagon box. She checked to make sure that the box of food, another box filled with clothes, the tools they may need if the wagon broke down, and of course the kids were all packed safely in the back of the wagon. Assured that everything was in order, Myrtle turned back around in her seat and started to relax. She let her mind wander daydreaming of the long-awaited visit she was going to have with her parents and friends.

In the secure broad bottom of the wagon, the children joked, laughed, and played with each other. Ray, being the younger brother, enjoyed aggravating his older sister Nera. After all, this would be the last chance he had to tease her, since she wouldn't be coming home with the family at the end of the week.

Chuckling, Rusty interrupted me, "You aren't implying that just because Uncle Ray was a younger brother, he was a pest, are you?"

"No, Rusty, I'm not. It's just that Ray and Nera were so close in age they each delighted in playing one-upmanship just to make the other hoot and howl. But deep down, they were going to miss each other in the years to come."

Dick sat quietly, her back resting on a pile of blankets, making a string quilt for her mother. A little sewing box that held a couple of spools of thread, pins, a pair of scissors, and a thimble lay close by her side. Ruby played with her homemade doll. The doll was made from a scrap of feed sack material. A walnut was used for the head. A pretty ribbon was tied under the walnut to hold it in place. The eyes, a mouth, and two little dots for the nose were drawn on the material. Short pieces of yarn were carefully sewn on the material for hair. It was a pretty little rag doll, and Ruby was taking extra special care of her. Fern, the youngest, was amusing herself by climbing over the outstretched legs of her brother and sisters. Mayme, forever the little momma, kept a close eye on her baby sister ready to leap toward her if needed. She was fearful Fern would tumble out onto the ground before she could grab her. Florence was lost in her own daydreams, with thoughts of being a fair maiden in some faraway land waiting on her Prince Charming to come and rescue her. Lonnie kept an even pace with the wagon as he rode on the back of his trusted horse, Nell. He was looking forward to catching up on the latest news, going to the dance, eating, and swapping stories with his friends. Everyone was in a festive mood.

The morning soon grew hot as the sun bared down on the family. Lonnie pulled the broad brim of his hat down lower on his brow to shield the brightness from his eyes. Heat waves were shimmering across the hilltops. The early morning breeze had stopped. Not a breath of air could be felt.

"How much farther?" Florence whined. "I'm hot and getting all dirty."

"When are we going to be there?" pleaded Dick.

After a few miles into their journey, Ray tumbled out of the wagon onto the ground. It felt good to stretch his legs as he ran through the meadow. Shortly there after, the other kids followed. As the mules trudged along, the children started looking for treasures.

"Hey, look at this! It's an Indian arrowhead," claimed one of the kids.

"But look what I found . . . a hair comb!" chimed in another.

"What's so great about that? I found an eagle's feather."

It didn't take long before the children were hot and tired of walking. One by one they climbed back into the wagon to marvel over their prize.

Myrtle looked up and saw the sun was directly overhead.

"Stop the wagon under that elm tree," she told Howard. The limbs of the big tree opened like a canopy to provide much-needed shade. A small stream with cool clear water ran close by. Climbing down from the wagon, Myrtle told Ray and Nera to get the food box from under the seat while she spread a blanket on the ground to serve as a table. "Florence," she said. "Take that stone jug and fetch fresh water out of the stream." The older girls helped their mom unpack the lunch things from its box, while Lonnie and Howard unhitched Jude and Red. Howard led the mules and Lonnie's horse to the stream. When the animals had drunk their fill and cooled off, Howard led them to the back of the wagon where the feedbox, full of fresh oats, was hanging.

After the family had eaten their lunch, Myrtle moved the blanket to the shade underneath the wagon. She took Fern, Ruby, and Mayme with her and stretched out for a short nap. They were soon lulled into a rest-filled sleep by the soft munching sounds the mules made as they ate. The older children were too excited to sleep until Lonnie insisted they lie down and be quiet anyway. It seemed as though they had just settled down when Lonnie yelled, "Time to pack up and get goin'." The mules were hitched up to the wagon as the family climbed back in the wagon box.

The hot sun was unrelenting, as it burned down on the traveling family. Soon everyone started to get irritable.

"Move over, it's hot."

"Get your leg off me."

"Hey, I didn't say you could have that. Give it back."

Complaints and whines of the children were coming regularly from the back of the wagon. Myrtle sighed to herself as she thought, *It won't help to quiet them. We're all hot and tired, but we'll be in Macks Creek soon.*

There was not a cloud in the sky. The mules were hot and sweaty and tired from pulling the wagon all morning.

"What in the devil was that?" exclaimed Lonnie, swinging his hat in front of him. Bees! They were swarming him and the sweaty mules!

"Kids, sit down back there. Nera, grab Fern and hold her tight," cried Myrtle.

Right before the spooked mules bolted, Howard shouted, "Hang on!"

The wagon jerked violently forward. All the children were thrown to the back of the box and landed in a big heap, legs and arms flailing. Their screams resounded in the heat of the day. Their hearts pounded in their throats as they struggled to untangle themselves. The noisy racket jolted the mules into even more of a frenzied action. The wagon careened down a steep hill. One of the wagon wheels hit a big rock. The wagon titled precariously on two wheels, threatening to tip over. Gasping, Myrtle grabbed the side of the seat. All the color had drained from her face, and the knuckles on her hand turned white. The only thing she could do was to hang on and pray. Howard's young muscles strained to rein in the frantic mules. Lonnie raced along side the runaway wagon, helplessly trying to talk to Howard and the mules at the same time. The scary ride lasted for several minutes, uphill and down before Howard got the mules under control. He continued to speak softly to the animals, while Myrtle talked quietly to her children in an effort to calm them down. A potentially disastrous outcome had been avoided because of Howard's masterful handling of the mules. Lonnie's heart swelled with pride at his young son's skill.

The sun was low over the western horizon when the family finally arrived in Macks Creek, tired and dusty but safe. Grandma Mat came outside to greet her oldest daughter. After giving Myrtle a warm hug, she helped the first kid out of the wagon. She gave him a gentle kiss on the cheek then reached up to help another kid out of the wagon. The lifting down and kissing ritual continued until she had all of her grandchildren out of the wagon. Running away from the wet kiss, they rushed into the store, where Grandpa Fred met them with a treat of candy.

The five-day stay with their grandparents had begun. Everyone was looking forward to a fun week and exciting anticipation of the circus coming.

11

The Circus ♥

In the 1920s, the circus led as America's number one source of entertainment. Brightly colored wagons, loaded with people, props, tents, and animals, slowly traveled across the United States performing under a Big Top tent in cities as well as the smallest of towns. One particular summer, the circus left Eldon, Missouri, heading to Macks Creek. Snaking across hills and valleys, the caravan traveled through Miller and Camden County. Drawn by teams of draft horses, the massive circus wagons could travel only fifteen to twenty miles per day.

Brightly decorated wagons doubled as homes for the performers as well as carrying large trunks filled with flashy costumes and props needed for the shows. Typical sleeping arrangements consisted of goose down mattresses kept tightly rolled up during the day, conserving space in the cramped interior of the wagon. The cook's wagon was loaded with pots, pans, kettles, and cast iron skillets hanging from the roof. You could always tell it was the cook's wagon coming because the noise arrived long before it did. The tailgate was lowered, held in place by metal chains on both sides, providing a much-needed worktable. A huge piece of canvas lay folded on a larger-than-normal flatbed wagon. When this material was stretched out and erected with wooden poles, it became the Big Top tent. A second flatbed wagon carried wooded bleachers with some assembling needed. Larger cages containing tigers, bears, and other exotic animals were fastened securely to wagon frames. Trainers followed close by to keep their animals calm. The elephants were too large to fit in cages so, entwining their trunks in the tail of the lead elephant, they swayed back and forth as they followed the parade of wagons.

People who lived in Macks Creek, Branch, and on Dry Ridge and Hack Ridge became excited when the local newspaper announced the circus was coming to town. Brightly colored posters, telling of the Big Top, wild animals, people flying through the air, and the unbelievable act of a human cannonball appeared on barns, fence post, and sides of buildings throughout the counties.

Every morning, local men folk gathered around the "liar's bench" in front of the Macks Creek café to talk about what livestock they had available to enter in the cattle, horse, sheep, and hog competition events. The women discussed with each other what they would be entering in the cooking competition. All the while, they secretly schemed on their own as to which one of their prize-winning recipes for jams, jellies, pies, or bread would end up as the judge's favorite. The children found it increasingly hard to keep their excitement in check so that they wouldn't overstep their discipline boundaries. The last thing they wanted was to be punished and not be able to attend to all the festivities.

Shortly after dawn, on the morning of July 3, loud shrill notes coming from a calliope announced the arrival of the circus. Lonnie, Myrtle, and their children hurried outside, joining the other spectators. They lined the hillside to watch the colorful and noisy procession of performers, brass bands, jugglers, and exotic animals come lumbering over the hill. The circus parade was one of the biggest and most anticipated events of the year.

Joeys, as circus clowns were called, dressed in big oversized shoes, brightly colored britches and juggling red, blue, and yellow balls, stopped in front of the Moulder children. As the clowns performed tumbling acts, the adults and older children laughed and cheered. Fern, held securely in her daddy's arms, giggled with glee. Little Ruby, frightened by their colorfully painted faces and wild hair, hid her face in the skirt of Myrtle's dress, peeking out through the folds. Once the clowns had passed, Ruby laughed out loud when she saw a man playing an organ grinder pass by. A small monkey, dressed in a red and green vest with a red top hat, sitting precariously on top of his little head, rode proudly on the organ grinder's shoulder, waving to the crowd of people.

The town council had predetermined the carnival would be set up in the field south of the newly built Highway 54. In order to reach that location, the parade had to cross an old sunken pole bridge. The bridge's maximum weight limit was that of a wagon and team of horses. An emergency council meeting was immediately called.

The mayor, voicing his concern, remarked, "I think the elephants, not to mention those massive wagons, are too heavy to cross the bridge."

"I agree," said the town's doctor. "I'm afraid that old bridge will crumble and fall in the river and maim someone, to say the least."

"And what in the world would we do without that bridge?" questioned the local banker. "The farmers coming into town would have to detour around until we got the funds to build a new one. That could take months or maybe even years. I vote NO! The wagons and elephants cannot cross the bridge."

It was a big concern for all the members of the council. The vote was unanimous. The circus caravan would not be allowed to cross the old bridge.

The driver of the lead wagon arrived at the water's edge. Climbing down from his seat, he carefully looked over the situation. The embankment in front of him was steep and rocky, the stream was low, and the bank on the other side was a gentle upward slope. Deciding they could do it, he climbed back on the wagon seat, clicked the reins, and called out, "Get along now! Easy does it!" The rest of the drivers followed his lead. Their faces turned beet red, as they pulled back on the reins, trying to steady the horses. "Whoa there. Slow now." The horses, almost sitting on the ground to keep from sliding down the bank, slowly pulled the wagons behind them. With the drivers carefully coaxing them forward, the horses and heavy wagons made it down the slope and across the stream without incident.

After the last wagon made its way safely across the stream, the elephants at a slow, steady, sure-footed pace made their way down the rocky bank and into the cool water. One of the lead elephants stopped to take a long drink. Then he filled his trunk. Turning to the crowd that had gathered on the bridge and was standing along the banks of the stream, he blew his trunk, spraying the onlookers. Squeals of laughter came from the crowd, as the elephants continued to spray the people and themselves.

Howard and Ray rushed on to follow the procession as it entered the empty field. To their amazement, the wagons were soon unloaded. The young men joined the workers, helping to attach guy wires to the huge piece of canvas. With the help of the elephants, the brothers used their strong young bodies to help raise the rigging. More workers were summoned to attach and secure the trapeze, aerial apparatus, and rope ladders. Using miles of rope and wire, the big top and all the props were soon secured. Howard then helped guide the horses, which were dragging the bleachers into the tent. Before long, the bleachers were standing upright around a large wooden ring lying on the ground in the middle of the tent.

While Howard and the "rowdies" were busy setting up the tent, Ray wandered to the center of the field to watch the animal trainers. He wondered, with immense interest, at how the trainer, using a chair and a bullwhip, was able to coax the big cats back into their cages. He noticed the trainer and animals had a mutual rapport for each other based on trust, respect, and affection. When Ray wondered to close to one of the cages holding the big cats, the trainer immediately stopped him. That's when he realized these cats were still wild animals. Even the trainer had to be very careful to keep them behind strong barricades when he wasn't working with them.

The next morning, Independence Day, the Moulder children were up and out of bed at daybreak. After they gobbled down their breakfast of johnnycakes, sorghum, and fried ham, they helped their mom and grandma put away the breakfast things and straightened their beds. They were anxious to be on their way to the circus, so after their chores were done, they tried to coax Myrtle into letting them go to the fair grounds by themselves. "There's too many rascals in town for you to go traipsing off by yourself. Just wait, we'll all go together."

Folks who lived in town, as well as in the outlying areas, were all excited about the circus. Mat, Myrtle's mom, was no different. She decided to close the café for the day. She helped prepare a box lunch with a round of cheddar cheese, crackers, fried chicken, baked ham, and a couple of fresh-baked cherry pies. Fred had left to go mind the store. With so many people in town, he hoped to cash in on some extra sales. Lonnie was soon out the front door and headed toward Main Street with hopes of getting reacquainted with some old friends he knew would be sitting on the liar's bench.

It was finally time for Myrtle and Mat to escort the children to the carnival. Picking up the box packed with food and grabbing an old quilt, the two women and eight children ventured out of the house for the short walk across the bridge. The noise of people shouting penetrated their ears as they came in view of the field. They were in awe of the big tents and numerous wagons now parked in what was once an empty field of bluegrass. Slowly, they continued to walk through the fairgrounds, taking in the sights.

It was difficult for them not to stare as they passed a very fat woman dressed in a bright pink outfit covered with ruffles and frills down to the tops of her long white stockings. She was walking next to a woman with a thick dark beard on her chin. The two strange-looking women were talking to a crowd of people, promising them great fun and lots of excitement. Continuing their walk down the midway, Myrtle nodded to a woman, standing over an open fire, stirring the contents of a big black kettle. The tantalizing aroma of brown beans, onions, and ham hocks rose from the steam. A dutch oven was on the ground beside her, and a big pan of fresh-baked corn bread was sitting on a makeshift table.

Next, they passed a wagon where the side had been pulled up to form a canopy over the opening. A young woman was sitting on a ledge dangling one leg over the side, while her other leg, bent at the knee, was in front of her. She was wearing a bright red blouse, slung low over her shoulders, exposing the tops of her firm young breasts. Her skirt, made from a large-flowered print material, draped around her tiny waist and fell to just below her knees. Her jet-black hair was pulled back behind her ears and held secure by a string of red flowers. Large gold hoops hung from her earlobes and strands of multicolored beads wrapped around her neck, hanging down low over her bosom. Every finger on both hands was adorned with gold or silver rings. Gray coal outlined her piercing black eyes, and her lips were painted red. Trinkets dangled from the ceiling of the wagon, sparkled in the sunlight while gaudy-looking vases of all shapes and sizes set on the ground.

"My goodness. What kind of lady is that?" asked young Florence.

"That ain't no lady. Now hurry on, young'uns," Mat said, rushing her grandchildren passed the gypsy woman.

At the end of the fairway, animals of all sizes were locked in cages or hobbled to stakes in the ground. "Pewy, they stink," commented Ruby, pinching her nose. A big pile of manure behind the last wagon had already started to attract flies.

Myrtle and her mother located an empty area far from where the animals were being kept. Spreading the quilt on the ground under a big oak tree, the two women made their selves comfortable to watch the activity as it was unfolding before them. All of a sudden, a little monkey dressed in a green vest came running into their midst, followed by the short squat man they had seen the day before. "Stop, I say. Stop!" he was yelling. Huffing and puffing, the man finally captured his runaway friend. "Pardon, ma'am," he said tipping his hat to Myrtle and Mat. "Don't mean to bother you none. I'll take my little friend, and we'll be on our way."

Downwind from where the animals were hobbled was a horse tank full of watermelons, floating in ice-cold water. A young man—dressed in a pair of red-and-yellow-striped britches, a green blousy shirt, and a straw hat sitting on top of his bright red hair—was calling to the fairgoers. He was trying to convince them to buy some of his melons.

Across the field from the carnival area, a long tent had been erected. Women were coming and going from inside the dark interior. "That must be where we're suppose to take our pies," Myrtle said. "Let's go look before Lonnie joins us, wanting something to eat."

It appeared as if a small city had sprung up overnight. Not only were there tents and wagons and animals, crowds of people were everywhere.

Independence Day was a time for remembering. The American flag, erected high on a flagpole, flapped in the morning breeze. Smaller flags were attached to nearby buildings and to every fence post as far as they could see. Lonnie had joined his family so they could all watch, listen, and pay respect to their country. While the adults listened respectfully to delegates from the State of Missouri deliver their patriotic speeches, the young ones, having been taught reverence and a deep respect for the flag, stood quietly by their parent's side. The speeches soon ended. The older children ran off to take in all the sights the carnival had to offer while Lonnie and Myrtle, taking the small children with them, found their designated spot under the big oak tree to lay down for their afternoon nap.

"Come one . . . Come all . . . The circus is about to begin!"

Lonnie, now awake, left the coolness of the shade to round up the older kids. He found Howard and Ray pitching horseshoes behind the big tent. He called out to Nera and Florence when he spotted them over by the merry-go-round. Myrtle, with the little ones in tow, joined her family. "Come on, let's go," called Lonnie.

Before entering the tent, they stopped by a concession stand where Lonnie bought each of the kids a small ice cream cone and Myrtle a cool cup of tart lemonade. With anticipated excitement, the Moulders entered the huge tent. It was dark and cool inside. The smell of canvas filled their nostrils. Finding seats on the bottom row of the bleachers, they were all mesmerized by the sights and sounds of so many people.

The crowd grew quiet. A man—dressed in a bright red jacket, gray pinstriped trousers and waving a black top hat—was strolling into the Big Top. He walked to the center of the ring, raised his hands high in the air, and shouted, "Ladies and gentlemen and children! Welcome to the circus!"

A big brass band started playing John Philip Sousa's "Stars and Stripes Forever." The audience stood, men and boys removed their hats, while the women and girls placed their hands over their hearts. A young man, riding on horseback, proudly carried the American flag around the interior of the tent.

A hush came over the crowd when two very pretty young women and one young man, standing on the backs of three white horses, came riding into the arena. Attached to the horse's bridles were red, yellow, blue, and green feathers. The riders were dressed in brightly colored fabrics, and the girls had plumes in their hair. For the next few minutes, they thrilled the crowd with their trick riding. The end of the act came when the riders made a human tower on the backs of two horses trotting around the ring. The male rider stood, placing one foot on each of the two horses. Once he obtained his balance, the girls, one on each side of him, put her foot on his hipbone. Holding on to his hand, they stretched their other leg high in the air to form a V. Loud applause erupted as the riders rode out of the arena.

Just then, three men, each carrying a three-legged stool, came running into the ring, while a fourth man rolled in a big metal hoop. After placing the stools and the hoop in their appropriate places around the ring, they quickly exited the tent. As the ringmaster was setting the hoop on fire, the men returned, this time rolling in the tiger cages.

A bullwhip snapped as the tigers were released from their cages. Shout of encouragement from the trainer had the wild animals jumping onto the stools to sit patiently as if they were common house cats. Another snap of the bullwhip sounded. This time, the trainer was coaxing the big cats, one at a time, to jump through the flaming hoop. Each time one of the cats jumped, ear-shattering applause rose from the crowd.

After the trainer had the tigers secured back in their cages, three clowns, dressed in bald wigs, big red noses, and comical masks painted on their face, came running into the center of the tent. Little black and white dogs, dressed in funny-looking hats and ruffled neck collars, followed them. One of the clowns performed tumbling acts while another one juggled red, green, and yellow balls. The third clown walked on his hands and played with the little dogs. A shrill whistle sounded. At the command, the dogs ran around and around the ring. When one of the clowns yelled, "Jump!" the little dogs took their turn jumping through a small hoop. The clowns finished their act with the dogs prancing and dancing, turning around and around on their hind legs. Ruby and Fern clapped with glee at the antics of the little dogs.

The ringmaster called out to the crowd, and all eyes turned upward. A young woman, her outfit all glitz and glimmer, was swinging on a bar suspended high above the floor. Gasps came from the wide-eyed crowd when she slipped backward, turned a flip, and then flew through the air. A man, swinging upside down from another bar, caught her and pulled her up to sit beside him. While the couple continued swinging high above the crowd, the spectators' attention was drawn to another young woman, also dressed in a glistening outfit, standing on a platform above them.

Everyone held his or her breath when she stepped off the platform onto a rope that was suspended high above the ground. Holding a bright red parasol for balance, she slowly walked to the middle of the rope and then stopped. Balancing on one foot, she teetered, swaying back and forth, before slowly continuing across the rope. As soon as she was standing safely on the second platform, loud applause exploded from the crowd.

"Hey, Ray, did you see those pretty girls?" Howard whispered.

"Sure did. Weren't they somethin'," winked Ray.

"Boys, mind your manners," scolded their mom.

Next, high above them, a young man took a unicycle and placed it carefully on a wire that stretched from one side of the tent to the other. Climbing onto the seat, and holding tight to a long pole to keep his balance, he started peddling. To the amazement of the crowd, he slowly peddled his way across the wire, turned, and peddled back to the safety of the platform.

As promised, a huge cannon was rolled into the center of the ring. The ringmaster climbed up a tall ladder, thanked everyone for coming, and then slid backward into the mouth of the cannon. One of the clowns took a flare and lit the wick. Quickly, he turned, bent down, and placed his hands over his ears. *Varooom!* An ear-shattering explosion resounded from the cannon as the ringmaster flew threw the air. The crowd cheered and yelled with excitement when he landed safely in a net strung across the backside of the big tent.

Before anyone was ready, the circus was over. What a great time they all had.

When the Moulders walked from the cool dark interior of the circus tent into the bright hot sunshine, they heard the tinkling sound of the merry-go-round. It was warming up, preparing for the onslaught of children. Myrtle gave her family permission to go to the carnival with strict orders to be careful. Off they ran in every direction. Dick and Mayme, holding secure to the dime their daddy had given them, rushed toward the swings and pony rides. Florence took Ruby and Fern to ride the merry-go-round, while Nera, staying close to her mom, headed to the tent where the food judging was just beginning. Howard and Ray left their parents, hoping to finish their game of horseshoes.

"Don't be long," Lonnie called to his children. "Your ma will be sittin' out supper soon. There's the dance tonight, and you'll wanna be ready to kick up your heels."

Early that evening, as the sun was starting its descent in the western sky, Grandpa Fred closed the store, crossing the field to join his family under the big oak tree where the adults then enjoyed an uninterrupted picnic. After Lonnie took a long cool drink of apple cider from a gallon crock jug, a long slow belch came from deep down in his throat. Then he stretched his legs out before leaning his heavy bulk against the tree trunk. His blue eyes twinkled as he watched his little wife.

When the supper things had been put away, Myrtle stood up on her tiptoes to search the mingling crowd for her children. Unable to locate them, she muttered, "Where do you suppose those young'uns are off to?"

"Oh, Ma, they're okay," Lonnie said convincingly. "Come sit by me and rest a spell before the dancing starts." Easing herself down on the ground beside her husband, Myrtle started to relaxed.

Together, they watched as three men, carrying guitars and a banjo, came walking over the hill. One of the men was about as round as he was tall. The second man was sporting a dark brown beard that reached to the middle of his chest. The last man was very tall and lanky. They were all bare foot; their feet dark and looked like worn leather. The three men made their way to a wooden platform. Carefully, they placed their musical instruments next to an overturned washtub that had a pole sticking out of the center. A taut wire was attached to the top of the pole and was threaded through a small hole in the bottom of the tub. A tall skinny man soon joined the group of musicians. He wore overalls, and on his head sat a well-worn straw hat, the brim bending low over his eyes. He had a corncob pipe clinched in his mouth. An empty crock jug was slung over his shoulder.

"This is going to be quite a hoedown," Lonnie told Myrtle with a little squeeze. "Are you gonna take a spin around the dance floor with me tonight like you used to?" he teased.

"Now, Lonnie, you know I have to watch the little ones. Besides, dancing with our girls will be more than you can handle in one evening," Myrtle giggled.

"We'll leave you young'uns to the night life. Me and Mat's gonna head on home. See you'ns in the morning," Grandpa Fred remarked, straining to get up from the ground.

When the musicians started to play, the Moulder children came running. The girls knew their dad was a dancer and a half and would enjoy taking turns spinning around the dance floor with him. Jig dancing, square dancing, Skip to My Lou, polka dancing, and waltzing were in store for the Moulders this evening.

The week passed all too soon, and it was now time to leave. Before the sun was up the next morning, the family said a tearful goodbye to Nera.

"You be good. Don't give your grandma any trouble," Lonnie told his oldest daughter. He turned away quickly before Nera noticed the catch in his voice and the tears that were starting to swim in his eyes.

Myrtle and Nera wiped away tears that were flowing freely down their cheeks as they gave each other a big hug. "I know you'll be okay now. The damp river air won't bother you anymore. You'll be safe here with Ma and Pa. God bless you, dear."

"Bye . . . bye . . ." called the children to Nera. Ray was acting very brave, but deep down he knew there was going to be a big void in his life without his older sister at home to pester and tease.

"Florence, I just know we can convince Daddy to let you come to Macks Creek in a couple of years. I just know we can," Nera promised, as she gave Florence a big tearful hug.

Lonnie and Myrtle safely tucked their tired children in the wagon box, along with the family's clothes, tools for the wagon, a boxed lunch of cold breakfast meats, cheese and slices of homemade bread, and oats for the mules.

Just as the sun was turning the eastern sky a soft shade of orange, Howard called to the mules, "Giddy up mules. Git on home now."

"Gosh, it sounds like they had a great time during their vacation," Suzanne said.

"I'm sure they did," I replied. "Mom's family was just like any other family in the backwoods. Even though they had to work extremely hard just to survive, they still managed to find time to have fun."

12

Life on the River ♥

Living by the Big Niangua River brought significant challenges to the family's very livelihood. Knowing the dangers the river sometimes presented, Myrtle wanted her children to be prepared for any dilemma that might arise. So with her gentle insistence, all of her children were instructed on the finer points of river navigation at a very early age. Learning to swim was their first order of business, right after learning to walk.

Adults and children worked long and hard during the week with seemingly endless chores of milking, threshing, housework, and other backbreaking labor to afford them with much free time. However, on those hot and sticky summer days, swimming in the river was exciting and a quick way to cool off.

One hot August afternoon, begging permission from their mother, the Moulder kids went swimming. Yelling to the neighbors up and down the river, "Last one in is a rotten egg!" kids came rushing to the water's edge from all directions to join in an afternoon of fun. Safely covered from head to toe by sturdy camisoles, bloomers, and long johns, the children stripped off their daily clothes, dumped them into a pile, and splashed into the river, innocent to the cares of the world.

Myrtle had decided to join her children. Bringing her small sewing basket, she sat in the shade provided by the tree limbs hanging over the water's edge. While her young children and their friends played in the water, Myrtle watched attentively. Silent and almost subconsciously, she would continually count the bobbing heads in the water. It never mattered whom the head belonged to as long as she counted enough. All the children felt safe under the watchful eye of Myrtle.

After an hour passed, Myrtle called out to Florence. Hearing her mother's summons, Florence immediately left the water and came to sit down by her mom. "Dear, it's time for me to go back up to the house and start supper. Mind the children while I'm gone." When there were no parents around, the oldest child present was given the strict responsibility of watching out for the others. This authority was never questioned out loud. There was no argument. In that day and age, one was never heard to say to another, "You're not the boss!" The younger ones were instructed to obey, just like they would if their mom or dad had spoken.

Florence, only a young teenager, had been given the responsibility of watching over the children while they played in the river. Taking her adult responsibility very seriously, she stood on the bank and watched as the water churned and bubbled with laughing and noisy children. She watched Ruby run to join her cousin Gaynel riding down the river on a log. Gaynel's daddy had cut down a big sycamore tree, and using about five foot of the trunk, he cut out a shallow indention along the top that resembled a saddle. The indention had been sanded smooth to remove all the small slivers. He nailed two strips of wood, one to each side of the log, to be used as footrests. Using her weight to navigate through the water, Gaynel moved the log close enough for Ruby to hop on. Sitting astraddle the big log, Ruby grabbed Gaynel around the middle and remarked, "We got too much water at our end of the river. You're lucky. You have just the Little Niangua." The little girls screamed with laughter when the current caught them, and they were whisked down the river at a breathtaking speed.

Florence sat on the bank watching the children play and splash around in the water. They were all having a good time when suddenly, Florence noticed Mayme's head disappearing, reappearing, and disappearing again, looking like a fishing bobber with a whopper on the hook. Her arms were flailing about like a bird preparing to take flight. Mayme, trying to get to shallow water, had stepped in a hole and went under. Frightened, she was unable to obtain her footing. Florence immediately rushed over to her younger sister and with one quick yank; she had her up and out of the water. Tucking Mayme safely under one arm, Florence helped her little sister to the shallow water.

After she was assured that Mayme was okay, Florence once again took vigil of the action in the water. She watched as Ray climbed to the top of a huge tree growing out of the bank. Grabbing a rope that was hanging from one of the big limbs, he pushed himself off. Swinging out over the water, he let go and dropped down, making a big splash. Swimming to the shore, he climbed out and headed back to the tree. When he got to the top, Dick was standing there holding the end of the rope, hesitating to swing out. So Ray pushed her. Dick managed to hang on for dear life until she was safely away from the tree. Then splash, down she went into the cold water. Landing on her back, she quickly disappeared. Dick kicked her legs hard and fast as she struggled to reach the surface. As soon as her head broke through, she spit out a mouthful of water and started to cough. By this time, the rope had swung back to the tree. Ray grabbed hold of it, jumped, and swung out over the water. Not realizing Dick was still below him, struggling to get her breath, he let go. Barely missing his sister, Ray surfaced and swam to shore. Florence was standing there, waiting for him. With hands on her hips and knitted eyebrows, she ordered, "Ray, you know better than to push someone in the water. You could have caused poor Dick to drown. And then, to make matters worse, you didn't pay attention to what was below you. You almost jumped right on top of the poor girl. Now, get out of the water. You're done swimming for awhile."

The children knew they had to be mindful to the ever-present dangers of the river. Safety came along with the fun. Their mother, Myrtle, was especially diligent in making them listen to authority. As her children learned, at a much-later date, their little mother could not swim a stroke.

"That reminds me of our own mother sitting on the banks of that same Little Niangua River, watching us swim when we were kids," commented Phyllis. "I'm sure the river was a constant worry for her, just as it was for Grandma. Don't you imagine that when the hot days of summer was over and the cool weather returned in the fall it was just one less thing that Myrtle and Mom had to worry about?" she asked.

"Speaking of fall," I continued, "Aunt Ruby told me that one year, it had been an exceptionally rainy fall season. On this particular day, rain continued to fall in a steady downpour.

Looking out the schoolhouse window, Ruby couldn't help but wonder how she and Mayme were going to get back across the river. By mid afternoon, the rain stopped, leaving dark gray clouds hanging low in the sky, threatening to open up again at any time. In their rush to get home, the sisters took a shortcut across Bessie Long's field. Soon they reached the river. As suspected, the current was strong and treacherous. The river had risen to flood stage; water was running over the banks and into the fields. Racing hearts beating in their chest, the girls looked up and down the river, searching for a good place to cross. A feeling of relief flooded through them when they saw Howard, standing on the opposite bank of the river. He was holding Nell and Molly by their harnesses.

Cupping his hands around his mouth, Howard yelled above the noise of the river, "Mayme, whistle for Nell. She'll come to you."

Puckering up her lips, Mayme let go of a loud shrill whistle. Nell's ears stood straight up. She was a mature horse and knew what was expected of her. She had crossed this river many times before. Responding to the command, Nell moved into the fast-moving water. Molly followed close by her side. Mayme and Ruby held their breath as they watched the big horse and little mule swim toward them. Reaching the other side, the animals had to trudge through mud to reach the girls.

"Good girls," Mayme said, patting the animal's necks.

Grabbing the halter, Mayme climbed onto the back of Nell, while Ruby used Molly's mane to pull herself up to sit astraddle the little mule. Mayme looked back across the river toward her brother. She was looking for reassurance that only he could offer. Once again, Howard cupped his hands around his mouth and yelled.

"Mayme, put Nell in first and let her lead. She will break the current for Molly."

Trusting her older brother's instructions, Mayme coaxed Nell back into the fast-flowing river, Molly following close to the flanks of the older horse. Hanging on tight, the girls could feel Nell and Molly's strong muscles constrict and then release as they began to swim. Several minutes passed before the animals found their footing in the soft mud on the washed-out riverbank. Howard ran to join his sisters. Leaping up on the horse behind Mayme, they all hurried back to the house before being caught in another downpour, should the clouds again open up, drenching the already-soaked region.

"Wow," Phyllis said. "Howard to the rescue again. What would Grandma and Grandpa have done without him?" she questioned.

"According to all our aunts," Donnis said, "Howard was a big help to Grandma when it came to caring for his younger siblings. He was no doubt a good guardian to those youngsters."

"He was also a huge help to his dad when it came to providing for the family. Like when they made molasses," I explained.

"What's molasses?" asked Matthew, crawling off his dad's knee to join his sisters Katie and Emily on the floor.

13

Molasses ♥

Winter was sending serious messages that a long cold spell was on its way. Coming into the house to get warm by the potbelly stove, Lonnie declared to his family that it was molasses-making time. He had been to the molasses patch behind the house and saw that the tops of the stalks were starting to turn brown. They needed to get the sugar cane harvested soon, or the sugar content in the sap would be useless.

Molasses is a thick syrupy liquid that is produced when the water content from the juice of sugar cane is boiled away. The savory sweetness of the all-natural molasses gives moistness and a delicate caramel aroma to cookies, pies, and brown breads. Molasses was a mainstay sweetener for the Moulders since white sugar was too expensive for everyday use.

The next few days were filled with hard work for the whole family. Lonnie spent the mornings cutting and splitting wood. Then Dick and Mayme placed it in a pile four feet high and three logs deep. After they finished stacking the wood, Lonnie and the girls carried a big metal pan out of the barn. The pan was six feet long, thirty inches wide, and six inches deep. Six-inch-high metal strips ran down the length of the pan, making five individual troughs. Each trough had a small opening cut in the end. A spigot, attached through a small hole, was on the outside of the pan. After a good cleaning with hot water, Lonnie lifted the pan onto a rock furnace. The furnace was a rectangular box constructed out of flat rocks cemented together. It was four feet tall and had a heavy metal grate lying on the top. There was a small opening in one end. A metal door was securely fastened by a set of hinges on one side and a metal latch on the other.

Howard and Ray carried an iron shaft out of the barn and set it on top of an old tree stump. The stump was approximately three feet in diameter and stood about three and a half feet tall. Next they rolled a large wooden wheel out of the barn. With a loud grunt, they lifted the wheel and set it on top of the shaft. Using a sledgehammer, Ray pounded steel stakes into the wood, making sure the hub of the wheel was securely fastened.

While Lonnie and his sons were outside setting up the boiling pan and getting the grinder ready, Myrtle and her daughters stayed inside the house, readying things that would be needed. Using strong lye soap, Florence cleaned the washtubs and all the empty glass containers her mom had. After the jars had been washed, Florence used a pair of tongs to submerge them into a kettle of scalding water. When a few minutes had passed, she lifted each jar back out of the water. Being careful not to touch the rims, she turned them upside down on a dishtowel to dry. Myrtle washed her old dishtowels and hung them up to dry behind the stove, all the while keeping a close eye on Ruby, Fern, and the new baby, Letha Beryl, born July 1, 1922.

The next morning dawned cold and crisp. The night before, Lonnie had told his children they would have to stay home from school the next few days until the molasses was made. Even at a young age, the children knew the importance of helping their dad with the hard work. They also knew what wasn't kept for the families own use would be sold to neighbors or the mercantile in Linn Creek and people that were traveling through. The money would help pay for certain necessities the family would need to make it through the winter.

There was a hint of snow in the air as Lonnie headed to the barn to hitch up the mules. A winter chill made him button up his overcoat and pull the carflaps, attached to his woolen hat, down low over his ears. The sun was just coming over the hilltops when Lonnie led Jack and Raleigh out of a warm stall and into the barnyard, where he hitched them to the wagon. Going back into the barn, Lonnie grabbed several pairs of rough leather gloves. He knew handling the stiff leaves of the sugar cane would cut his children's tender hands if they didn't wear the shucking gloves. Tossing them into the back of the wagon, he climbed onto the seat and snapped the reins. Driving the team of mules around to the back of the house, Lonnie saw Howard and Ray waiting for him at the end of the long rows of cane.

The combination of the hot sun that summer and the damp soil aided the cane in growing over six feet tall and bigger than two inches in diameter. Using a cane knife, similar to a machete, the blade twenty-four inches long and slightly curved, Lonnie and Howard cut down the tall stalks, leaving the staub (stalk) five to six inches tall in the ground to produce next years crop. Ray followed close behind his dad and brother, bundling several of the cut stalks under his arm. When he could carry no more, he returned to the wagon where Dick and Mayme were waiting. Dropping the cane on the ground, he returned to the field to collect more.

Lonnie was known as the best molasses maker in the county. "Make sure you git all the 'feathers' off," Lonnie called to his daughters. "We don't want the molasses dark or bitter." Dick and Mayme pulled on the shucking gloves and started the tedious task of pulling the blades or "feathers" from the cane. When the wagon box was full of the stripped cane, Ray climbed up onto the wagon seat. Waiting patiently for his sisters to climb on the backs of the mules, he slowly drove the team and wagon back to the barn.

Myrtle was watching for her family to return to the house from the molasses patch. When she saw Ray and the girls, she called out the back door, "Girls, dinner is ready. Come on in and wash up. Ray, go get your dad and Howard. Tell them it's time to eat."

Before Lonnie came in for dinner, he started a fire in the rock oven. He knew exactly how hot to make it and that it needed to burn slow and even, or the molasses would scorch. When the fire was burning to Lonnie's satisfaction, he shut and latched the small metal door, controlling the heat inside the furnace.

After a hearty dinner, Lonnie left the house and headed toward the wagon full of sugar cane. Howard was already there, tethering the mules to the wooden wheel. With a giddy up, the mules plodded around and around. Inside the shaft were two iron cylinders. They were laying one on top of the other. Fine grooves going around the circumference were cut into them. When the mules turned the wheel, a spindle attached to the cylinders would cause them to turn.

One by one, Lonnie fed the cane into an opening on one side of the shaft, where the rotating wringer stone would squeeze the sticky juice out of the cane, causing it to run down a small U-shaped funnel into a five-gallon barrel. After the juice had been extracted, the cane fiber would slide out another small hole. When the barrel was full of sticky juice, Ray and Howard carried it to the metal boiler pan. With a mighty heave, the boys poured the liquid into the rectangle pan where the juice would cook and bubble for about six hours. The hot liquid would rise in little mounds before exploding, sending out a sweet aroma into the air. As the water evaporated, the heavier liquid would snake through the individual troughs and slowly turn to molasses. Keeping vigil over the hot liquid, Lonnie used a special strainer made to skim off a green foamy substance of impurities that bubbled to the top. The strainer, made of wood, was a flat plate like scoop with a long handle attached. He would run the scoop under the foam and lift it away from the molasses. When the green substance turned yellow, and the bubbles began to look like frogeyes, the molasses was done. Lonnie would open the spigot and drain the molasses through a muslin dishtowel that was stretched tight over the top of a washtub and secured with clothespins. Hot and sticky, the strained molasses was then dipped out of the tub and poured into the sterilized mason jars. Lonnie knew molasses had to be canned while it was hot so it would not cool and harden.

Out of fifty gallons of juice, Lonnie would render only about seven gallons of molasses. After Lonnie's work was done for the day, Myrtle saw to it that the straining cloths were thoroughly washed, making them ready for when the whole process started over the next morning.

Just at dusk and just a bit before quitting time, Myrtle would appear with a few peeled apples and some fresh hot biscuits. It was a treat for everyone, who helped with making molasses, to dip the hot biscuits and peeled apples into the boiling pan to sample the new season's fresh batch of molasses. Yummmmm!

"I've never tasted molasses before, but boy it sure sounds good," Matthew told his dad.

14

Winter Comes to the Holler ♥

Dad had been sitting on the couch listening to the stories when he suddenly spoke up. "You know," he said, "your mom once told me out of all the seasons, she liked winter best. She said after the trees had lost all their leaves, you could look out and see deep into the woods."

"Go on," I said, trying to coax him into telling us about when winter came to the holler.

"Git up, kids," Lonnie called to his children, waking them from a sound sleep. Shaking their big toe, he laughed, "It snowed last night, and everything outside's white. Looks like winter came early this year." Opening the door of the potbellied stove, he slid in another log. The popping, crackling fire soon had the little house nice and warm. "With it snowin' this early, I'm afraid it's gonna be a long hard winter. Howard, Ray, git out of bed. We need to git the stalls in the barn cleaned and filled with fresh straw. Flossie and her calf are gonna need a warm place to stay. "Git up, kids. We have a lot of work to do."

As the young boys slowly crawled out of bed, the girls jumped up and raced to the windows. The eastern sky was just turning a soft shade of orange, blue, and pink as the sun crept over the hills. Snow clung to the sides of the riverbanks and coated the overhanging tree limbs. A glistening brightness lay soft over the whole lower valley. Every tree and bush looked as though they were strung with diamonds and feathery white covers.

Running back to the warm side of the room, the girls hurriedly put on their woolen dresses. Before pulling on their heavy oxford shoes, they tucked the tops of their long cotton stockings underneath the leg opening of their long bloomers, securing them with a narrow piece of rubber. The boys, trying to wipe sleep out of their eyes, finally managed to pull on their flannel shirts and faded blue overalls over their long johns. Their thick woolen socks would help keep their feet warm inside their leather shoes.

"Settle down and eat," Myrtle said, spooning hot grits into bowls. "This hot cereal will keep your insides warm. It's going to be a cold walk to school."

After breakfast, the youngsters put on their coats, mittens, and hats. They wrapped gunnysacks snuggly around their shoes to keep their feet dry. Bundled up so tight they could hardly move, the children ventured out into the cold morning. "Mind your sister," Myrtle called out before closing the door.

Ruby's friend Gaynel met them at the edge of the river. The best friends, locking arms with each other, trudged through the deep snow.

They hadn't gone far when Ruby yelled, "Bet I beat ya!"

Both girls raced off toward a big white snowdrift. Spreading their arms wide, they fell flat on their backs, sending plumes of snow glistening into the air. Slowly, they moved their arms up and down, then very carefully got up. They were standing side by side admiring two little snow angels in the soft white snow when Florence walked up behind them.

"My goodness! Would you just look at you two?" Florence scolded. Trying to brush the snow from her sister's coat, she exclaimed, "Oh my, your clothes are all wet. Might be the death of you yet. Mother is going to be so mad if you catch cold." Feeling no remorse for their act of defiance, Ruby and Gaynel raced off toward the little school.

The children were excited about the first snow. They knew that when the temperature dropped, the river would freeze over. The adventure of ice-skating and sledding down the snow-covered hills always brought a new source of entertainment to the holler. It was hard for the classroom of children to keep their minds on their studies. Daydreaming while looking out the window, the bright snow beckoned to them all. During noon recess, Ms. Woods[*] joined her students outside.

"It seems to have gotten a little warmer since this morning. Let's go for a walk," the teacher said. They hadn't gone far when they located fresh tracks, made by a small herd of deer, and followed them down the hill to the edge of a pond. "Careful now," she cautioned. "The ice only looks solid enough to hold you. Boys, I said stay back. Don't get so close!" The children skirted round the pond, admiring the crystals forming on top of the ice. Two of the older boys took off on a run, chasing a rabbit they had scared out of its nest. "Don't be tardy," Ms. Woods called after them. Soon, it was time to go back inside the warm schoolhouse and resume their studies. As the day wore on, the temperature continued to rise. By mid-afternoon, it was a little above freezing. Finally Ms. Woods dismissed her students from school and bid them all goodbye.

Florence and Dick stood on top of a hill looking down into the valley. The glare caused them to squint and have to shield their eyes with their hands. They were amazed at how bright the meadow looked, with fresh-

---

[*] Ms. Wood is a fictitious name.

fallen snow that had yet to be destroyed by kids throwing snowballs and building snowmen. Walking down the hill through a small cluster of trees, the girls marveled at how overhanging tree branches were encased in ice. Following rabbit tracks that crisscrossed the meadow, they soon reached the river. Both girls stopped walking and fell silent, their eyes wide, as they looked at the beautiful sight before them. The river had been transformed into a winter wonderland. Ice crystals hung low over the indentions of the banks, almost touching the ground. Iridescent colors of pink, blue, silver, and gold shone from them. "Look at that," Florence whispered to Dick. "We can actually walk under that ledge of ice." As their older sisters stood admiring the beauty around them, Ray, Mayme, and Ruby raced toward Morris's pond.

Stopping a few hundred yards from the pond, Ray yelled, "Come on, let's go!"

"No, we can't," cried Ruby. "Daddy told us not to go near the pond without permission."

"Oh, scaredy cat. It'll be okay. Just stay close to the edge."

Walking out on the ice, the children were careful to mind their brother and stay close to the edge where the water was still frozen. Slipping and sliding, falling on their backsides, standing back up, and sliding again. They were having the time of their life until . . . *CRACK!* Ray jerked his head toward the center of the pond.

"Get away from there, stupid! That ice isn't thick enough to hold you!" he shouted.

Jimmy,* a neighborhood boy, was in the center of the pond struggling to get away from the crack in the ice. *Craaaack! Splash!* Down he went into the icy cold water.

"Get back, all of you," Ray shouted. "Harold* get me that long stick over there. Now stay back." Ray lay flat on his belly as he crept toward Jimmy and the hole in the ice. Stretching as far as his fourteen-year-old body frame would allow, Ray extended the limb to the thrashing boy. "Grab hold," he yelled. His friend grabbed the branch and hung on as Ray tugged and pulled with all his might.

"Hurrah! You can do it," cheered Ruby.

"Yea!" squealed Mayme clapping her hands and jumping up and down. "Pull harder!" The children waited anxiously, watching Ray pull Jimmy out of the water and to safety.

Lonnie happened to be coming around the corner of the house just as the cold wet boys entered the yard. The girls ran to meet their dad, both talking at one time. "Hold on, hold on. What this all about?" Looking

---

* Harold and Jimmy are fictitious names.

directly at Ray, Lonnie questioned his young wet son. "You best speak up, boy." About that time, Myrtle came out of the house to see what all the commotion was about. "What in the world?" she exclaimed when she saw the kids.

"We were skating on Morris's pond," explained Ray. "I told them to stay close to the edge. But Jimmy got out too far and fell in. I had to pull him out."

"Oh my! Ray, that was a very brave thing to do," praised his mom.

"It was also a very stupid thing to do," admonished Lonnie.

"But I saved him," Ray countered.

"That's no excuse. You kids have been told time and again not to go near Morris's pond unless you git permission. Girls, git in the house, your ma will take care of you. Jimmy, Harold, git on home before you freeze to death. Ray, go change your clothes and meet me behind the woodshed."

"It's cold in here," Anetta commented.

"It's a hospital room. It's supposed to be cold," whispered Suzanne.

Anetta, who was taking her turn sitting with Mom, took Mom's hand into her own. Looking over the bed at her sister, she frowned, saying, "Mema's hand is cold. And so are her feet. You know how she hates to be cold. I'm going to get her some slippers." When she returned a few moments later, she was carrying a pair of soft cotton stockings. Gently, she slipped them on Mom's small feet. "There, Mema. That should help keep you warm."

While Anetta had been out of the room, Suzanne had located a thermal blanket in the closet. Spreading it gently over Mom's still body, she told her sister, "Your right. Mema doesn't like being cold. She never went anywhere without her blanket."

Tucking the blanket up around Mom's shoulders, both girls gently took her cold hands, placing them inside their own warm ones. Standing quietly beside their Mema, they each thought about the baby blankets Mom had lovingly made for each one of their own babies.

15

It Can't Be Done ♥

"Gee, living back then sure sounded like fun but a lot of hard work too," commented Samantha.

"It was," Dad told her. "But the Moulders were just like every other family that lived around them. They knew they all had to pitch in with the daily chores just to survive. Each of the children had a job to do. And it was done before playtime," he said. "You kiddies continue on. I'm gonna sit with Mommy for a while." He slowly stood up and walked out of the room.

"Let's back up just a few years," I said.

It wasn't long after Lonnie and Myrtle were married, rumors started to circulate through the Ozarks that a dam was going to be built across the Osage River causing the Big and Little Niangua rivers to flood. "That's a bunch of hogwash. It'll never happen," was the general consensus of the local people. But many miles away in Kansas City, Missouri, the idea of damming the Osage River was being studied. The enormous amount of water in Missouri and its potential for supplying electrical power to the southeastern part of the state was being noted. Big businesses had a vision of harnessing all this waterpower and putting the rivers to work for the citizens of southeastern Missouri.

When rumors finally turned to fact, Lonnie and his neighbors were shocked and not at all pleased. When the lake was filled, Linn Creek would be forty feet underwater. "It can't be done" was the cry heard echoing through the hills. Its citizens couldn't understand why their entire way of life had to be destroyed for people in other parts of the state.

In November 1924, as the lazy river continued its course past the Moulder home, Hydro-Electric Company bought the land between the three rivers. A few years later, the electric company sold their holdings and options on fifty thousand acres in Camden County to Union Electric of St. Louis, Missouri. Union Electric then offered a sale price to each landowner based on the size of his property. Unfortunately, the price offered was pretty low even for those days. Thousands of people lost their homes and farms. Some families made plans to move as faraway as Kansas

City and St. Louis to start their livelihood over. Uncle Elmore and Uncle Vander Moulder, along with other members of the Moulder and Gerhardt families, started packing their possessions for the move. Friends, finding jobs in other communities, were preparing to leave.

The Moulder farm was located less than four miles southwest of where the Niangua River merged into the Osage. Lonnie was going to have to move. The Ozark Hills had been his home for generations, and the thought of leaving was extremely disturbing. The river and surrounding woods provided for his family's well being. The abundance of fish swimming in the river had helped to feed his children. And with the money he made from selling animal furs, Lonnie was able to buy necessities his family could not reap from the land. So he resisted.

Moving to a large city was totally out of the question, while moving to a small town posed another problem. Not only how would he provide for his family, but also where in the world would he find a house large enough to move his wife and ten children?

After many months of dealing with sleepless nights, anguish, and a great deal of coercion, Lonnie finally agreed to sell his property. He knew he had no choice. His home and the land on which it stood were to be destroyed; the valleys between the Niangua River and the site of the dam to create the Lake of the Ozarks was going to be flooded. On July 11, 1925, before Will Easter, Lonnie and Myrtle optioned to the dam company at Linn Creek, Missouri.

"What happened to them?" Chandi questioned.

"Well," I said. "Lonnie and Myrtle stayed as long as they could, maintaining their day-to-day life. But always in the backs of their minds, they knew this valley would someday be flooded, forcing them to leave their beloved river."

16

Florence's Dream Comes True ♥

Now that Nera was living in Macks Creek, the duty of helping Myrtle with the daily chores fell on Florence's young shoulders. She soon acquired the nickname of Mother's Little Helper. Day after day, she worked beside her mom cooking, cleaning, washing stacks of dirty clothes, and keeping a close eye on her younger sisters. Her back would ache as she leaned over a tub full of hot water, scrubbing the family's clothes on a washboard. And after each meal, there was always a huge stack of dirty dishes waiting to be done. Her tender young hands turned red and chapped from the harsh lye soap. As she worked, she dreamed of leaving the river. She wanted a life that was rich in prosperity and wealth with no more piles of laundry, no more dirty dishes, and no more snotty little noses to wipe.

During the evenings, after all the supper things were done and the little ones tucked safely in their beds, Florence would escape to a quiet corner of the small house to read articles from the *Caper's Weekly* and the *Grit* newspapers. By the dim light of the coal oil lamp, she eagerly tore through any printed materials she could get her hands on. Through mail-order catalogs, the wonders of the urban department stores were introduced to the young girl. Florence wanted more than anything to be able to experience all the changes that were happening outside of her small world. She yearned to wear pretty dresses and nice shoes, silk stockings, and fancy hats. Florence knew in order to make her dreams come true, she would have to sway her dad into letting her continue her education. And in doing so, she would have to move away from home.

Lonnie was aware of Florence's yearnings. Every evening, he watched as she sat in the corner of the living room, pouring over the new catalogs that had come in the mail. However, he remained unyielding in his belief. An eighth-grade education was plenty of schooling for a girl. Not only that, but it would also cost twenty-five dollars in tuition, money Lonnie didn't have. Higher education for his children was simply not within his reach.

During the summer months, Nera came back to the holler to be with her family. Florence was excited to have her older sister home. She was eager to hear what it was like living in Macks Creek and attending high school. The two young girls lay awake late into the night, whispering and talking, trying to figure out how to convince their dad to let Florence go. No matter what they said or did, Lonnie remained steadfast in his belief about higher education. And besides, he already had one daughter away from the farm, and that was enough. Florence was needed at home to help her mother.

The summer passed quickly. All to soon, it was time for Nera to return to Macks Creek. With a big hug and quiet tears, she promised to do what she could to help her sister. Florence stood on the front porch watching her dad and Nera drive off in the wagon. She tried to squelch the mixed feelings that were welling up inside her. Oh, how she loved and missed her sister. How she yearned to be in that wagon going off to school. But her feelings of love and respect for her parents were stronger. She knew they needed her here at home to help care for the family.

As the months passed, Florence never gave up her dream of someday leaving the river. But knowing her dad was a proud, stubborn man, she realized that he knew what was best for her. And she respected him for that. She trusted his judgment. Someday though, when she was older, she would leave the river. Florence continued to study hard at the Arnoldt school. At the end of her eighth-grade year, she passed her state-offered test and received her eighth-grade school certificate.

After a year of watching his daughter scour through every book and magazine available to her and listening to her talk about someday going to the city, Lonnie finally relented.

"Florence," he called to his daughter one evening. "Your ma and me's been talkin'. After this years cannin' is done, you better get your things ready. I'll be taken you to Macks Creek before school commences in the fall."

Florence couldn't believe what she had just heard. Running over to where her dad was sitting, she knelt at his feet and hugged him tight. "Oh, Father," she cried. "I promise to study real hard and make you proud of me."

Taking his young girl by her shoulders, he looked deep into her eyes. With tears glistening in his own, he whispered, "I already am, daughter." Florence's dream of attending high school and moving from the holler was becoming a reality.

Dick, who was a beautiful seamstress, helped her sister with mending and sewing a few new articles of clothing Florence would be taking with her. The days flew by while young Florence continued with her daily chores. Before long, summer had arrived, and it was time to help with the canning.

"Child," Myrtle called softly to her daughter. "You are gonna be sorely missed around here." Florence looked over the kettle of stewing tomatoes at her mom. "You be good, mind your manners, and study real hard," Myrtle continued. "There's nothin' better than a good education."

"I promise," was all Florence could murmur.

"We better get back to work now. Don't want those tomatoes to get mushy."

Soon it was time for Florence to leave. She packed her Sunday dress, shoes, and the rest of her meager belongings in an old worn suitcase. After making sure her school certificate was safely tucked away in her purse, she climbed up onto the wagon seat beside her dad. Howard, Ray, Dick, Mayme, Ruby, Fern, and Beryl stood waving and shouting goodbye to their older sister. Standing on the porch, Myrtle held baby Thomas in her arms. "Giddy up," Lonnie called to the mules. Florence turned around in her seat. Her voice choked with tears as she called out, "Goodbye, Mother. I love all of you." Florence's dream was coming true. She was moving off the river and out of the Happy Holler home.

Hearing the good news that Lonnie had finally agreed to let Florence join her, Nera moved out of Grandma Mat's house. The two young women rented a room on the second floor in the home of Mr. and Mrs. Ralph Miller, a local Christian couple.

Along one wall, inside the small room, was a bed covered with a colorful homemade quilt. A small oval rope rug, made from braided old rags, lay on the floor. There was a dresser, with four small drawers, standing beside the bed. A porcelain pitcher and bowl, with two white towels, sat on top of the dresser. A small table, covered with a red checked tablecloth, stood beside the door. There were two chairs pushed underneath it. In the center of the table set a hot plate. White curtains, with little blue flowers embroidered across the lower edges, hung over the only window in the room. A cord, used to turn on a single white light bulb, hung down from the center of the ceiling.

To help pay for her living expenses, Florence located a job doing light housework in Dr. Moore's office building. When school started, she included janitorial work at the school to help pay her twenty-five-dollar tuition.

One Saturday a month, Lonnie would make the long trip to Macks Creek to bring goodies to his daughters. Florence would glance out the window at Dr. Moore's office, waiting and watching for her dad. When she finally saw the family wagon coming over the hill, she raced across the street to meet him.

"Hey, young'un, how ya been?" he asked, climbing down from the wagon seat. "Here you go, girl," he said, handing his daughter a bushel basket. As he turned back to the wagon to retrieve a large wicker basket, he heard his oldest daughter, Nera, join them. "Well now. You girls been a minded your teachers?" he asked, as the three of them walked across the street and into the rooming house.

Holding the door open leading into their little room, Florence asked, "What's in the box?"

"Did Mommy send a letter?" cried Nera.

"Hold on, girls. Let me sit a spell," Lonnie said, as he put the box on the table and lowered his big body into one of the chairs. "That's quite a climb up those steps."

Respectful of their dad's request, Nera and Florence sat quietly on the edge of the bed. Soon, a gleam shone in Lonnie's blue eyes. He beckoned to the girls. Jumping up, they raced across the room to see what was in the box. It was almost as exciting as opening their present on Christmas morning. They found a slab of smoked bacon wrapped in brown paper. There were jars of sauerkraut, vegetables from the garden, and canned chicken. A dozen eggs lay in the folds of a large red hanky. There were turnip greens and potatoes in the bushel basket. Lonnie held out a brown paper sack filled with fresh-baked cookies. But the most welcomed item of all was a letter from their mom, telling of all the news from back home.

Phyllis's daughter Chandi interrupted me, "That must have been so exciting for Florence and Nera. Nowadays, most kids are eighteen years old before they go away to school."

"I'm sure it was exciting. And probably a little scary too," I commented. "After all, Florence would have been only about thirteen years old during that time."

Donnis spoke up, "Grandma Myrtle kept a diary and would note everything that was taken to Nera and Florence while they attended school. One entry read, 'October 20, 1926, to the girls, ½ gal. molasses, ½ gal. kraut, 1 doz. eggs, ¼ bu. turnips.' Another entry said, 'November 7, 1926, shoulder of meat, peck of meal, 10 qts. of fruit.'"

After Donnis had finished talking, I continued . . .

In May of 1926, Nera graduated from Macks Creek High School and moved from the Millers home. That fall, she started teaching at Rag School in Prairie Holler, close to the Little Niangua River. Fulfilling the promise she had made to Florence a few years back, Nera used part of her wages to help her younger sister with the remainder of her school tuition.

After Nera moved back to Prairie Holler, Florence was unable to afford living at the Miller's home. So she moved into Flora Bonner's boardinghouse, where she was able to work for her board and keep. Florence enjoyed her independence as she matured into a beautiful young woman. She studied hard at school during the weekdays and took care of Mrs. Bonner's children after school and on Saturdays.

One Saturday morning, while Florence was sweeping the kitchen floor, she spotted a bright new penny lying under the table. She looked around as she bent over to pick it up. Mrs. Bonner was standing at the kitchen sink.

"Is this your penny?" Florence asked, holding out her hand.

"Why yes, dear, it is," replied Mrs. Bonner.

Lowering her eyes to the floor, Florence remarked, "I want to write to Mother, but I don't have the money for a postcard. May I borrow it?"

"Of course, you can."

Believing Mrs. Bonner had probably dropped the penny on the floor for her to find, Florence realized she already had more than money could buy. She was blessed with good friends, and she was happy!

After a long week of school and work, Florence was anxious for Saturday evenings. She looked forward to attending school events and Saturday evening socials. During her high school days, she had her choice of young suitors. But all the while, Florence never forgot her childhood dreams. She continued to study hard while she watched and waited for that special man who would come to town and whisk her away.

Florence graduated from Macks Creek High School in the spring of 1928. Relying once again on Nera for financial assistance, Florence moved to Boliver, Missouri, to study for her teaching degree.

17

Crane Holler ♥

A warm, balmy wind blowing from the south signaled spring was on its way. The trees in the dense woods, surrounding the Moulder's home, stretched toward the sky as if trying to reach the warm sunshine. Gentle breezes blew, sending dancing shadows through the leaves that were just unfolding from their buds to the soft green cushion of grass lying in the meadow below. Wild flowers added colors of red, yellow, blue, and pink hues to shades of green, as Mother Nature returned once again to the holler.

The young Moulder girls Mayme, Ruby, and Fern were also noticing the change of the seasons.

"Settle down and eat your breakfast," Myrtle scolded her young daughters. "It's almost time for you to leave for school."

Just then, Lonnie walked into the house. "Sure's gonna be a beauty of a day," he remarked. That's all it took. The three girls jumped up from the table and ran outside. They were excited to once again be able to romp and play in the new spring grass under the wide blue sky. Returning to the house—where Myrtle had just finished packing their lunch pails with leftover side pork, a hard-boiled egg, and a cold biscuit with plum jelly spread on it—they ran back outside and across the yard toward the riverbank.

"Don't tarry on your way home. You have chores to do before it gets dark," Myrtle called after them. "Mayme, make sure you get those young'uns home right away after school. Don't go losing track of time in the meadow."

"Okay, Momma," Mayme called over her shoulder.

After crossing the two rivers, the girls entered Crane Holler, a long cool meadow. The children had the range of several acres of woods and ponds where they came into intimate contact with the world of nature. Mayme cautioned her younger sisters to whisper, so they wouldn't disturb the serenity of the morning. The only sounds heard were an occasional *whip-whip-whip-poor-will* joined by the soft whistle of a quail. Softly echoing through the hills was the tapping noise of a redheaded woodpecker breaking the uniform tranquility. The girls walked deeper into the meadow. Passing a blackberry thicket, they heard a wild hen turkey's irate chatter. "Stay back," she seemed to be warning. Underneath the thicket, Ruby spotted a nest with three white turkey eggs lying in the center. Keeping a wide berth, the girls continued on their way to school.

The sun had climbed higher in the sky. Shadows on the ground were being chased away. The morning chill was gone, and the warmth from the sun soon had the girls removing their shoes and stockings, hiding them in an old tree stump until after school. The new soft grass tickled their feet as they ran and skipped through the meadow. A sneaky ole possum, hiding in a tall clump of grass, watched with beady little eyes as the noisy girls skipped passed him. Sitting on a lily pad floating in a pond was a big old bullfrog. Fern watched as air filled the frog's throat, causing his neck to expand like a balloon. *Burump, burrrump,* he croaked. Stretching his long legs, he jumped. Sailing through the air, the frog landed gracefully on another nearby lily pad. The cool darkness of the deep woods and the bright sun-filled valley beckoned to all creatures, enticing them to come out and witness nature at its best.

Ding, dong, ding, dong. Hearing the school bell ringing through the hills, Mayme called to her sisters "Hurry up, we're gonna be late." Running, the girls soon reached the little country school. Racing up the front steps two at a time, they quickly walked into the dim interior of the building, sliding into their assigned seats, just as the teacher Ms. Woods welcomed them.

"Good morning, children."

"Good morning, teacher," twenty small children called out in unison.

"Settle down now. I have some exciting news for you. At the end of the school year, we will be having a spelling bee," shared Ms. Woods.

This was very exciting news to the youngsters, especially to Ruby. She could spell any word that was given to her. She could even out spell the oldest kid in school.

The morning wore on, and it was soon time for lunch. Joining her friends, under a big shady elm tree, Mayme let her eyes wonder toward Crane Holler. A cold chill ran down her back as she remembered her momma's cautioning words that morning. "Don't go losin' track of time in the meadow," she had said.

I have to remember to get straight home. I don't want to be in the holler when the cranes come, Mayme told herself. After finishing her lunch, she jumped up, shaking the cold shiver away. The ill feeling was soon forgotten as she joined her friends in a game of baseball. Jimmy slid into home base, just as the teacher stepped out of the schoolhouse ringing the bell, signaling noon recess was over.

Walking single file, through the door of the one-room schoolhouse, the children quietly found the way back to their seats. Fern sat on the front row with the other first graders. Ruby and her best friend Gaynel, the only third graders, hurried back to their seats, while Mayme joined her friends in the back of the room. After Ms. Woods started the older kids on their studies of writing, arithmetic, and geography, she joined the little ones, listening as they read from their primary readers. Everyone tried hard to contain their excitement as their minds wondered, thinking about the fun they would have racing back to the meadow. The afternoon passed ever so slowly. Finally, the teacher dismissed another day of learning.

"Let's go!" The children raced to the door and leapt down the steps, pretending to jump on to the backs of their beautiful imaginary mounts.

Mayme joined the others on the back of her stick horse. "His name is Prince. Look at him prance and boy can he run," she squealed to her friends. In her imagination, Prince was a beautiful horse with a star on his forehead.

As the children entered the meadow, they skipped and frolicked in the warm spring sunshine. They chased imaginary rustlers, saved wagon trains, and fought Indians. They ran yelling, pointing their finger as if it were a gun. With a loud bang they called out, "You're dead, you gotta drop dead" until every kid in the meadow was facedown in the grass. Buck Jones, Tom Mix, nor Hop-a-Long Cassidy never had a thing on them. Riding their stick horses, Ruby and Gaynel chased a furry little gopher until it located an opening to an underground maze. A little boy crawled along on his knees, his face close to the ground, and his rump sticking up in the air. He inched along, stalking a soft shell turtle. A herd of cows leisurely chewed their cud, as they dozed in the afternoon sunshine, while a white tail deer ran and jumped with graceful leaps. Mayme laughed out loud when she saw two curious little ground squirrels scampering and frolicking with each other in the lower branches of a hickory tree. A red fox, with its furry tail held high, stopped just short of taking a nosedive into the ground while in hot pursuit of a rodent.

The children spent the afternoon dreaming away the remnants of a poor and hard life. Mayme was so caught up in the fun she was having, she failed to notice the sun as it slowly descended down the western sky.

A low rumble, far in the distance, could barely be heard. It was soft and soothing as though a spring thunderstorm was brewing. Mayme looked up, searching the blue sky for the ominous dark clouds that could be heralding in a spring rain. She was surprised to see the sun had sunk low behind the hill. Cold chills ran down her spine. Her heart began to pound. Fear swept over her when she looked out across the valley and noticed long shadows spreading dark fingers out across the meadow. Realizing it would soon be dark, Mayme frantically searched for her sisters. Failing to locate them right way, panic set in.

"Ruby, Fern, where are you?" Her voice cracked with fear.

"Here we are," Ruby answered.

Looking in the direction in which the voice had come, Mayme spotted her sisters on the other end of the valley. Struggling to take a deep breath, she yelled, "Ruby, Fern, run! We have to go. Now!" As Mayme ran toward her sisters, she was aware of every sound of nature that, earlier in the day, had been pure beauty but now seemed to make her young heart skip a beat. The welcoming call of the whip-poor-will had turned into a sorrowful moan. The boding cry of the tree toad and the dreary hooting of the screech owl made the little hairs on the back of her neck stand straight up. Finally, Mayme reached her sisters. Not hesitating, even one step, she yelled, "Come on. The cranes will be here soon."

The darkness of the deep woods was now a place of dread. However wide-awake and brave she had been when she entered Crane Holler that morning, Mayme was now inhaling witching influences, as she began to grow imaginative. The sun slid farther over the hillside. Shadows cast down by tall trees seemed to reach out to the frightened girls' every step. As the youngsters raced by a briar thicket, frightened birds rose from their roost. Panic penetrating from Mayme seeped into Fern and Ruby, making their legs pump higher causing their hearts to race, until it threaten to beat clean out of their chests. Tree limbs reached out as if to grab them. Small animals raced to find shelter among the grasses and cut banks. With a shiver, Mayme vaguely heard her momma's cautioning words echo through her memory, "Be far away from crane holler before it gets dark."

Spring had indeed arrived. And with it came the big blue heron cranes. The birds came from miles around to converge in the branches of tall sycamore trees surrounding the meadow. The stillness of the late afternoon grew deafening with the swishing sounds of large wings, flapping up and down. Dark shadows, silhouetting the birds, passed over the green grass, as an ear-shattering roar, coming from the moaning and screeching voices of the birds, penetrated the once-serene valley. Fearing the cranes were getting closer, Mayme looked back over her shoulder, just in time to see huge birds fly over the crest of the hill.

"Faster, run faster," cried the frightened young girl.

"They're here," cried Ruby. "I don't like that noise."

"Me neither," echoed Fern.

"Stop talking and run!" Mayme yelled to her sisters. Holding fast to Fern's hand, Mayme's feet hardly touched the ground as she nearly drug her little sister behind. All of a sudden, the sky turned a dark ebony color, as hundreds of the large birds flew over the hill. The noise intensified as the cranes circled lower and lower. The lower the birds got to the ground, the faster the girls ran.

"Wait for me," called Ruby, after her sisters.

"Hurry up!" Mayme replied. "We have ta get outta here before they come down and see us."

Just as Mayme, Ruby, and Fern reached the safe refuge of their own yard, the sky turned from pitch-black to a hazy pink hue. The huge cranes had finally come to rest in the trees. Myrtle was outside, waiting and watching for her young daughters. When the frightened little girls saw their mom, they ran straight into her welcoming arms.

Softly, she scolded her young daughter, "Mayme, you lost track of time, didn't you?"

"Yes, ma'am. But the meadow was so beautiful." Then sobbing, she added, "I didn't mean to be bad."

Myrtle's soft words had a soothing effect on her daughter. "I know. But you're safe now." Knowing her fear was punishment enough, Myrtle gently swatted Mayme on her backside and said, "Go on now and wash up. Supper is ready."

18

Treed Possum ♥

Hearing someone walk down the hall, we turned to look toward the door. In unison, we breathed a sigh of relief when Dad walked into the little waiting room instead of the nurse. He reassured us there was no change in Mom's condition.

"Is Mom alone?" I asked.

"No, Phyllis and Chandi are with her," Dad replied.

"Good." I stood up and walked over to look out the hospital window. It was now midmorning. The sun had climbed higher in the sky, and it was undoubtedly going to be a hot August day. Standing by the window overlooking the city of Wichita, I remembered so many times before standing at the hospital window, while Mom lay in bed. "What's it like outside?" she would ask. I would tell her whether it was warm or cool, if the wind was blowing, or if it was a calm day. Some days though, while she lay sleeping or just staring into nothing, I would stand quietly looking out the window praying to God, as I was doing right then.

"So far we have heard about Mema's brothers, sisters, and Mom, but we haven't heard much about her dad," remarked my nephew Lonnie, who had been named after Mom's dad. "Are there any stories there?" The younger Lonnie was about as exact match as you could get between grandpa and great-grandson. Broad shoulders, big round belly, bristly chin hairs growing on his plump cheeks and chin. He was almost a mirror image of Mom's dad, standing there in his blue-striped bib overalls.

"Sure there are," Donnis said.

"Well, what are you waiting for? Let's hear them."

Lonnie had a difficult time scratching out a living in the early 1900s. In the summertime, they would live off the land. He fished in the Niangua River, hunted raccoon, squirrel, possum, wild turkey, quail, and duck. He raised corn in the bottomland to feed his family as well as fodder for his cows. Early in the fall, Lonnie would hitch up the wagon for the drive to Linn Creek to buy staples, items they could not grow themselves. He would buy salt, baking powder, soda, and coffee with the meager few dollars

Myrtle had earned from selling eggs, berries, and molasses. But he would have to go in debt in order to get his children's shoes and coats, along with his gunpowder and shot. A man was as good as his word, so after a firm handshake and a promise to pay up in the spring, Lonnie returned home with his purchases.

To help supplement the family's meager income, Lonnie trapped all winter long collecting, stretching, and curing animal hides and pelts. He was always on the lookout for signs of beaver, muskrat, otter, and mink leading to burrows and dens in the riverbanks. When he located an animal's hideaway, a heavy cage was set into a cutout of the bank. To conceal the gray-colored metal, the cage was covered with mud. Hooking one end of a long chain to the trap and the other end to a sturdy overhanging tree trunk, the cage was secured to the riverbank. For bait, a piece of rotting meat would hang from a short piece of twine inside the cage. Then he propped the door open with a stick. When a varmint found its way inside the cage, slam! The door of the cage would come down, capturing the animal. The children were instructed to check the traps as they walked to and from school. Whenever they found a trapped animal, they were to holler out across the fields. It was amazing the distance a child's yell could carry and echo throughout the hills. It could certainly be heard a mile or two away.

While Lonnie was busy working around the farm, he would listen with an attentive ear in case something was found in one of the traps. He had told his children to grab the end of the chain and pull with a gentle tug. He warned them though to let go of it right quick if the chain tugged back! Lonnie knew, from the sound of their voices, where on the river they were and which trap had something in it. He would go directly to that trap to help the children capture the animal.

Lonnie also kept hound dogs, a coon dog, and a foxhound. Ole Slim was a coonhound. Making a certain yelping sound, Ole Slim would give chase until the coon found a sturdy tree. Up the trunk, to the safety of the branches higher than Ole Slim could jump, the coon would run. The expression for this chasing and treeing a raccoon is called *treed*. Lonnie claimed that he could tell by the sound of a dog's bark whether the dog was running after an animal or whether he had an animal treed. Not only could Lonnie identify the individual sound of a dog's bark, but he also said he could tell what animal his dog had up a tree by the sound his dog was making.

At the first sound of Ole Slim's barking, Lonnie tucked his ax in his bib overalls, grabbed his rifle, and chased out, running as fast as his bulk would take him, following the sound of the dog's voice through the woods. When the dog eventually treed the raccoon, Lonnie would rush over to the base of the tree. If the tree was small enough, he took his ax out of his bib and chopped it down. If the tree was too big, Lonnie would clamor up it, shake the limb so the animal would fall to the ground where the dog was waiting for the quick capturing chase. Lonnie trained Ole Slim to chase the animal, pin, and hold it down. He resisted shooting the animal since a bullet hole in the skin reduced its value. He would knock it in the head, killing it.

Ole Speedy, a foxhound, Lonnie's other hunting companion was appropriately named. She would chase a fox through the meadows until the wily old fox found a hole and darted down into it. Ole Speedy would stand watch until Lonnie arrived to make the capture. Using a barbed wire, he would stick one end inside the hole and gently twist it until one of the barbs became tangled in the fur. Tugging on the wire, Lonnie soon had the fox out of its hole.

Riding on horseback, it was all Lonnie could do to keep up with the dogs, as they ran through the woods and into the meadows. Lonnie had trained his dogs to case, capture, and then hold the animal until he could get to them. He didn't want the dogs to kill or do any other damage. Pelts with teeth marks were less valuable than pelts without holes. Otter, raccoon, and muskrat brought a lower price, usually a dollar for a prime pelt. He could get up to four dollars for a good beaver pelt. If Lonnie was fortunate enough to trap a fox or a mink, he knew its pelt would bring more money than several hundred of the others.

Lonnie would take his kill behind the house and deep in the woods. Nailing the front paws to an old walnut tree, he would use a sharp knife to cut through the skin around the animal's neck and down through the soft skin of its underbelly. Being very careful so as not to damage the pelt, he peeled the hide away from the animal, then tacked it down flat onto a board made of hewed oak. Using a metal scrapper, he scraped the hide clean. Then he cleaned all the entrails and fine membranes from inside the carcass. Removing the skinned animal from the tree, Lonnie put the meat in a barrel of water to be cleaned and salted for supper that evening.

Dad interrupted. "I remember one time sitting on the porch with your grandpa talking about his dogs. Lonnie bragged that he had his dogs so well trained, all he had to do was show Ole Slim and Ole Speedy a dry'n board, and away those dogs would run. He had boards for drying the pelts of raccoon, fox, and beaver. After a short amount of time, the dogs would come back home with a varmint clenched in their teeth, just the right size for the board. However, one day while Lonnie was out fishing, Myrtle carried her ironing board out to the porch. The dogs took one look at that board, took off on a dead run, and was never seen again." Dad's telling of grandpa's story had the younger children wide-eyed, wondering if that was true or was this just another "papa" story.

Donnis continued . . .

Early in the spring, after the rivers thawed, furrier agents could be seen rafting down the Osage and the Niangua rivers. Advertisements appeared in the *Reveille*, advertising furrier agents were setting up appointed buying times in Linn Creek. Furriers designed clothing for warmth from animal pelts. Beaver hides were commonly used for hats. Minks were used for collars, muffs, and coats while the full body of a fox, including head, paws, and tail were used by ladies of high society for garment accessories. They were willing to pay descent money for good pelts. And Lonnie was willing to sell to whomever offered the highest bid.

Winding down after a long day's work, Lonnie was relaxing in his rocker in front of the potbellied stove, a chaw of homegrown tobacco securely tucked in his cheek. He was reading the *Reveille* when he heard Ole Slim and Ole Speedy bark. "Mayme, Ruby, head on up the hill and get that possum." By the sound of their bark, Lonnie knew what animal his dogs had treed. Mayme, age twelve, and ten-year-old Ruby had been hunting with their dad enough times they knew how to shake an animal out of a tree.

Following the dog's bark, the girls located the treed possum. They shook the tree as hard as they could until the possum fell to the ground. Ole Slim, knowing his job, chased and pinned it down. Running to where the dog was holding the possum, the girls did just as their daddy had instructed them to do. After ordering Ole Slim to get back, Ruby laid a strong stick across the possum's neck. Straddling its head, she stood with one foot on each end of the stick. Mayme grabbed the possum's tail and jerked as hard as she could. The possum fell limp, sprawled on the ground. They were really proud and knew their daddy would be pleased. It took both girls, one on each side of the possum, to tote it back to the house. Each girl held onto the possum's tail, with one hand and with their other hand, secured the possum's hind legs, its head dragging and bumping along the ground.

About halfway back to the house, just big as can be, that ole possum decided to come alive! The girls had not been strong enough to break its neck; they had simply knocked it silly. The possum gasped, shook to clear its head, and then started to struggle, squirm, and fight attempting to free itself from its captors. Using its front claws to attach itself to Mayme's and Ruby's clothes, it clawed and climbed up the little girls, trying to get free. Startled, they went to screaming and carrying on. Throwing her hands in the air, Mayme yelled, "It's alive!" Ruby was so frightened she started jumping up and down. She jumped so hard, she peed her pants. The possum, groggy from its recent ordeal, drunkenly tried to stagger out of reach of the girls and the dogs. In a controlled panic, Mayme grabbed a big stick and with one fell swoop knocked the possum in the head and killed it. Unharmed but with dresses torn and muddy, the little girls dragged the possum's lifeless body back to the house. The dogs, following behind, kept vigilant watch over their charges, making sure the possum was really dead! Lonnie was very proud of his two daughters, and they were real proud of themselves also. They had got their first treed possum!

Lonnie cared for his dogs almost as if they were members of his family. He never neglected the well-being of his children, but even when there was a scarce supply of fresh meat for the dinner table, Lonnie always made sure there was enough leftover for his dogs. After all, if it weren't for Ole Slim and Ole Speedy, Lonnie would have been unable to provide for his family's well being.

19

Fishing ♥

Every family up and down the river was extremely poor. But very few families ever went hungry. Relying heavily on the woods and streams for food, most men would fish, shoot, trap, or catch animals to bring to the family's dinner table. On occasion, it wouldn't be unusual for the Moulders to share a big old raccoon for dinner. Myrtle could dress a coon with baked sweet potatoes, carrots, and onions as good as she could a Thanksgiving Day turkey. Most of the wild game the family used for food could be obtained only certain times of the years. But not fish. Living on the river, fish was in abundance, enabling Lonnie to put food on the table all year long. Lonnie and his sons fished many of the streams and rivers that ran through Camden County. They caught fish by using traps, trout lines, by noodling, and with gigs.

Each evening, if the rivers weren't frozen over, Lonnie and Ray would climb into the little johnboat to float down river checking their trout lines. Using the light from a coal oil lantern, they would check the fish lines that were hanging down into the water from low-hanging branches. If the line were hanging straight down and not moving, they would float on by. But if the line was moving in a circular motion or back and forth, they knew something had taken the bait. Rowing the boat closer, Lonnie would reach out to retrieve his catch. Re-baiting the hook with a glob of stink bait or blood bait, made from raw silage and animal blood, he would drop the hook back into the dark water with hopes of catching another big catfish.

In the spring, along about late May or early June, when the rainy seasons were over and the water had receded, potholes and eddies were formed in the riverbeds. Hoping to catch some of the fish that were in these holes, Ray would take his trap to the river. The young boy would place a few cornballs, made from corn kernels, corn flour, and water, into each trap before lowering it into the water. The fish would swim into the trap, through a large opening in a wire funnel to get the bait. Once inside, they were too large to get out through a smaller opening in the other end of the funnel and were trapped. Ray would check his traps every evening, releasing his catch for the day in the dammed-up portion of the branch. What fish the family didn't eat, travelers from all around would come to the Moulder farm to make a purchase.

Not only did Lonnie and his boys catch fish using traps and trout lines, they also noodled for them, which is fishing by hand. Lonnie would spot a cut bank along the river with some low-hanging limbs dipping into the water. This was usually a likely hiding place for female catfish to lay their eggs. He would slowly wade into the murky brown river until the water was up to his chest. Rolling up his sleeves, he would reach under the limbs and into the side of the bank. He wanted to noodle the female fish before she had a chance to fan out her tail and lay her catch of eggs. Once that happened, a male fish, which would be swimming close by, would chase her away. After he spawned (fertilize) the eggs, he would remain on guard, biting and fighting anything that got to close, including a human's hand. Big cats have upper and lower rims of little fine teeth resembling course sandpaper, which enables them to hold their prey. He would not gash nor hold and shake to tear. He would simply give you a very quick and hard snap pinch. It was never a serious bite, but it made an evident and very uncomfortable sore.

Hoping he wouldn't disturb a beaver's den or stir up an ornery muskrat, Lonnie felt around the interior of the hole looking for fish. Most of all though, he hoped his submerged hand wouldn't come into contact with a snapping turtle, just waiting for food to happen by. Quicker than the blink of an eye, a turtle could latch onto a finger and snap it right off. Once Lonnie was sure it was a fish he had grabbed, he quickly hooked his fingers through the gills and lifted it up and out of the water.

After receiving several nasty fish bites on his hand and forearm, Lonnie devised a better way to noodle the thirty-to-fifty-pound fish. He took an old cotton sock, wrapped it around a large gaff hook, and then attached it to the end of a stout wooden pole. Wading into the water, with a firm hand on the pole, he reached under the murky brown water and into the cut bank. When Lonnie felt a fish nosing around the sock, he would jerk up and outward to set the hook. This proved to be a very useful as well as a painless way to catch several pounds of large catfish.

For most of the year, the waters of the Niangua River ran rough and muddy. But on a cold, clear day, you could see down twelve to fourteen feet. One year, in late November, Lonnie called his cousin who lived about twelve miles away. "Hey, Foster," Lonnie said into the mouthpiece of the crank telephone. "The river's runnin' clear. I can pirt-n-near see clean to the bottom. Git that kid of yours and come on over, bring your gigs and don't forget your trammel net." A trammel is a fishnet with three layers;

the outer two are coarse mesh, and the loose inner layer is a fine mesh. When fish try to swim through the outer mesh, they become entrapped in the fine inner mesh. And Foster owned the only one in the whole county. "We can get some good fishin' in as long as the weather holds."

The next day, Foster and his son hitched up their horses to their wagon, put in some hay and corn, the gigs, a spear like pole with a sharp barbed hook, and most certainly, the trammel net. After arriving at the Moulder's late in the evening, they made plans to start out at dawn.

The next morning was cold and clear. Lonnie, Foster, and their boys got into Lonnie's boat and rowed down the Big Niangua to a shallow eddy just above the Old Arnold Mill Pond. After they strung the big trammel net across the narrow end of the eddy, Lonnie continued to row the boat into the pond, which was about twenty feet deep and full of fish. To drive the big fish out of the deep water and back up to the eddy, the men rattled their gigs on the gravel of the nearby banks. Before long, hundreds of red horse, buffalo, drum, carp, and bass were fenced in between the trammel net and the fishermen. Then the gigging set in. Lonnie was a master at gig fishing. It didn't matter how fast a fish swam by; Lonnie could pitch the gig and hit the fish right behind the head. After the boat was filled with fish, Lonnie rowed to shore, where they threw them out on the bank before going back for more. That morning, the four fishermen gigged about five hundred pounds of fish. "I think we've got enough! Let's go get that big catfish that's been hiding in deeper water," Lonnie suggested.

Reaching the deepest part of the pond, about thirty feet deep, Ray anchored the boat with a big rock. Cupping their hands around their eyes—Lonnie on one side, Foster on the other, and one boy on each end to help steady the boat—they leaned over the sides, until their faces were close to the water. They were looking for the old fish, stirring up mud as he swam on the bottom.

Suddenly, Ray hollered, "They're right under us!"

The fishermen quickly grabbed their gigs, throwing them straight down in the clear water. About every other throw they made, the gig handle came up with a big fish on the barbs. After a couple of hours, they had speared about two hundred pounds of blue cats. "We're gonna have to git the wagon down here to get all these fish back to the house," Lonnie told his cousin.

Leaving the boat, trammel net, and the boys at the river to guard their catch, the men walked back to the house. Returning with old Nell, pulling the wagon, the men soon had the wagon filled with fish. It took several trips to get them all back to the house.

Foster and his son stayed another night discussing the fish that got away. With each story, the fish grew bigger and bigger. With each swig of moonshine whiskey, the tale got funnier and funnier. Early the next morning, Lonnie's cousins headed home, taking with them as many fish as they could carry in their own wagon. Lonnie set the larger fish loose in a pooled area of water that ran from the springhouse while Myrtle canned and smoked the smaller fish.

A few days after the great fishing expedition, Bill King, the mail carrier, stopped by for a visit. Lonnie wanted to show Bill the whoppers he had caught and were now swimming in the pooled area of the branch. Impressed, and hankering for a good fish fry, King bought the largest of the fish. A week later, when the *Reveille* came in the mail, Lonnie's family was surprised to see a front-page picture of King, holding a humongous fish he had caught out of the Niangua!

Just as Donnis finished telling about the fishing trip, my nephew laughed. "Is that really true?" he asked.

"It sure is," she replied. "And there's a picture to prove it."

---

* Contains excerpts from the book, 'That's The Way It Was' by Buford Foster.

20

Christmas Program ♥

"Christmas time was much different during the early nineteen hundreds than it is nowadays," I said, as I returned to my place on the couch. "There were no bright city lights, busy department stores, or food banks to help feed the poor."

"Bummer," mumbled my three little nieces lying in the middle of the floor.

"That's right," I continued. "Each day was just like the day before. That is, until just before Christmas."

Thanksgiving was over, and Christmas was fast approaching. The first snowfall had come early, and everyone in the holler was in a festive mood. Young children, who were living along the riverbanks and in the woods, were anticipating the yearly visit from Santa Claus. They wondered if they had been good enough that year for St. Nick to visit them on Christmas Eve. And if they hadn't, was there enough days left before Christmas to make amends? The Moulder children were no different. Ruby was concerned about the time she threw a rock and broke out one of Fern's front teeth. Had Santa forgot how Fern ran to their mom with a bloody mouth, tears streaming down her face? What about the time Beryl and Mayme got into a scuffle and Mayme got pushed through a fence. The barbs on the wire cut her leg so bad she would carry a scar for a lifetime. Did Santa see that? Questions from the older children as to whether or not Santa really existed were quickly squelched, just in case.

Christmas Time, a public program, was customary at the schoolhouse and was one of the biggest highlights of the year. Everyone in the valley pitched in with the preparations while enjoying the camaraderie they had with his or her neighbors.

A few days before the program was to be held, women who lived in the area would get together to hold a "bee," a time for women to spend the day enjoying each other's company. One of the ladies would welcome the other women into her home to prepare refreshments for the Christmas program. After drinking a cup of hot coffee by the heating stove, the women would roll up their sleeves, tie on their aprons, and go to work, baking cookies, making candy, and popping corn. It wasn't long before the first batch of gingerbread men were baking in the oven, sending warm spicy smells of cinnamon, cloves, and ginger throughout the house. Myrtle stood at the wood cook stove, with spoon in one hand and the other hand on her hip, all the while visiting with her friends. Instinctively turning back to look in the cooking pot sitting on the stove, she gave the hot mixture a quick stir. As soon as the liquid started a hard rolling boil, in went a heaping spoonful of sweet home-churned butter. With great care, the blistering pot was carried to the table and the hot liquid poured into a shallow pan to cool. When the candy was cool enough to handle, Myrtle slathered her hands with butter so they wouldn't burn. Pouring the hard candy onto the tabletop, Myrtle rolled it into hundreds of little bite size pieces. By lunchtime, the women had put in a full day's work.

After the kitchen was clean, Myrtle looked around the living room for a nice comfortable chair. Now it was time to really get down to catching up on the latest news. She noticed there were several different conversations going on at the same time. The noise coming from the living room sounded as though a bunch of well-meaning magpies were all trying to be heard at the same time. Locating an empty chair in the corner, Myrtle sat down for the first time that day. Joining her friends, she took her needle and thread from a small scrap of material that had been safely tucked away in her purse and started stringing fresh popped corn. By the middle of the afternoon, all of the treats were ready for the annual Christmas program.

During the week prior to the Christmas holiday, the students enjoyed making decoration for the little country school and the Christmas tree. Children in the first and second grade colored sheets of white paper using bright red and green crayons. When several pieces lay in a stack, the teacher Ms. Woods cut each sheet into narrow strips. Using paste made from water and white flour, the youngsters took one strip and glued the ends together making a loop. Taking another narrow strip, they inserted one end through the opening of the first loop. The ends of the second loop were glued together to make two joining loops. They continued adding loops until several red and green paper chains lay across the teacher's desk. While the small children stood beside the desk admiring each individual chain, Ms. Woods walked up behind them. They didn't have to turn around to know she was close at hand. Even during the dead of winter, their teacher had the sweet smell of lavender about her. "You children should be very proud of those paper chains. They will look very nice on our tree."

Ms. Woods gave each of the children in the third- and fourth-grade class a piece of cardboard that had been cut into ten-by-twelve-inch rectangles. A big bold letter had been printed on each card. Using their imagination, the nine- and ten-year-olds decorated each card with a Christmas scene, before coloring the big letter black. Construction paper was used to cut out little red bells and yellow stars. A short piece of yarn was threaded through a small hole that had been punched through the paper. The teacher then gave each child a piece of white paper instructing them to fold it into a triangular shape, several times over. She helped the youngest of her students make tiny cutouts around the edges. They were delighted when they unfolded the plain piece of white paper and saw that it was now a beautiful snowflake. After instructing her students to print their names on the back of their snowflakes, Ms. Woods gave each child a small piece of cellophane tape so they could hang their artwork in the window.

The much-anticipated day of the program finally arrived. During lunch period, Ms. Woods asked a couple of the older boys to go into the woods and get a Christmas tree. Normally, the boys would take advantage of the time they could spend outside and away from their studies. But feeling extra proud the pretty young teacher had singled them out for a special job, they hurried through the woods to find the perfect tree.

"There's one," called out Charley.*

"Nah, that's too scrawny," replied Harold. "Let's go this way."

It didn't take the boys long to find a beautiful five-foot cedar tree, its limbs full of sharp pointy little needles. With skill they had acquired from hours spent cutting wood for their own family's use, the boys took turns chopping away at the trunk, sending bits of rough bark flying through the air. Finally, the tree lay on the snow-covered ground. Grabbing hold of the trunk, the boys drug the tree into the schoolhouse and set it in a big wooden bucket filled with dirt. The fresh smell of cedar filled the small classroom.

Ms. Woods sent the little girls out to the edge of the woods to gather bright red holly berries. With their buckets filled to overflowing, they returned to the schoolhouse, giving the berries to the older girls, who were waiting with needle and thread in hand to string them together. After the decorations were complete, all of the children participated in trimming the tree with the colored-paper chains, little red bells, shiny pointed stars, ribbons, and bows. Strings of popcorn and red holly berries were the last decorations added. Just before school was dismissed, Ms. Woods stood behind her desk and gazed around the room. Looking back at her were twenty-five young children, their eyes filled with pride. "All of you have done such a beautiful job decorating this room and the tree. Your parents are going to be so pleased," she said in her gentle voice. "Now, there's

---

* Charley is a fictitious name.

only one thing left to do." The teacher reached into the center drawer of her desk and brought out a big silver star. "Ah, it's so beautiful," cried the children in unison. Not caring that the star was just a piece of cardboard covered in tin foil and carefully rubbed until all the wrinkles were gone, everyone thought it was the most beautiful star they had ever seen. The tallest boy in school was selected to place the big shiny star on the very tip-top of the tree. The handmade decorations that had so lovingly been made magically turned the cedar tree into the prettiest Christmas tree ever. "Now, children, don't forget. You need to be back here with your families at seven o'clock," reminded Ms. Woods. "Yes, ma'm," they answered, racing off toward their homes.

The annual Christmas program was held the Friday evening before Christmas. Parents came from all around. It was a good time to cease with their daily work to enjoy the Christmas spirit with their friends and neighbors.

A short time after sunset, men, women, and children arrived at the schoolhouse. Riding in wagons and horse-drawn buggies or coming on foot, they called out holiday wishes to each other as they hurried into the little building. The smell of fresh cut cedar and the crackling of the warm fire lent to the annual festivities as everyone started to find their seats. Little girls with big bright ribbons dangling from their pigtails and young boys with clean faces and hair slicked back, so that you could hardly recognize them, sat up straight and tall on the very front rows. Each child had selected a piece out of the teacher's book of Christmas poems he or she wished to recite. The verses had been practiced over and over again until the children were ready and confident enough to proudly perform them in front of their parents.

Ms. Woods stood up. The overly crowed room became silent as she read the most beloved story of the birth of the Christ Child from the Holy Bible. After a short prayer, the Christmas program started with the youngest of the children. Each class took their turn coming to the front of the room to say their Christmas poem. Proud mommas and daddies beamed when their little boy or girl stepped forward to perform. The last of the program was when the third- and fourth-grade children gathered up the cardboard squares. Turning to face the crowd of people, each child, in its turn, held up their card and recited the short verse that he had memorized. "Christ was born on Christmas day, in a manager low he lay." When all of the children said their verse and held up their card, the word "CHRISTMAS" was spelled out in big letters. The room erupted with clapping hands and cheers.

Voices resounded through the hills when parents joined their children in singing, "Joy to the World" and "Jingle Bells." The annual Christmas program was over for another year. Everyone lingered in the little schoolhouse to visit, eat cookies, and drink hot apple cider, all the while offering glad tidings and Christmas cheer to each other. Soon, it was time to go. Ms. Woods stood by the door handing out small bags of popcorn, peanuts, and hard-rock candy. By the light of the full moon, everyone headed homeward, as night settled over the Ozark Hills.

21

Christmas ♥

Christmas Eve day dawned bright, clear, and cold. Myrtle had a warm fire going in the cook stove when Nera and Florence, who had returned from Macks Creek for a few days, joined her in the kitchen to help prepare a hearty warm breakfast for the rest of the family. "Make sure you'ns bundle up good," Myrtle told Dick and Mayme. "It's bitter cold out this mornin'." The two girls put on their coats, mittens, and hats before venturing out into the brisk morning air. Their feet made a crunching noise on the ice-crusted snow as they made their way to the warm barn. Once inside, Mayme grabbed a pitchfork, scooped up a load of fresh sweet hay, and put it in the manger for the cow. Convinced that Flossie was now preoccupied with her morning meal and with the chance of being kicked eliminated, Mayme sat down on a three-legged stool and started to milk.

Dick grabbed a bucket and filled it with kernels of corn from the corn bin. Securing her scarf tighter over her head, she went back outside. "Here chick, chick, chick," she called, tossing the corn to the chickens. Returning to the barn, she retrieved a small straw basket hanging from a nail on the wall and filled it with fresh straw. Once again, she left the warm barn, this time running to the henhouse. When she entered the dark interior of the little building, she noticed that some of the chickens were still setting on their nest. Taking a deep breath to steady her nerves, Dick slowly slid her hand underneath the hen and gently removed the eggs. Myrtle's chickens were good layers and adequately provided the family with plenty of fresh eggs. What wasn't eaten, Myrtle would send to town with Lonnie to sell.

Inside the snug little house, Lonnie sat at the table, pouring hot coffee from his cup into a saucer. Putting the saucer below his bottom lip, he gently blew across the liquid to cool it before slurping it down. Scratching his chin hairs, he said more to himself than anyone else, "I saw a flock of wild turkeys roostin' in the draw yesterday. Think I'll go see if I can get one for Christmas dinner."

Directly after a hearty breakfast of fresh eggs, biscuits, gravy, side pork, fried nice and crisp, and a cup of warm milk, Ray and Howard bundled up in their coats and boots, preparing to venture out into the woods to chop down a Christmas tree. "Don't forget your gun. I heard from a neighbor that there's a cougar in the area," Lonnie told his boys.

The boys hadn't gone far when they noticed big cat tracks in the snow. The tracks were going toward the steel rabbit traps the boys had set out the day before. "It's a good thing we brought our guns. From the size of those tracks, that's gotta be a big cat," remarked Howard. Hurrying through the snow, they arrived at the first rabbit trap. Nothing. Checking to make sure the bait of turnip stems were still there, they hurried on to the next trap. Hearing a frightened squeal, they knew the second trap held a rabbit. Carefully raising the door, Ray clobbered the rabbit in the head with the stock of his gun. Throwing the dead animal over his shoulder, the boys continued on through the woods looking for the Christmas tree. Reaching the crest of a hill, they stopped and looked down into the valley. They were squinting their eyes against the brightness of the snow when they spied the cougar. He had caught a young deer and was engrossed in eating it. Taking careful aim, Ray sighted in on the big cat. *Boom!* The cougar fell dead, as the sound of the rifle echoed through the hills. It took just a few minutes to skin out the cat and be on their way.

"This hide ought to bring a fair price," beamed Ray.

"Shore will, I expect," replied Howard.

Locating the tree that had been picked out a few days before, they took their ax and chopped it down. Grabbing the tree trunk, the boys carried it along with the cougar's hide and the rabbit back to the house. Once they had the cedar tree inside, they stuck the trunk in a galvanized tub filled with sand. Lonnie was warming himself by the stove when the boys came in. A dead turkey lay on the sideboard in the kitchen.

"Was that you doin' some shootin'?" asked Lonnie.

"Yea, we got us a cougar down in the holler," replied Ray. "We hung the hide in the barn. Got us a hare too. Maybe Ma will make us some rabbit stew for supper."

"Maybe so," remarked Lonnie, looking at his sons with pride in his eyes.

It was Lonnie's responsibility to take the team and wagon to town once a week to do the marketing. But twice a year Myrtle would go. She went in the early spring to get her canning supplies and again, the day before Christmas. After donning her hat, coat, and gloves, she tied a woolen scarf around her head while giving strict orders to Nera to watch the young ones while she was gone. She wrapped an old cotton towel around a rock that had been heating on top of the cook stove. Carrying the hot rock to the wagon, she tucked it deep into the foothold to help keep her feet warm. She hitched the mules to the wagon, climbed up onto the seat, and with a gentle snap of the leather reins, Myrtle skillfully drove the wagon across the shallow river, then through the meadow to the mail-route road.

Turning onto the road, she followed it along the edge of the woods to Linn Creek. The wheels of the wagon scared up a couple of jackrabbits that had been burrowed down in a hollowed-out tree trunk. Startled, Myrtle stopped the wagon to watch the rabbits run off through the woods. She chuckled to herself, *You little devils. Scare me like that again and I'll see you on my supper table.* It was so peaceful and quiet. The sunshine shown down through the trees with such brightness that Myrtle had to squint to keep her eyes from hurting. As a ray of light filtered over her, it gave off an illusion of warmth. She noticed the long pointed icicles hanging from the tree branches were starting to melt. As water dripped from the tips, little indentions were made in the snow. She thought the temperature must have been above freezing, even though she didn't feel any warmer. Tightening the scarf around her head and drawing the collar of her coat up snug around her neck, she snapped the reins. "Giddy up, mules," Myrtle called out softly. "We best be goin' before we freeze." Continuing down the road, the only sound around her was the clip-clop of the mule's hooves hitting through the crusted layer of snow. The brick at her feet had grown cold, and she began shivering deep down to the bone. Going around the last curve in the road, she was sure glad to see smoke coming from the chimney of the general store, beckoning her to the warmth inside.

Myrtle quickly found her way to the center of the little store. Removing her gloves, she warmed her cold hands with heat radiating from the potbelly stove. "Good morning," she called to the storekeeper. "Howdy, Ms. Moulder. What can I get for you today?" The merchant was standing behind a counter that stretched the full width of the little store. Shelves made from planks of wood were built into the back wall behind the counter. They reach from floor to ceiling. Vegetable cans and fruit jars were neatly lined across some of the shelves. One-pound bags of salt and five-pound bags of white sugar were wrapped in brown paper bags. On the lower shelves, behind the counter, were twenty-five-pound bags of flour. Stamped in big red letters on the cloth were the words Kansas Best. In front of the counter were barrels of soda crackers and peanuts. Nail and gunpowder kegs stood in the corner. Bolts of colored prints and calico material were neatly lying on a wooden table. Glass jars filled with jellybeans, balls of cherry-flavored sour candy, and peppermint sticks sat on top of the counter.

"I need about a half a pound of sugar, a pound of coffee, five pounds of white flour, and six sweet potatoes. Lonnie's needin' some oats for the mules, and we'll be needin' some kerosene. I also need to pick up some Christmas gifts for the kids," Myrtle replied.

"Go ahead and look around. I'll get your things sacked up for you,"

Leaving the chore of sacking her few groceries to the storekeeper, Myrtle walked around the interior of the small room admiring all the new items that had come to adorn the shelves. There was so much more than she remembered; it was hard to look at everything. So she concentrated on Christmas gifts for her ten children. She knew she had limited funds to spend, so she chose the gifts wisely. A nice hair comb would do for the girls, a pocket comb for the boys, and a shiny new toy for baby Thomas. When she returned to the counter to pay her bill, she included a peppermint stick for each one.

"Here you go, Ms. Moulder. Tell Lon Merry Christmas."

"Bye and Christmas cheer," Myrtle called over her shoulder as she left the store.

By the time Myrtle arrived back home, the Christmas tree was decorated and stood in the corner of the living room. Little pieces of tin foil had been crumpled and tied with quilting thread. Hanging from the branches, they glistened like little stars. Red berries had been strung and draped precariously around the tree. Cotton stockings were hung on the wall behind the wood burner stove.

Ruby had cut the toe out of an old worn out cotton stocking. After she had found just the right spot, she nailed it to the wall. Then she put a cardboard box directly underneath it.

"Well, I'll swan," commented Dick. "What'd you do that for?"

"I'm gonna fool Santa," Ruby answered. "He'll start filling up my stocking, and the presents will fall through this hole into the box. He'll just keep putting in presents, and my stocking will never get full. But the box sure will. Boy, will I ever get a lot of presents."

"It won't work," Dick told her sister. "Besides, it's not nice to trick Santa."

"Will too. Just wait and see," beamed Ruby.

All through the day, Fern had been contemplating about a secret she had. After much thought, she decided to tell the others at supper. So with a sly grin on her face, she joined her family as they all sat down around the table for their evening meal of rabbit stew. Supper was just starting when ten-year-old Fern, sitting up straight and tall in her chair, puffed out her chest and boastfully announced, "There's no such thing as Santa Claus. He's not real. He's just a myth." All eyes shifted to look at Fern as if she had lost her mind. Myrtle's mouth dropped open, the children gasp all at once, and Beryl started to cry. Except for Beryl's tears, Fern had received the reaction she was hoping for. However, the reaction she got from her dad was quite different. Seeing the frown lines suddenly appeared across Lonnie's forehead, Fern lowered her eyes, embarrassed by her outburst. She knew that look. As with all the Moulder children, all it took was one of Lonnie's looks to know they were in big trouble. Taken aback by his daughter's declaration, Lonnie firmly scolded her, "That's quite enough out of you, young lady. We'll just see what you git in your stocking tomorrow mornin'. No Santa Claus! Now that just beats all."

After the supper things were put away, Myrtle called out, "Time for bed. You'ns need to get to sleep so Santa can come." After crawling under the covers on her side of the bed, Fern lay awake, wondering if her dad would still be mad at her in the morning. Or worse yet, what if there really was a Santa Claus?

"Christmas gift," Lonnie called out in a booming voice, waking his family from a sound sleep. "You better git over here and see what Santa left."

"Good mornin' and merry Christmas," Myrtles soft voice greeted her children as they climbed out from under their warm quilts.

Before their feet could hardly hit the cold floor, they raced to the warmth of the fire burning in the stove anxious to see what Santa had left. Inside the cardboard box, below Ruby's stocking, were a beautiful blue hair comb and a stick of peppermint candy. In her excitement over her gifts, she completely forgot about the trick she tried to play on Santa. Nera, Florence, Dick, and Mayme marveled over their presents also. Howard and Ray quickly used their own brand-new combs to try to calm their unruly hair before sticking them into their shirt pockets. Raising one eyebrow, Lonnie watched as Fern peeked inside of her stocking, a stunned look creeping across her face. "Well now, young lady," Lonnie remarked. "Maybe next time you will think twice before you go and blurt out words that will cause hurt to others." The only thing inside Fern's Christmas stocking was just a fair-size gift of calf manure.

After wishing his family a very Merry Christmas, Lonnie went outside to join his neighbors in welcoming Christmas morning by shooting several rounds from his shotgun in the air. Myrtle and her girls spent the rest of the morning in the kitchen preparing a tasty Christmas dinner of baked turkey, corn bread dressing, gravy, mashed sweet potatoes, stewed turnips, canned green beans, and home made white bread with freshly churned butter. For dessert, Myrtle mixed together cookie dough, using one-cup sour cream, one cup white sugar, one-quarter teaspoon soda, one egg, and one-teaspoon baking powder. Using her rolling pin, she rolled the "doe" real thin. With a metal cutter, she cut out cookies about the size of a small dinner plate. While the cookies were baking, Myrtle filled a kettle with dried apples, flour, and a small amount of water and had it simmering on the stove. Steam rose from the kettle sending a tantalizing aroma of cooked apples throughout the house. When the apples were soft, she smashed them with a fork, making an apple filling for the cake. Stacking one of the baked cookies on top of another with the hot apple mixture in between each layer, she completed the cake by icing it with one cup sugar, a half cup cream, cocoa, just enough to add color, and a tablespoon of melted butter. At the end of the meal, Myrtle carried the dried apple cake to the table. She knew it was her family's favorite dessert. Myrtle told her children that the cake was always better after it had set overnight. With sticky fingers and icing smeared across their lips, no one heard a word she said.

Katie, my niece, was now sitting on her dad's lap. With a puzzled look on her face, she inquired, "Was that really all Aunt Fern got in her stocking?"

"Kids back then were taught to respect their parents and others," Rusty explained to his young daughter. "When they did something wrong, they were punished. Leaving only calf manure in Aunt Fern's stocking might seem pretty harsh to us today, but Lonnie evidently knew what he was doing because Aunt Fern is one of the most loving, kind, and respectful people I know."

The subject changed rapidly from Aunt Fern's Christmas present to Mom. "Why haven't you told any stories about Mema?" questioned Katie.

"Because she hasn't been born yet," I replied.

"Oh," was all she said, settling back down on the floor to lean against her dad's knee.

22

Beryl's Whipping ♥

"I remember another time Aunt Fern got into trouble. This time, she had an accomplice—her younger sister Beryl," Donnis said, as she continued with the story.

The New Year arrived with a vengeance. It had snowed almost every day since the beginning of January. One particular day, it snowed really hard. The wind made a mournful howling sound as it blew around the house, catching the snow and swirling it around and around leaving sculptured white drifts piled high. The temperature had dipped below zero. Old rags had been stuffed around the windowsills to keep out cold drafts. Looking toward the river was like looking into a blinding white light. You couldn't see the broad side of the barn. It was much too cold and dangerous for the Moulder girls to cross the river and walk over the hills to school, so they stayed home. However, good weather or bad, there was livestock to care for and chores to be done.

After breakfast, Lonnie put on his heavy winter coat, pulled the earflaps of his hat down low, wrapped a woolen scarf snuggly around his head and neck, and pulled on his overshoes. Finally, he put on his thick warm gloves. His little girls laughed at the sight of their dad. All you could see was his twinkling blue eyes. Bracing himself for a blast of cold air, he opened the door, stepped over the threshold, and quickly shut the door behind him. Readjusting the woolen scarf around his nose and mouth, he grabbed one end of a stout rope that was hanging from a nail on the outside wall of the house. Making sure the rope was securely fastened; he trudged out into the yard and into the snowstorm. The wind was blowing so hard he had to lean forward to keep from being pushed backward. Ice pellets, feeling like little bee stings, glanced off the exposed part of his face. Holding tight to the rope, he wrapped his arms tighter around his body trying to keep out the cold wind. As his scarf slipped down around his chin, his breath instantly froze creating little icicles in the air. After several minutes, the dark brown color of the barn dimly came into view. Making his way across the final few yards to the barn, he took the end of the rope that he had been carrying and fastened it to the wall before stepping inside.

Watching from the window, the older children soon lost sight of their dad through the blowing snow. Opening the back door just a crack, Howard watched for a gentle tug on the rope. When it came, he knew his dad had made it to the barn. It was now safe to join him to help with the chores. Wrapped up in their coats, scarves, and hats, they tied tow sacks over their shoes to keep them dry. Making their way outside, they quickly took hold of the rope. Using it as a lifeline from the house to the barn, they made their way through the storm.

While the blizzard raged outside, the small Happy Holler house was warm and cozy inside. Myrtle had built a blazing fire in the cook stove leaving the oven door ajar, so the warmth could radiate throughout the room. She was occupied at the stove preparing a big nourishing dinner for her family who would soon be coming in from the cold. Baby Thomas had been breast-fed his morning meal and was peacefully asleep in the center of Myrtle's bed, cocooned by a feather tick mattress. Seven-year-old Fern and five-year-old Beryl happily played on the floor beside the warm stove, entertaining themselves with their dolls. So it was just the four of them inside their little house. As children are prone to do when they are cooped up inside together for too long, Fern and Beryl became bored. They were tired of playing with their dolls. They started to whine and began squabbling. "There's nothin' to do," cried Fern. Little Beryl was getting underfoot when Myrtle told her to just go find something to do and leave her to her chores.

Dragging a wooden kitchen chair across the floor to a nearby window, Beryl climbed up on the seat to look out. The snow was still coming down, but the wind had subsided.

"Can we go outside now?" Beryl asked.

"No," answered her mom. "It's too cold." But they were bored!

In addition, the little girls had another problem. Even at their young age, Fern and Beryl knew the importance of taking care of their shoes. Shoes had to last in order to be handed down to a sister who could wear them the next year. Only the girls who couldn't wear their sister's hand-me-downs got new ones.

With Fern as the ringleader, she soon convinced Beryl that they could sneak away from the house and have some fun. In her young mind, Fern reasoned that their mom was too busy fixing the meal to notice they were gone. Soon a plan was hatched. Knowing that it would be easier to gain forgiveness than to get permission, Fern and Beryl pulled off their shoes and socks and went out into the snow barefoot. By this time, it had quit snowing, and the sun was shining. The girls ran out through the yard gate and headed toward mail-route road. When Fern turned around to make sure Beryl was following, she noticed Lonnie coming out of the barn. Just as he spotted them, he bellowed, "Myrtle, git them brats back in the house!"

Frightened by the sternness of Lonnie's voice, Fern and Beryl hightailed it back up the mail-route road, through the yard gate, and up to the house as fast as their little legs could carry them. Myrtle met her daughters at the door, a stern frown on her face and a rolled-up newspaper in her hand. "What do you girls think you're doing?" Myrtle questioned her two young daughters. "I swan, if you don't catch a death of a cold by this," she sternly yelled. Dutiful daughter that she was, Fern presented herself to take her whipping like a big girl. Holding securely to one of Fern's arms, Myrtle let fly with the newspaper at her daughter's backside. Even though it didn't hurt all that much, Fern threw a little fit and bawled out like she was being killed. She was really having a good one.

Meanwhile, Beryl had squatted and backed into the corner of the room, like an old hen squats over her brood of chicks, protective like and still. She peered out into the room, thoughtfully watching her mother discipline her sister. Fern spotted Beryl in the corner and thought, *Wonder what she's up to. Knowing her, she must be hatching up something.*

And she was! When Beryl's turn came to get her whipping, she began skipping and dancing, jumping and giggling, laughing and singing, all aimed at distracting Myrtle from what she was about to do. Beryl put on such a show that her mother was overcome with laughter. She got so tickled that she forgot her duty and joined her daughters, laughing and whooping it up in the warm glow from the big fire in the stove. They had a big time!

"Did Aunt Beryl ever get her whipping?" asked Torrie.

"No, Grandma never did whip Aunt Beryl. And years later, Aunt Fern remembers, 'I took the whippin' for both of us. I haven't got over it all these years. I don't guess I ever will!'"

23

Unexplained Happenings ♥

It had been a long morning. I felt stiff and tired and needed to stretch. Using the wall to lean on, I felt the coolness from the tile penetrate through my blouse. I closed my eyes and thought about Mom. The last time I held her hand, it felt cool. I heard whispering voices. Opening my eyes, I looked down the hall in the direction of Mom's room. Phyllis and Jeff were walking toward me. Jeff's arm was around Phyllis's shoulder. "How's she doing?" I asked. Jeff slowly shook his head. I left my sister and her son-in-law outside the waiting room and walked down the hall toward Mom's room. My legs seemed so heavy. It was a struggle to put one foot in front of the other. But no matter how hard it was to go see Mom lying there lifeless, I couldn't stay away for very long. When I entered the dim interior of the intensive care room, Chandi was standing beside the bed, brushing mom's hair. What a beautiful act of kindness I thought. I walked up behind my niece and gave her shoulders a loving squeeze. She turned to me. Neither one of us could hold back the tears any longer. Standing there beside Mom's bedside, we both cried as we held on to each other. While Chandi and I kept an attentive watch over Mom, Donnis was back in the waiting room, continuing with the stories.

The encyclopedia defines "superstition" as "belief, half belief, or practice for which there appears to be no rational substance." Some people think they are just old wives' tales or made up nonsense. But many people believe them to be true and would base their entire lives around them. Strange tales of spirits, eerie lights and uncanny sounds have been passed down through the years to the Moulder children told to them by older family members.

People of Linn Creek were fortunate to have a country doctor living close by. He lived in a large two-story white house on Main Street. A wraparound porch circled the outside walls. His office was located in the back rooms. Lining the interior walls of the small room were metal file cabinets filled with medical records of several generations of local families. Near the only window in the room sat a roll top desk. Little pigeonhole compartments were stuffed full of loose papers. On the top of the desk sat a hurricane lamp, notepad, and a bottle of black ink.

The only interior door led to an examination room. A wooden table covered with a clean white sheet stood in the middle of the second room. Bottles of ether, alcohol, laudluam, penicillin, and other various medicines were placed on a nearby shelf beside rolls of bandages and sticky medical tape. A porcelain water pitcher, stacks of clean white towels, and a bar of strong surgical soap sat on a smaller table. The only light in the room was a single light bulb that hung from a wire over the table. This room was used for extreme emergencies when the patient was injured or too sick to travel eighty miles to the nearest hospital.

No matter what time of day, when someone arrived at the doctor's home seeking medical assistance, the doctor would grab his small black bag and run out the door. Hitching his carriage to a team of sturdy long-legged horses, he would race off into the country to care for his patient. Many people did not have the money to pay for medical treatment. Accepting a couple of fat hens, a country ham, or a pound of fresh churned butter, the doctor was always grateful for whatever his patient could offer. Some never did pay, but he treated them anyway.

"Boy, have things changed," commented Lonnie. "Nowadays, I doubt if any doctor would even look at you without medical insurance."

"You're probably right."

With the nearest doctor five miles away, Myrtle saw the need to administer her own medical remedies. Skunk oil, caster oil, and boiled roots were used to cure almost any ailment her family came down with. Due to the lack of iodine in the soil, a common ailment in Missouri in the early 1900s was goiter, which is the swelling of the thyroid gland. To cure goiter, Myrtle carefully poured one-eighth ounce tincture iodine (a liquid from boiled walnuts), added one-half ounce potassium, and five ounces of rainwater into a glass vile. After a vigorous shake, she would apply this mixture night and morning with a brush to ease the swelling.

Many dreaded diseases invaded close-knit communities at the turn of the century. An epidemic of measles or cholera would cause families to close their doors to neighbors in order to quarantine the sick. Sickness like these traveled quickly, leaving death and mournful crying in its path. In the 1900s, over twenty-five thousand people in the United States died from another dreaded illness called typhoid fever. Typhoid was caused by germs entering the body through the mouth, usually from impure drinking water and the lack of a proper way to destroy sewage.

While the Moulder family was living at the Happy Holler farm, a neighbor boy became dreadfully ill. He had contracted typhoid fever. After many anxious days watching over their young son and unable to control his raging temperature, Roy's family had become exhausted. Lonnie and Myrtle remembered the help they had received in their time of need when their own son Ray had come down with the typhoid, so they were among those who volunteered to help Roy's family.

By the time Myrtle arrived at her neighbor's home, the boy was lying deathly still in his bed. His cheeks were flushed beet red with fever, and his face was extremely warm to the touch. Myrtle encouraged Roy's parents to get some rest before they too were stricken down with the fever. Leaving Myrtle to care for their son, Roy's parents took her advice and retired to their bed.

Myrtle applied a cool wet cloth to the young child's forehead. Wet dishtowels lying on the boy's arms, legs, and torso were soon warm from heat radiating from his skin. Myrtle tried in vain to cool him off, but his temperature continued to rise. After a few hours of tending to the sick child, Myrtle took a moment for herself. She moved a rocking chair close to the window and with a sigh lowed her tired body down and began gazing at the full moon rising over the crest of the hill. It was a huge white ball in the pitch-black sky. She sat staring at the moon but couldn't help hearing Roy's parents toss and turn in a fretful sleep. While Myrtle was remembering the long nights she and Lonnie had sat with their own sick child when he was so desperately ill, Roy's fever continued to rage to the point of delirium.

While Myrtle was desperately trying to help the young boy, Lonnie was home holding vigil over the safety of his own family. He sat by the stove waiting for his wife to return and for the long night to end. Ole Slim and Ole Speedy lay on the floor in front of the door, their muzzles resting on folded front legs watching Lonnie. *Thump, thump, thump,* came the sound as both dogs beat their tails against the wooden floor. Their ears perked up and then relaxed as if waiting for a command from their master. But none came.

The full moon continued its steady travel across the sky, sending beams of light through the window. Ten-year-old Ruby crawled out of bed, wrapped a bed quilt around her shoulders, and tiptoed to the warmth of the stove, kneeling at her dad's feet.

"Can't sleep?" Lonnie softly asked.

"No. The moon's too bright. It's keeping me awake." After a few moments, Ruby whispered, "Is Ray gonna die?"

"No, he's gonna be just fine. His fevers broke, but he's still weak. He'll be up and around soon," Lonnie said in a gruff but soothing voice.

"Is Roy gonna die?" asked the frightened little girl.

"I don't know. It's in God's hands."

After a few quiet moments, Ruby spoke again, "Can't the doctor do something?"

"Child," Lonnie tried explaining to his young inquisitive daughter, "some people think doctors can perform miracles, but it's not like that at all. All they can do is help nature along. No one can change the course of things no matter how long or hard they pray. Nature will always take its course. Now quiet before you wake the others."

Rocking in rhythm to the ticking mantle clock, both Lonnie and Ruby jumped when twelve midnight struck. Before the last dong faded into the night, they distinctly heard the piteous bleating of a lamb. Then all was still and quiet. Lonnie looked down at Ruby, cuddled up tight against his leg. His little girl's large brown eyes filled with fright were looking up at him. A silent thought passed between the two of them, but both were afraid to voice the thought out loud. Without a sound, Ruby crawled in to the safety of her dad's big lap.

While Lonnie continued to gently rock in rhythm to the ticking of the clock, the remainder of the family slept soundly in their beds. A soft purring noise made by their breathing was the only sound coming from that side of the room. Lonnie's eyes shifted upward as a creaking noise was heard coming from the upstairs attic. "It's only Ray turning over in bed," he explained to the startled little girl. *Crack! Sizzle!* With the little hairs on the backs of their necks rising, Lonnie and Ruby jerked to look in the direction of the potbelly stove. Realizing it was just a log that had burned through, cracked and fell, sending little orange sparks up and out of the stove, they relaxed as they watched the embers fall back into the depths of the hot stove.

The hours crept passed. Finally, the welcome sound of the wagon coming from the yard signaled Myrtle's return. Lonnie rose from the chair and went to open the front door. Without saying a word, Myrtle came into the house and went straight to the kitchen to get her self a cup of warmed-over coffee. Slowly she walked to the rocking chair, looking tired and haggard. With a huge sigh, she lowered herself into the chair. Ruby crawled into her mom's lap. Myrtle tucked the quilt snug around her daughter's neck as she held her tightly in her arms.

Softly she told Lonnie, "It's over. Young Roy's dead."

"What time did he die?" Ruby asked, her eyes opened wide as saucers.

"Just at midnight," Myrtle replied.

Lonnie looked at over at Ruby just as the little girl looked back at her dad. Their eyes locked as they realized that their fears had been confirmed.

Years later as Ruby related this story, a strange faraway look would come to her hooded hazel brown eyes, and she would say, "And children, no one had sheep for miles and miles around." Lonnie was not superstitious, but he always vouched for the truth of this unusual occurrence. Ruby remained very superstitious and respectful of the night full of creepy sounds. And she was especially restless when the moon was full as she related tales of unexplained happenings.

Not a sound or a movement was made in that waiting room as Donnis finished telling the story about a little boy named Roy.

Back in the hospital room, Chandi and I were holding our own vigil. Looking down at Mom, lying so still, I wonder, *Mom, where are you? Do you know that we're here for you? Can you hear me?*

Chandi's voice interrupted my thoughts. "Why's Mema fighting that tube in her mouth? Do you think she knows what's going on?"

Trying to convince myself as well as comfort my niece, I said, "I don't think so. I think it's just her muscle's involuntarily moving."

"Oh."

Just then, a slight movement occurred underneath mom's closed eyelids, as if she were watching something. Chandi and I held our breath. We took Mom's hands in ours. Suddenly, Mom's eyebrows raised; the movement stopped behind her eyelids, and she smiled the most beautiful smile I had ever seen across her face. She had stopped fighting the tube protruding from her mouth. As we stood silently watching, a look of total peace came to this beautiful woman. I glanced at the monitor that was registering her breathing and her heartbeats. They were still functioning normally. She was still alive. I now know in my heart where she is and whom she saw deep down in the depths of her soul.

24

The Flood ♥

During the month of April 1928, torrential rains caused serious damage to homesteads, livestock, and crops along the principal streams in Camden County. The greatest damage was along the Niangua River where water rose eighteen feet. While below the mouth of the Niangua, the Osage River rose twenty-three feet. The losses around Linn Creek were considerable.

Early in the spring, about the same time the rains started, Myrtle received word that a neighbor lady had come down sick with the fever, and her help was needed. Thinking she would be home by dark, Myrtle left Dick to care for the family. Putting on an old oiled slicker to keep away the dampness, Myrtle left the warm, dry farmhouse. Locating Ray in the barn, she told him to come with her. She needed someone to put her across the river. The rain started to let up as Ray skillfully rowed the boat across the Big Niangua. Myrtle sat in the bow looking up at the dark gray clouds hovering overhead. She tightened the slicker snug around her head and shoulders as she stepped out onto the bank on the far side of the river. "A storm's abrewin'," she told Ray. "Better git on home." It started to rain again as she walked across the lower end of Uncle Elmore's farm. The ominous dark clouds were getting heavier. Lightning streaked across the sky. Bowing her head to ward off the big raindrops, Myrtle crossed the meadow that ran close to Vander Moulder's fields.

Myrtle finally reached the path that led a short distance up a hill to her friend's home. Thunder rumbled overhead followed by another streak of lightning, lighting up the dark sky. Myrtle searched through the trees for a welcoming light she knew would be coming through the window of her friend's home. She caught the pungent smell of burning wood about the same time she saw smoke curling above the trees. Hurrying the last few yards, Myrtle was ushered into the house by her friend's husband. "How is she?" Myrtle inquired.

The man just stood there. She noticed his hair was askew on top of his head, and several days' growth of whiskers covered his pale cheeks. His eyes had sunken back into his face from lack of sleep. Slowly, shaking his head, he turned to look across the little room. Leaving her wet slicker hanging on a nail by the door, Myrtle walked over to the daybed that was along the far wall. Turning up the flame of the coal oil lantern, Myrtle immediately assessed her friend's condition. She was laying so still, her face an ashen color. Her breath was very shallow as she breathed the death rattle. While Myrtle took over caring for the sick woman inside the drafty house, she listened to the heavy rains continuing outside.

After several minutes sitting beside her friend, Myrtle realized that this was going to be a long night and needed to call home. Slowly she walked to the telephone hanging on the wall. She picked up the cone-shaped earpiece and placed it to her ear. Then she gave the handle on the side of the phone box a quick turn. A few seconds passed before Myrtle spoke into the mouthpiece. "Hello, this is Ms. Moulder." There was a short pause, and then she said, "Family's fine, thank you. I'm kinda in a hurry. Would you connect me with my house?" There was another short pause while the two phones were being connected. "Hello, Howard?" Myrtle finally said. "I can't get home tonight. You'll have to bring Thomas to me. And bring Ruby too. She can hold him while you row the boat."

"I'll be there as soon as I can," Howard replied to his mom.

Howard bundled Thomas and Ruby in their heavy woolen coats. Carrying Thomas and leading his little sister by the hand, the three of them went out into the soggy wet day. After making sure the children were safe and secure in the bottom of the boat, Howard started to row, dodging logs and trash that were coming down the river. They floated over a small piece of their dad's farm and then floated up to Uncle Elmore's property, where Myrtle had walked just a few hours before. Howard and Ruby were amazed and stared in awe at all the water as they left Vander Moulder's farm in a boat. Arriving safely at the bottom of the hill leading to their neighbor's home, Howard saw his mom standing in her oil slicker, waiting on the bank. Taking the small children from her son, Myrtle told him to get on home now. She would call when her friend no longer needed her assistance. Leaving Ruby and Thomas with Myrtle, Howard started back home.

The next morning, the woman was dead. While Myrtle waited for Howard to come back for her and her young children, she prepared her friend for burial.

A few days later, after the water had receded back between the riverbanks, Lonnie was out assessing the damage to his crops when he noticed Mayme, Ruby, Fern, and Beryl coming home from school. The girls were trudging through the wet soggy bottomland to where they had tied the little wooden boat that morning. But during the day, the rains had come again. The rivers were already full, causing the rising water to flood above the banks and once again into the fields. Not finding the boat where she had tied it that morning, Mayme was getting concerned that the rope had come loose, and the boat had drifted away. Standing knee-deep in water, Mayme, not sure what she was going to do looked around her. To her immense relief she saw her big strong daddy across the river waiting for them. He was pointing at something. Following his guide, Mayme located the boat bobbing up and down in the middle of the river. The rope had held secure but was straining tight between the boat and a tree stump.

Mayme was now thirteen years old. It was her responsibility to get her sisters across the river. Lonnie cupped his hand around his mouth and yelled, "Mayme, use the rope and swim out to the boat." Being a strong swimmer, Mayme waded into the fast-rushing water. The current was swift and strong. Using the rope to help keep her afloat, she finally reached the boat. Dragging herself into the semi safety of the craft, she rowed it back to collect the rest of the girls. Her daddy calmly called to Mayme once more, "Take the boat upriver to the eddy. The water will turn you around and bring you back."

Knowing this was a dangerous situation; she did not question her daddy's words. Aware of the responsibility that was placed on her young shoulders, Mayme followed them faithfully. She loaded her sisters into the boat. After telling them to remain seated, she shoved off. Paddling with all her might, the boat slowly moved upriver against the strong current. Skillfully dodging sticks that were being carried along in the fast-moving river, she finally came to the eddy where she relent the boat to Mother Nature. The boat spun halfway around, and then darting forward with such a force, the young children had to cling to the sides of the boat for dear life. True to Lonnie's words, they raced toward the safety of the landing spot and into the arms of their dad waiting for them. Being able to read the river, Lonnie had once more saved the lives of his children.

That spring, Lonnie lost his entire crop. Only one shock of corn remained standing in his fields. Myrtle's truck garden down by the river had been destroyed. Devastated, Lonnie came home to his family. "There's nothing left of the crops, and the garden has been washed away. The flood took it all," he said. "Myrtle, pack up the kids and go to your ma's for a while. There's nothing left to do here."

Within the next hour, Myrtle had packed a few clothes for her and the children in a worn wicker basket. She wrapped ham and cold biscuits that were left over from breakfast that morning in a tea towel and laid them on top of the clothes. After Mayme, Ruby, Fern, and Beryl climbed into the back of the wagon, Lonnie helped his pregnant wife up and onto the wagon seat beside Dick. Taking Thomas from Lonnie's outstretched arms, Myrtle told him, "We'll be gone a week or so. This baby's gonna be here soon enough, and I need to get the gardens in." Lonnie stood watching as

Myrtle drove off with his daughters and young son toward the mail-route road. When they were out of sight, Lonnie turned and called to Howard and Ray, "Come on, boys. We're going to have to get those young pigs butchered since there's no corn left to feed them. And the garden's gonna need tilled again. Better git started."

That summer, Myrtle gave birth to her eleventh and last child. A daughter, Martha June, was born on June 22, 1928.

"That's Mema," Katie cried.

"It sure is, sweetheart," I said walking back into the room. "Speaking of Mema, I believe in my heart that she has made her peace with God and that Jesus is with her, waiting to take her home." With tears in my eyes, I told my family about what had happened just a short time ago as I stood beside mom, holding her hand.

25

Thomas and the Ash Hop ♥

Thomas Fredrick, Lonnie and Myrtle's youngest son, was born on April 24, 1926. Howard and Ray were now strapping young men, and after raising five daughters, Lonnie was overjoyed with the birth of his third boy.

One September morning after the girls had left for school, Myrtle was minding to her morning chores. Thomas, about two years old, was playing on the kitchen floor. Myrtle didn't become overly concerned when she could no longer hear Thomas because she knew his daddy was also in the kitchen. But Lonnie was all too consumed with his own chores to pay much mind to the little boy. Lonnie had finished filling a metal bucket with gray ashes he had taken from the cook stove and had left the house headed toward the river. A wooden barrel sat between the river and the branch. Lonnie emptied the bucket full of ashes into the barrel, scooped water out of the river, pouring just enough into the barrel to cover the ashes. Over time, the ash and water combination would meld together causing a chemical reaction, making lye. Laying the bucket upside down on the ground, he headed toward the barn to tend to his mules. Lonnie was unaware that Thomas had followed him outside.

All of a sudden, back in the house, Myrtle got a worrying sense that something was wrong. Rushing back to the kitchen, she immediately noticed the back door was open, and Thomas was gone. Frantically, she ran outside and yelled, "Thomas! Where are you? Answer me!" Seeing Lonnie exit the barn, she called to him. "Have you seen Thomas?"

"Nope" was the sober reply.

Searching throughout the yard and around the chicken coop, Thomas was nowhere to be found.

"Momma. Momma." Myrtle heard a frightened voice coming from the direction of the river. Lifting the skirt of her dress above her knees, Myrtle raced toward the water. As she neared the ash hop, she stopped, straining to listen. The small scared voice reached her ears once again. This time it was a little louder. "Momma!" Running toward the sound, she saw a small gray hand reaching above the rim of the wooden barrel.

"Oh my God!" she gasp. Grabbing Thomas's arm, Myrtle gently lifted her little boy from the ash hop. Thomas was covered from head to toe in gray ash.

Rushing back to the house with the toddler in her arms, Myrtle prayed that he had not gotten into the lye. Putting Thomas down on the floor beside her, Myrtle used the crank telephone to call Dr. Moore, the town doctor. After explaining what had happened, the doctor's reassuring voice came through the earpiece.

"Now calm down, Ms. Moulder. Did the boy get into the lye?" he asked.

"I'm not sure," was Myrtle's reply.

"Okay, here's what I want you to do. Give him a bath in apple cider vinegar. And pay particular attention to his eyes and mouth. He will smell like vinegar for a while but should be okay."

Hanging up the phone, Myrtle followed Doc Meyer's orders to a tee. But in her excitement, she forgot to wash his hair. The toddler soon recovered from the ordeal. A few days later, to the dismay of the family, Thomas's hair fell out. It took a few weeks for it to grow back, but his blond baby curls were gone. Straight dark hair now covered his small little head.

"Why was Lonnie making lye?" Suzanne asked.

Store-bought soap was considered a luxury and was therefore financially unattainable. To make lye, Lonnie would add ashes and water to a barrel, causing a chemical reaction. The harsh liquid would run down a spout, which had been inserted into a small hole, and into a gallon bucket. Myrtle warned her family to take great care of those ashes and had better not be caught spitting into them because clean ashes make better soap.

In the fall, after a hog had been butchered, it was time to make soap. Myrtle heated water in a big round kettle over an open fire pit. Using a wooden paddle, she added hog fat and a few leftover scraps, as she continued to slowly stir. The contents came to a gentle bubbling boil resembling a pot of cream gravy. Bubbles rose then burst on the surface, creating little mounds. After about fifteen minutes, Myrtle poured the hot liquid into her galvanized washtub. Stirring in a small amount of pure lye, the mixture cooled, thickened, and turned opaque in color. Scooping up a small quantity of soap in her spoon, she dribbled it back onto the surface. Quickly, she drew a line through the small mound, checking to see if it traced. If a trace of the line remained for a few seconds, the soap was ready. Filling several small bowls, she placed them in the springhouse to harden. By freezing, the soap would contract slightly and easily release from the sides of the containers. Myrtle waited a couple of weeks for the soap to cure and become mild enough so it wouldn't burn or irritate skin.

During the curing time, a fine ash formed over the cakes. Myrtle simply cut away the ash. Essential oil, a pleasant-smelling additive, was a luxury Myrtle's family had to do without. So the end result was a fine, if nasty-smelling, bar of soap.

"What did they use the lye soap for?" my inquisitive daughter asked.

"Well, since this was the only soap the family had, they used it to wash dishes, clothes, and even for Saturday night baths," replied Donnis.

"Oh yuck!" Suzanne replied, curling up her nose.

26

Changes Are Coming ♥

What seemed to be only in the imaginations of many became a reality when the construction of Bagnell Dam started on August 6, 1929. The Great Depression had the country in a tight grasp, so news of the thirty-million-dollar project quickly spread. The building of the dam was the largest construction project going on anywhere in the United States. Every day, hundreds of men, women, and children would arrive to assist in clearing the land of all trees and existing structures that would soon be flooded. They came on foot, horseback, floating down the river, and in automobiles packed with everything they owned.

At the dam construction sight, Union Electric had started clearing the area making way for the construction of mess halls, warehouses, and sleeping quarters. There was a camp hospital along with a commissary, where the workers could buy boots, shoes, clothes, pots and pans, and food. A barbershop and a laundry service were also available. A notice in the local newspaper was posted asking for a list of every available house in the nearby towns. Every homeowner was asked to make arrangements to rent at least one room in their home to the workers.

Closer to the Moulder farm, lumberjacks swarmed the nearby woods cutting down trees. What was, at one time, the sound of prosperity and re-growth with the rebuilding of Linn Creek, now the zinging, whirring sound of saws that rang through the hills meant only destruction and huge changes for many families. Small tent cities invaded the area, as canvas lean-tos dotted the valleys, woods, and riverbanks. Men, women, and children came to cut down trees that had stood for thousands of years. When the huge trees fell, they were set on fire where they lay. If they were too big to burn, they were left to rot in the dirt. The smell of wood burning and decay was a constant reminder of the changes that was coming to the Moulder family's little piece of the world.

Travel conditions weren't the easiest, and scores of men, women, and young boys had to walk a considerable distance to find work. One morning, on their way to school, the Moulder girls happened upon a lumberjack standing at the edge of the river. His broad shoulders and big hands was a tribute to the fact that he worked hard and long, swinging an ax for a living. His weatherworn face resembled tan leather. Short stubby whiskers stuck out on his cheeks and chin. He wore a red flannel shirt tucked partway into his brown heavy cotton trousers, the legs tucked into his dirty boots. Dark oily hair protruded from under a sweat-stained felt hat perched on his head. Bushy eyebrows shaded his brown eyes. The handle of his saw slung over one shoulder, and a strap, hooked to a rife, was over his other shoulder as he stood at the edge of the river looking for a way to cross.

Remembering her daddy's cautioning words, "You'ns be careful in the woods. A lot of riffraff has moved in lookin' to make an easy buck," Mayme cautiously called out, "Howdy, stranger." Keeping a close eye on the man, Mayme took a key out of her pocket. "You from around here?" she asked.

"Nope, down south. I have a woman back up the road. She's settin' up camp for me and the young'uns whilst I look for work," the man explained.

Unlocking the padlock from around a sturdy chain, she inquired, "Need a ride across the river?"

"Would be obliged," replied the man.

"Well, climb in."

Ruby, Fern, and Beryl were already seated in the boat. After the man set down beside them, Mayme climbed in and laid the chain at her feet. She skillfully rowed the little johnboat across the Big Niangua. Reaching the far bank, Mayme retrieved the chain from the bottom of the boat and climbed out. She wrapped the end of the chain around another tree truck and closed the paddle lock. After all, they didn't want the boat to become the property of some woodsman. When the man was back on dry ground, he dug deep into his trouser pocket and pulled out a shiny dime. "Here you go, missy," he said, tossing the coin to Mayme. "Thanks for the ride." The young girls watched the back of the retreating man until he was around the bend and out of sight.

With all the strangers in the area, there was never any news of harm coming to a young woman. The young Moulder girls knew that their dad would kill any man that harmed one of his daughters.

There was enough work cutting down trees and shoring up the nearby riverbanks to employ more than twenty thousand people. They worked twelve hours a day, making between thirty-five cents and one dollar and twenty-five cents per day.

27

Florence Teaches School ♥

The population in Camden County exploded as men who came to find work brought their families with them. Local schools opened their doors to the onslaught of children. The state offered minimal funding, but mainly it was a matter of the local communities enduring this hardship until the project of building Bagnell Dam was complete. Florence had been hired to teach at the Arnholdt School, which was located northeast of Linn Creek. Receiving the salary of sixty dollars a month, which was a lot of money in those days, Florence was able to rent a small room at Sherman Roger's boardinghouse and still have a few dollars left to pay back the debt she owed her sister Nera for paying for her schooling.

On the first day in September 1929, Florence stood in the dim light of a coal oil lamp, looking into a mirror hanging on the wall. Taking a deep breath, she tried to steady her nerves as she secured the hat on top of her head with a long pointy hatpin. Picking up her schoolbooks from the nightstand, Florence turned down the flame, waiting patiently for the light to flicker and go out. Slowly opening her bedroom door, she quietly tiptoed down the stairs. The light of the full moon filtered through an open window in the kitchen, illuminating enough light that she could see to fill her metal lunch pail with a small piece of ham, a cold biscuit with jelly, and a piece of cake left over from Sunday's dinner.

Leaving the security of the house, Florence walked down the hill into the valley below. She watched the dim glow of lamplights flicker through open windows of the outlying homes, as people awoke to another day. Leaving the valley and climbing another hill, Florence entered the woods. The moon was bright and shining through the tall tree branches playing hide-and-seek with her as it chased away eerie shadows.

The sun was just beginning to peek over the hills as Florence came to the edge of the woods. There, in the middle of a large clearing, stood a small-whitewashed one-room schoolhouse. Narrow wooden steps led up to a small landing in front of the door. Tall skinny windows, three on each side of the building, had been opened to allow breezes to blow through removing the musty smell of hot summer days. Slowly, Florence walked around to the back of the building. A large stack of cut wood was piled near the side door. A baseball diamond, made by children from previous years, was worn in the thick carpet of bluegrass. An A-frame structure, made from steel pipes with two wooden swings hanging by chains from the vertical and horizontal pipes, stood in the center of a large area of rock-hard dirt. A plank board teeter-totter and a metal slipper slide stood near the swing set. Two narrow buildings, with a single door leading into each one, were on the far side of the schoolyard. A cutout in the shape of a quarter moon was carved below crude white letters that had been painted on the door, spelling "boys" and "girls."

Returning to the front of the building, Florence walked up the wooden steps. Opening the front door, she peered inside. Sunlight was streaming through the open windows. Dust particles glistened in the air. A wood-burning stove stood in the center of the room. The smell of dry cedar penetrated Florence's senses as she spotted a metal storage bin in the corner filled with kindling. A galvanized water bucket was sitting on a small table right next to the side door. And the ever-present dipper hung on a nail directly above.

Taking a few steps inside, she noticed that three rows of school desks took up most of the floor space. She counted six desks in each row. Each seat had a desk attached to the back. The desktop could be raised providing a place for pencils and books. The youngest of the children would sit in the front rows with the older ones farther back. There were makeshift benches made from planks of lumber lining the walls to accommodate the overflow of students. Florence walked to the front of the room. Laying her textbooks and lunch bucket down on a big wooden desk, she let her mind wonder back to when she was just a young girl, sitting by the coal oil lamp looking through catalog after catalog as she dreamt of a better life.

The feeling of butterflies flitted inside her stomach as she removed her hat, laying it on the desk beside her books. Gently rubbing the palm of her hand over the cool smooth desktop, she looked around the little schoolroom. Sunbeams lay across the hardwood floor, remnants of a slight musty smell penetrated her nostrils, and gentle breezes blew through the open windows. Tears swam in Florence's eyes as she realized that her hopes and desires were now becoming a reality. This was to be her desk, where she would instruct and educate the young minds of her students. For the next few months, she would teach reading, writing, arithmetic, literature, English, history, agriculture, and geography to all eight grades. Assured that everything was in order, Florence stepped outside and stood on the wooden porch. Ringing a small handheld bell, the sound echoed through the hills. Children came running out of the woods from all directions.

There were thirty children attending class that year, ranging in ages from five to twelve years old.

Shortly after the school year started, Uncle Alfred Moulder met Florence in the schoolyard. "There's a boy belonin' to that riffraff that's moved in down the river," Uncle Alfred informed his young niece. "And he's threatin' to get the teacher. He's as big as you. Better look out for that one." She assured him that she would not get careless and forget. Florence was never really afraid, but whenever she left the safety of the Roger's boardinghouse, heading to school or left the little country school headed for home, she was constantly looking back over her shoulder.

The days passed, and nothing seemed to be amiss until one night, after Florence was safely in her room, Mr. Rodgers accosted a rough-looking large boy outside Florence's bedroom door. When he called out to him, the boy turned and ran away. Not wanting to frightened Florence, Mr. Rodgers suggested she make arrangements to rent a room from the parents of one of her students. This would enable her to be closer to school, and she wouldn't have to walk through the woods each day.

The days turned into weeks. By midterm that year, the incident was all but forgotten. However, with so many strangers in the surrounding area, Florence continued to be aware of her surroundings and never let her guard down.

Fall arrived once more to the Ozark Hills. The leaves on the great maple, walnut, and sycamore trees turned brilliant colors of orange, red, and gold making the hillsides look like a painting right out of a New York City art museum. On pleasant days, Florence would go outside with the children during lunch period, taking with her a sack lunch and a stack of papers that needed grading.

One day she was sitting on the ground beneath the canopy of a tall maple tree, grading school papers, when she found herself distracted by the beauty around her. On the far hillside, multicolored leaves, still hanging on to tree limbs, were mixed with shades of green, ranging from deep dark emerald to bright Kelly and finally a pale yellow. Suddenly, a cool breeze blew in from the north sprinkling her with a cascade of leaves falling from the tree limbs overhead.

Returning to her task of grading papers, Florence heard her sister Fern boast to a group of friends. "I am too the best at playing marbles. I can beat anybody, even you, Willie."

"Can you prove it?" challenged her young cousin.

"Sure I can," retorted Fern as she knelt down on the hard ground.

Surrounded by a group of onlookers, Fern used her finger to draw a crude circle in the dirt. Taking five marbles from her pocket and five marbles from Willie's outstretched hand, she laid them in the center, making an X. When she had them just right, she leaned over the circle. Resting on her elbows, butt up in the air, head cocked to one side, tongue sticking out over her upper lip, and with one eye closed, Fern took careful aim as she flipped her favorite "shooter" with her thumb. Watching the marble roll across the dirt, she held her breath until it found its target. With a sharp click, her marble hit the other marbles, sending them rolling in all directions. Two marbles belonging to Willie rolled outside the circle. She continued to shoot her marble, hitting the rest of the marbles, until only hers were left. A loud cheer erupted from the group of friends that had witnessed the competition.

"Okay, Willie, I'll take that cat's-eye," Fern said as she rose to her feet, dusting the loose dirt from the knees of her cotton stockings.

"Ah gee, that's my favorite," the young boy replied.

"Well, it's mine now."

Fern was very good at playing marbles and would beat Willie every time.

Each day after lunch, when all the children were back in their seats, Florence would ask one of the older boys to go fetch some fresh water. Feeling proud that the pretty young teacher had singled him out above all the rest, he would take the metal bucket from the table and hurry outside. There was a red cast iron pump jack mounted on a slab of cement just outside the door. In order to prime the pump, he would pour a little bit of water left in the bottom of the bucket directly down into the center of the pump jack. Grabbing the long handle, he would start pumping. Up and down he went until a small stream of water flowed from the spigot. The faster he pumped, the bigger the stream of water became. After the bucket was filled, he slowly walked back to the school trying not to slosh water all over his trousers. Retrieving the long-handled dipper from the nail on the wall, he walked up and down the aisles passing the water bucket to the children. The only rule was "don't drink over the bucket."

Winter was fast approaching. Almost daily snowflakes floated down from overcast skies, bringing with them the promise of a very cold and wet season. About mid-December, the days had that cold, low overhanging heaviness, signaling a major winter storm was brewing. One night it snowed, and the winter winds howled through the hills, down in the valley, and up in every holler leaving almost insurmountable snowdrifts. Florence awoke with a pressing feeling that she needed to be at school early that day. She asked her landlord for the use of one of his mules. Sitting astraddle the animal, Florence hung on as the mule slowly and skillfully trudged his way through the deep snow.

Arriving at the schoolhouse, Florence quickly went inside. Thank goodness she had the forethought of banking the fire before leaving the day before. She knew the children would be arriving with wet feet and cold hands and would need a good hot fire to quickly dry and warm them. Not only was she their teacher but also their guardian. She did whatever she could to help prevent her students from coming down sick, especially with pneumonia, which could be a deadly illness. One by one and in small groups, the children arrived at the little schoolhouse. Coming inside to the welcoming glow radiating from the stove, Florence greeted them with a warm fire, warm hugs, and a warm smile. The fire burned hot in the center of the room warming everything that was close to the stove. However, the warmth failed to reach the drafty corners where the older children were sitting. They had to huddle together in order to generate their own warmth.

While the wind continued to howl outside, Florence and the children remained busy inside the little school with their studies. All of a sudden, the sound of dynamite exploding intruded the quiet clearing. The noise was so immense it caused the glass windowpanes to shatter and fall to the floor. Chaos erupted in the small room as another explosion sounded in the distance, followed by yet another. Florence, just as frightened as her students, tried to remain calm. Corralling the children around her as a mother hen does to protect her chicks, they all cried out at once, "What happened?"

"I don't know, children, I don't know," replied Florence, huddling together in the center of that little one room schoolhouse.

"What did happen?" Marla's son Jessy asked. Looking at my family, I noticed several pairs of large brown eyes looking back at me.

"The progress of building Bagnell Dam had made it to Prairie Holler. Contractors, who had been hired by Union Electric were dynamiting the land, making way for the lake," I explained.

After the windows had blown out of the school building, the Arholdt school closed its doors forever. Florence and her students moved to the Moulder School, located on higher ground southeast of Windermere and Cedar Point in central Camden County. Florence continued teaching until the spring of 1930. The dam project was almost complete. Men that had migrated to the area, working at clearing the land, were moving on in search of employment elsewhere, taking their families with them. Moulder School closed its doors two months earlier than was scheduled, leaving Florence unemployed.

28

Gravediggers ♥

Jessy was anxious to know more. "What were they dynamiting?"
"From what I was told, old graveyards."
"Graveyards? Why?" asked his wife, Jennifer, who had recently joined us.
"Over several hundred years, old graves in that area had been covered with layers of sandstone that eventually turned into solid rock. The rocky ground had to be dynamited so the graves could be found and moved."
"But why move them?"
"If the newer graves remained at the bottom of the lake, bodies could be dislodged and float to the top. In order to keep that from happening, the graves had to be moved to higher ground. And out of respect for the families that still lived in the area, older graves were also moved."

Generations of families had lived their entire lives in the backwoods of this region. They succumbed to their death through years of hard toiling work, accidents, and illnesses. Diseases such as measles, cholera, and typhoid fever were common occurrences. Once an epidemic started, the disease would rage through tightly knit communities. Young children, along with the aged, were usually the primary targets of these deadly diseases. The only thing that could be done was to try and isolate the sick and then pray. Sometimes God's will was to be done, and the disease would claim the entire family. Graves bearing the same family name had been dug side by side throughout local cemeteries.

In addition to hard work, accidents, and disease, deaths during complicated childbirths claimed its share of infants and mothers. Most of the children were born at home. So when a woman's time came to deliver, doctors were notified only if the child could not be delivered by normal means. Depending on the severity of the situation, the life of the unborn child, as well as that of the mother, could be in jeopardy.

People living in homes scattered through the woods and along the rivers sometimes buried their dead on private property in small family cemeteries.

Whether the cemeteries were in town or on the family farm, some of the graves had been left undisturbed for generations. Now, those lying in what was to become the lake basin had to be moved.

One evening just about dusk, a thick fog moved into the valley, making its way toward the river. It rolled around the bend like a snake slithers along the top of water, and soon the whole area was blanketed with a thick gray mist. The woods were thrown into complete darkness when the fog covered any glimmer of light the moon provided.

"Come inside before you catch your death," Myrtle called out to Mayme, Ruby, Fern, and Beryl. The young girls, standing on the back porch, were so intent on what was happening outside they failed to hear their mom calling. They were listening to a low, far-off rumbling noise. Standing arm in arm, they strained to look through the fog, in the direction where the sound was coming from. The noise steadily grew louder. Suddenly, two small pale yellow circles came over the crest of the hill, penetrating through the fog.

"Here they come," Beryl whispered.

"Move over, I wanna see," Ruby cried, giving her sister a little shove.

The girls continued to watch as the small beams of light grew into an eerie glow, the fog causing them to waver and become distorted with each bump in the gravel road.

"They're here again," Mayme stuttered.

Closer and closer, the lights moved toward the house and the frightened young girls. Slowly, cutting through the fog, a flatbed truck came into view. The girls held their breath as the truck crept passed the Moulder home. They continued to watch until all that was left were two little red taillights being swallowed up in the mist. The steady rumble of the truck's engine slowly faded in the distance. Standing still, and with wide frightened eyes, the girls jumped when a deep-throated croak of a big bullfrog called out, seeming to say, "They're coming, you better run" sending the girls scurrying back in side the safety of the house.

Not wanting to attract the attention of the local people, the gravediggers, who had been hired by Union Electric to dig up graves, worked under cover of darkness. However, they did have the full attention of the Moulder children!

"Okay, girls, calm down," Lonnie scolded. "Git to bed."

Soon the family was settled down for the night, all except Mayme. With covers pulled up around her neck, she lay wide-awake listening to the sounds of the night. She heard a night owl screech in the distant. "Who, who, who are you?" he seemed to be saying to the gravediggers, as they started their gruesome task.

The trucks came to a stop at the edge of a cemetery. The gravediggers climbed down to the ground, carrying their pickax and shovel. They had only the dim glow of their oil lantern by which to work. They started digging at the base of the tombstones. Some of these graves were over a hundred years old. The pine box caskets had long since deteriorated. Opening one grave at a time, the gravedigger would sift through each shovel full of dirt. Being ever so reverent in their search, sometimes just a small piece of cloth would be uncovered. Or maybe a ring, a ladies broach, or man's cufflinks would be lying in the overturned dirt. There would be no visible remains of a body. A handful of dirt placed inside a shoebox-sized container, along with the objects found, was sufficient. Sometimes, the gravedigger would uncover a few bones or fragments of a skeleton. These pieces of what was once a human being were placed in a larger pine box. As each grave was uncovered and the remains put in a new coffin, the name of the deceased would be marked on the wood and put on the trucks along with the tombstone or grave marker.

It was a long night for Mayme. She had laid awake for hours thinking about the gravediggers. The sounds of night normally lulled her into a peaceful sleep, but this night was different. So much was happening in her small world. There were strangers cutting down the familiar woods surrounding her home. Her relatives and childhood friends were moving away. And now the gravediggers had come. It was a sad time for the young girl.

"Git up, young'uns. Old Flossie's been out in the barn raisin' a ruckus. There's wood that needs to be split and hauled to the house. Day's awasten, git up I say," Lonnie called out to his family.

Before Mayme opened her eyes, she heard the crackle of wood in the potbelly stove. The morning chill that had penetrated the little house during the night would soon be gone. The smell of side pork sizzling in the cast iron skillet let her know that her mom was already in the kitchen cooking breakfast. Slipping out of the warm bed and wrapped in a blanket, Mayme stumbled to the window to look out. The fog had lifted. The glare of the early morning sunrise caused her to squint. It didn't take long before she once again heard the rumbling noise. A shiver ran down her spine when she spotted the old truck coming back through the woods. This time, the flatbed was loaded down with small pine boxes on top of medium-sized pine boxes that were lying on top of bigger pine boxes. Gray-colored tombstones and grave markers that had turned black with age were lying haphazard on top of the stack and strapped to the sides of the truck bed. Mayme felt her mom's hand touch her shoulder. She had come to join Mayme at the window.

"They're taking them to a graveyard up on higher ground," Myrtle's soothing voice whispered low in her daughter's ear. "They're headed to their second and final resting place, where they'll be safe from being washed away when the floods come. Now sit down and eat your breakfast."

Several months passed, and still trucks carrying caskets could be seen traveling from one graveyard to another. With each passing truck, the feeling of sadness grew deeper.

Late one night in early fall, the family was sleeping soundly when all of a sudden a terrifying scream shook them all straight up.

"What's that?" asked Thomas, scampering to his parent's bed. Baby June, lying in the wooden cradle at the foot of Myrtles bed, started to cry.

"Quiet down. It's just a cougar looking for his mate." Myrtle tried to convince her family that a big cat crying out in the middle of the night was just another part of nature. However, in her heart, she wasn't so certain. The scream sounded again.

Huddled with Thomas in the middle of her parent's bed, Fern cried, "It's an awful sound. It sounds like a woman screaming."

Awakened by all the commotion, Lonnie scowled as he ordered his kids back to bed. When Thomas and Fern were settled down and almost asleep, Lonnie told his wife, "I saw tracks down by the river when I was checkin' my traps. The boys and I will go hunting tomorrow."

Soon the family became sleepy again. Myrtle, unable to sleep, pulled her rocking chair closer to the wood-burning stove, covered her shoulders with a shawl, and set down to watch the fire burn low. As she rocked, she thought about her family, her friends, and that old cougar crying in the woods. *Where would her family go when the time came to leave?* she wondered. *Would she be able to keep in touch with her friends?* Her own frustration began to build. It wasn't right, she reasoned, to be forced out of the home where she had raised her children. And Lonnie was worrying so about finding a house big enough for all of them, let alone one they could afford. A last lone cry came from somewhere deep in the woods. Myrtle's thoughts turned to the wild cat. Is he too feeling frustrated about being run out of his home or burned out of the woods? In her mind, it was wrong that not only people, but also wildlife, had to be displaced from their homes in order for a lake to be built. Maybe, just maybe that was why this cougar was crying out in the middle of the night.

The next afternoon, Lonnie, Howard, and Ray came around the barn, dragging a very big cougar. After depositing the cat in the yard, they came inside the house for a cup of coffee. Lonnie started telling a story he had heard from a nearby neighbor. "I heard tell those gravediggers was up the river diggin' up a grave when one of them stepped on his shovel to pick up a load of dirt and the blade hit something soft. He commenced to use his hands to finish the job. Lo and behold, he found a man's body in a shallow grave directly on top the old grave. Like to have scared the crap out of him."

"Who was it?" Mayme asked, coming to sit by her daddy's side.

"Don't rightly know," Lonnie told his daughter, "probably one of those strangers that are nosin' around the woods. He hadn't been there long because he was still fresh. And coyotes hadn't found him yet."

Lonnie was interrupted by Myrtle's cautioning tone. "That's enough. There are some big ears close by. And they are taking in every word you say."

"Oh, Mom, I wanna hear about the man in the grave," whined Mayme.

"It's not proper for you to hear such things. Now go on. You have chores to do." After the child was gone, Lonnie confided in Myrtle, "This used to be a God-fearing land, but now, with all the strangers here from all over . . ."

"Did they ever find out who he was?" asked Torrie.

"According to Aunt Mayme, no they didn't," I explained.

"If all the graves had to be moved, where did our ancestors go?" he inquired.

"Our great-great-grandmother, Eliza Jane Gerhardt, was moved from Old Coelleda to a cemetery outside of a small town called Roach. Lonnie's parents, Thomas Hart and Martha Jane, who were buried at the Moulder Cemetery near Cave Pump Post Office at Windermere, Missouri, were moved to a cemetery on Upper Prairie Holler road. The Parracks, a God-fearing Christian family, donated land for the sight of Prairie Holler church and its cemetery. The church and Parrack Grove Cemetery are located in a peaceful little grove of trees tucked back in the woods.

29

The Move ♥

By the time Lonnie and Myrtle had been given their final notice to move off the river, their four oldest children had reached adulthood. On August 18, 1928, Howard had married Lillie Degraffenreid, a young woman whose family lived in the backwoods. Howard and Lillie were living near Lower Prairie Holler, and Howard was helping his father-in-law farm the Degraffenreid place. The following year on March 30, 1929, in Buffalo, Missouri, Nera married Henry Ricker, a man from Camden County. The couple moved to north central Missouri, where Henry found employment making bridge trusses. Ray also moved away from Linn Creek. His move took him north to Liberty, Missouri, where he worked with a crew shoring up the banks of the Missouri River. Florence was still employed by the school board, teaching at the Moulder School. She had become engaged to Ralph Morgan from Roach, Missouri.

Times were very somber for Lonnie. Day after day, vast changes were taking place around him. The entire town of Linn Creek had been demolished and rebuilt a few miles southeast of where it had once stood. It didn't matter to Lonnie that the relocating of an entire town, causing its residents to give up their homesteads, was one of the most disturbing aspects for Union Electric. Or that the purchase of property and razing of buildings was one of the most difficult tasks the new owners also had to endure. All he knew was that the tall sycamore, maple, walnut, pine, and cedar trees that had reached toward the sky for centuries providing shelter, as well as fuel, lumber, and a way of life were now reduced to short squatty stubs. Deer, turkey, possum, raccoons, and other wildlife Lonnie had relied on, not only for a means of support but food for his family, was now forced to find shelter in other parts of the county or succumb to a certain death. Valleys and hills now lay barren. Meadows of green grasses and wild flowers, where his children had romped and played for years chasing imaginary Indians and riding stick horses, were now dotted with raw piles of overturned soil where the gravediggers had conducted their gruesome task.

After years of denial that a dam was going to be built across the Osage River, flooding the Big and Little Niangua rivers, Lonnie finally accepted the inevitable. All of this land was soon going to be swallowed up under more than forty feet of water.

Moving day arrived with a cold chill in the air that seemed to penetrate to the very bone. Or was the chill in their hearts?

Lonnie and Myrtle, along with their younger children, were up before the crack of dawn. They were just finishing packing household items into crates and cardboard boxes when Florence and Ralph came riding down the road in Ralph's truck, followed by Nera and Henry who had moved back to a farm north of Macks Creek. Over the hill came Howard, Lillie, and their two young sons riding in a buckboard wagon. Myrtle was surprised to see Ray driving his new car into the yard. He had come back to help his family move. Lonnie and Myrtle once again had all of their children home.

After a short while, Lonnie interrupted the steady stream of conversation coming from around the kitchen. "Okay, time's awaistin'. We got work to do."

"Hasn't changed a bit, has he?" Ray asked his older brother.

"Nope," Howard spoke only one word, as the boys followed their dad out the back door.

It didn't take the men long to carry the packed cardboard boxes and crates, filled with dishes, pot and pans, flatware, clothes, and beddings from the house to Ralph's truck, where Howard was waiting to carefully stack them on top of each other. Using a strong wire, Ray secured the old washtub and water bucket, along with the dipper, to the running boards on the side of the truck. Howard's wagon had been loaded down with the bedposts, trundle bed, feather tick mattresses, kitchen table, and chairs. Myrtle had caged her laying hens in wooded cages, which were now fastened to the frame of the wagon. Last but certainly not least, Lonnie and Myrtle's big oak rockers were safely tied inside the wagon box. Myrtle returned to her home, taking one last look around each room to make sure nothing was being left behind.

Union Electric had sent out a declaration that only personal items could be removed from the property. However, one friendly agent advised Lonnie to take whatever he wanted, since whatever was left was going to be burned anyway. So a few days prior to moving, Lonnie had removed the oak siding from the barn. Fearful that the electric company would find out that he had taken what was no longer his, he set the barn on fire.

Lonnie clicked to Jude and Kate, the only two of his trusted old mules he hadn't sold. Leaving the holler one last time, the family traveled up the mail-route road to the high ridge overlooking the river. Getting out of the cars and down off the wagon seats, the family stood huddled together.

Holding on to one another, they watched in silence as a bright yellow orange hue crept along the riverbanks and up through what used to be the woods. Flames as far as they could see were leaping up with long fiery tongues, reaching high in the sky. Tears flowed unchecked as they watched the fire consume their home before it crumpled to the ground. In a shower of sparks, flames shot into the gray blackness that was starting to surround them. Smoke curled upward, forming long wavy columns, as it signaled a torched building lost somewhere below. The fire continued to creep along the water's edge reaching Uncle Elmo and Aunt Anne's farm. "This is one of the saddest times I can ever remember," Nera told her mom. With tears overflowing from her dark brown eyes, she continued, "Our dear neighbors, our aunts, our uncles, our friends are all gone."

Heat from the raging fire soon reached the family as they stood there on that high bluff. But the heat could not penetrate the cold lonely feeling that each one of them felt. Lonnie's frustrations rose as a sour taste came into his mouth from the pit of his stomach. He was feeling utterly lost, having to give up his home and his livelihood in order to relocate to another place far from the river. Swallowing hard to keep down the bile that was building in his stomach, he stood there and watched a thick gray blanket of smoke cover the river. Lonnie stood on top of that bluff, clinching his jaw and balling his worn hands into fists, as he remembered all the hard work over the years just to make ends meet. As the fire reached Albert Moulder's farm, the acid stench of smoke and burning wood rose from the basin of the river. Myrtle looked down into the flames leaping higher and higher. *For better or for worse is what I promised my man many years ago*, she thought to herself. *For richer and for poorer. Well, we sure have been through the poor part. Hopefully this move will be for the better. Lonnie will provide for us, just as he always has.* Dick and Mayme cried, remembering the fun times they had going to parties and picnics with their girlfriends and boyfriends. Now they were being forced to leave those friends behind. Ruby, Fern, and Beryl watched a small herd of deer racing ahead of the flames, desperate to reach the safety of the river. The young girls held on to each other, sobbing, as they remembered racing toward that same river to cool off on hot summer days. Little Thomas stood solemnly between his parents. In his young mind, he knew something big was happening to his family. He just couldn't grasp the hugeness of it. Baby June, held securely in her mom's arms, looked from one person to another, oblivious as to what was going on. All she could understand, at her young age, was that everyone she loved was crying. And this made her sad.

The fires continued to creep along the barren land consuming the buildings belonging to their neighbors and friends as it consumed their hearts. On a bitter cold January day in 1931, Lonnie Moulder's family bid a final goodbye to their beloved river. The lonesome sound of a lone whip-poor-will cried in the night as the family turned away from the bluff. The old home place and the once-thriving community of Linn Creek were slowly disappearing into history.

30

Goodbye ♥

"It's time. You need to hurry." Hearing a strange voice, I looked up and saw a nurse standing in the doorway of that small waiting room. The room had become my refuge during the past several hours. What was she doing intruding on my family? And why was everyone racing into the hallway? I thought to myself. All of a sudden, the air went totally out of my lungs. I couldn't breath. I felt as if someone had slugged me the gut. Realizing what the nurse had said, I told myself, *It can't be time. Marla's not here; she and her husband, Steve, are still in Phoenix. They won't be back in Wichita until ten o'clock tonight. And their daughter Mandi is on her way. She should be here any moment. It can't be time. I'm not ready! Oh, God please. I'm not ready.* I silently screamed to myself.

Not knowing how I got there, I found myself standing outside Mom's room looking in. As if in a dream, I saw my family surrounding Mom's bed. Each one was holding on to the person standing next to them. One of their arms was stretched out, their hands gently touching Mom, as if holding her safely until she passed into Jesus' loving arms. I took my place between Dad and Phyllis at the head of Mom's bed. As we stood there, touching mom, the monitors above her head started to click. Mom's breathing slowed. And then stopped. The respirator was the only thing that was now forcing air into Mom's lifeless body. For a few more seconds, the heart monitor continued to register a faint beat. One, two, three, four and then nothing.

It was time. Mom was no longer in pain. She was no longer struggling to live in a worn-out body. I couldn't cry. I couldn't even feel. How can her life be over? She looked so peaceful lying there, as if she were only sleeping. I felt Dad move. He slowly reached out and patted the top of Mom's head before leaning down to kiss her pale lips. I caught a faraway look in his wet eyes. It was as if he were reliving the last fifty-five years.

My family stood touching and caressing Mom for a while longer. Then one by one, we left the room. As soon as I stepped into the hall, I heard my niece Mandi, Marla's daughter. Jessy, her brother was whispering something in her ear. I saw her legs buckle. Jessy reached out, just in time, to keep her from falling. I was aware of my own daughters, Anetta and Suzanne, close by my side. I thanked God that I had their strength to lean on. Lost in our own thoughts, we left the hospital for the last time.

My family gathered together once again that night at the airport to welcome Marla and Steve home. We were all waiting at the door of the Jet way when my little sister walked through the opening. Dad was the first one to meet her. She fell into his waiting arms. "Oh, Daddy," she cried. "It was such a long way home."

Lonnie and Myrtle

Certificate of Marriage
State of Missouri

This is to Certify that on the Fifth day of March in the year of our Lord One Thousand Nine Hundred and Five at my Home in the County of Camden and State aforesaid I the undersigned a minister of the Gospel by authority of a license bearing date the Fourth day of March A.D. 1905 and issued by the Recorder of Deeds of Camden County, Missouri, did join in

HOLY MATRIMONY

Lonnie Moulder
of Linn Creek
County of Camden
State of Missouri

Myrtle Gerhardt
of Coelleda
County of Camden
State of Missouri

In the presence of
Omer Judon
Jessie Jackson

Witnesses
John H. Osborn
a minister of the Gospel

Marriage Certificate

Happy Holler Home

Ruby & Gaynel

Ruby's Spelling Certificate

Ray & Howards 65 lb fish

Sketch of House on Dry Ridge Artist Unknown

Lonnie and his 700 lb. hog

Earl, Donald & June

Moulder Family; Left-Right, Front Row: Nera, Mayme, June, Myrtle, and Lonnie: Back Row: Florence, Ruby, Fern, Dick, Ray, Beryl, Howard, and Thomas

Dry Ridge School June 2nd row 2nd from the right

June & Friends on Greens Mill Bridge

June's Graduation

June's Graduation Picture

Max Slusser

Howard, Lonnie, Thomas and Ray

Myrtle & Lonnie Moulder in Macks Creek

Lonnie & Myrtle's 50th Anniversary

Left to right: Howard, Nera, Ray, Florence, Zilpha (Dick), Mayme, Ruby, Fern, Beryl and June

Howard & Lillie Moulder

Nera & Henry (Sug) Ricker

Ray & Florence Moulder

Ralph & Florence Morgan

Zelphia (Dick) & Leon Ricker

Mayme & Onie Woodall

George & Ruby Kincaid

Eldon & Fern Clemmons

Beryl & Ethridge Rash

Thomas Moulder

Max & June Slusser

Macks Creek Centennial

Left to right: Fern, Ruby, Florence, Nera, Howard, Myrtle (seated), Beryl, Zilpha(Dick), Mayme and June

Part Two

Dry Ridge

31

New Beginnings ♥

    Tom, my brother, and his family arrived from Illinois the day after Mom died. Once again, my family gathered to support and help each other deal with the most difficult task we had to ever encounter. For the next few days, we stood strong beside Dad helping him make Mom's funeral arrangements.
    The day of Mom's funeral dawned hot and dry without a cloud in the sky. Family and friends filled the sanctuary of the church to bid her a final goodbye. It was overwhelming to witness how this small-town girl had made such a positive impact on so many people. After the funeral concluded, I returned to my parent's home along with my dad, brothers, and sisters. The steady stream of longtime friends and other family members that had come by to offer their condolences were now leaving us alone to mourn and grieve for our loss.
    Sitting in the last empty chair at the dining room table, I looked across the living room. I smiled when I saw my two daughters, with their husbands, and my grandchildren join my brothers, sisters, and a score of nieces and nephews settling down on the chairs, the couch, and some were even stretched out on the floor. There were so many of us that every available space in the room was filled. While I sat there, watching my family visiting with each other, a feeling of emptiness came over me. I left my place at the table and went to the kitchen. Stopping in the doorway, I listened, expecting to hear all the familiar noises that used to come from this room—pots and pans rattling, cabinet doors softly closing, water splashing in the sink, and Mom's nonsense humming. Standing there, I remembered an incident that happened a long time ago.
    In my memory, I was a little girl standing in this very doorway. Mom was puttering around the kitchen humming a little tune as she made supper.
    "Momma?" I asked. "What are you humming?"
    "Nothing, dear, why?"
    "That song, what is it?" my inquisitiveness peaked.
    "Oh that. Its just noise that makes a little nonsense tune."

Not realizing what I was doing, I started to hum my own little nonsense tune while I put a slice of chocolate cake on a plate and poured me a glass of iced tea.

Returning to my place at the dining room table, I sat down. The room grew quiet.

"Can you tell us more of Mema's stories?" Emily spoke up, breaking the silence.

"Yeah, what happened to Mema's family after they left the river?" asked Danielle.

"We've heard about Mema's brothers and sisters but not much about her. Can you tell us about when Mema was a little girl?" chimed in Samantha.

"Sure, I'd be happy to," I said. "Let's see now, where was I?"

Chris, my great-nephew reminding me said, "Mema's family was standing on a bluff overlooking the river."

"Yeah," replied his sister, Samantha. "And everything was burning."

"Everybody was so sad," cried Katie.

"Okay, okay. I remember," I chuckled.

32

Starting Over ♥

Bagnell Dam was now complete. Electrical service to St. Louis and southeastern Missouri began on Christmas Eve 1930. Some of the workers, who had been hired for the project, returned to their homes. Others moved on hoping to find employment elsewhere. Old-time families, who lived along the river and in the community of Linn Creek, moved away to surrounding towns. But the majority of Lonnie and Myrtle's neighbors purchased property in or around the newly erected town of Linn Creek. With so many families being forced to move, houses soon became scarce. However, Lonnie managed to find a small farm with a house large enough for his family one and a quarter mile south of Macks Creek, Missouri.

There was a lease on the property that had yet to be fulfilled. Lonnie negotiated with the current tenant, getting permission to move his cows and pigs to the wooded land that surrounded the house until he could move his family into their new home. In the meantime, Lonnie rented a small house in Macks Creek. It was exciting for the Moulder children to be able to actually live within the city limits of a town, if for only a couple of months.

Macks Creek is a modest little town that lays nestled in a small valley approximately twenty miles southwest of Linn Creek on U.S. Highway 54. A small sparkling stream runs through town and was one of the main attractions of the settlers who came to this area many years ago. For generations, the local Baptist church used the water in the stream for baptisms. Over the years, people have enjoyed its pleasant waters for fishing and swimming on hot summer days. And at least three times in the history of Macks Creek, water from the stream has saved the town from being completely destroyed by fire.

The stream was named Mack's Creek for a man who trapped and fished along its banks. Mack was simply referred to as Old Man Mack. On June 28, 1872, a post office was established under the same name of Mack's Creek. Twenty-one years later, on September 22, 1893, the town's name was changed to Macks Creek.

Macks Creek was a small but thriving town. Located on the far western side of town were the Masonic Lodge, a doctor's office and a general store. Down Main Street was the barbershop, a favorite meeting place for local men to visit and catch up on the news. Not only did the barber offer a shave for ten cents and a haircut for a quarter but was also often called on by the undertaker to make pine coffins. A post office, with mail-delivery service from Macks Creek to Lebanon was also located on Main Street, along with Fred Gerhardt's and, his brother-in-law, Bob Eidson's local mercantile. Mat Gerhardt owned and operated Macks Creek café. The Bank of Macks Creek stood on the southwest corner of Main Street. Up the road, on the corner of Baptist Street and county road N, was the Baptist church. Farther up N road was the schoolhouse.

As travel increased on Highway 54, Creach Hotel was a popular place to get a room and a family-style meal. In 1932, a year after the Moulders moved to town, three new mills began operation. Due to the repeal of prohibition, wooden staves, or slats as they are now more commonly called, were needed to make barrels for storing and shipping whiskey and beer. White and Bur oak trees were cut down, hauled, and sold to these stave mills.

With all its progress and growth, the small town of Macks Creek has endured during the last century. The stream that flows along the west side of town has remained constant, winding its way through the hills and valleys, changing only as Mother Nature so willed it to do before finally emptying its spring waters into the Niangua River.

33

Moving to Dry Ridge ♥

Two months passed. March 1, 1931, Lonnie and Myrtle moved their family into the new home up on Dry Ridge.

"Why was it called Dry Ridge?" Rusty asked.

"No one in the family really knows for sure. But speculation has it that Dry Ridge, an area that spans several miles, was fittingly named because the small river named after Old Man Mack that snaked its way through the countryside and down in the meadows was more than a mile away," I replied.

The farm was a mile and a quarter south of Macks Creek on county road O. Going south from Highway 54, the road wound its way up and down the hills through the valleys and meadows. After crossing a rock slab, spanning a narrow creek, the road meandered up a hill, turned slightly to the southwest, ran between the house and the barn before rounding a curve to head back south toward Mill Creek Road.

The Moulder's new home was the most beautiful house they have ever seen. It was a big two-story home with windows in each of the six rooms. A wraparound porch encased the side and back of the house. Dick, Mayme, Ruby, Fern, Beryl, and Thomas crowded through the front door and into the parlor. Standing awestruck with their eyes opened wide and their mouths agape, they tried to take in the entire house all at one time. Myrtle, holding two-year-old June, stood behind them, equally astonished.

"Well, I'll be," commented seven-year-old Beryl. "We sure are livin' high on the hog now."

There was a door to the left of the parlor that led into a large master bedroom. Light was shining in from one of the windows making the dust particles in the air glisten. On the right side of the parlor was a wide archway leading into the living room. A bay window on the south side of the room was big enough someone could sit on the inside ledge to look out over the countryside. On the east wall, a small fire was burning in a potbelly stove, chasing away the morning chill. Six-inch-high baseboards lined the shiny hardwood floors. Each door was trimmed with molding four inches wide. Carved into the top of each door facing was an intricate pattern. Directly in front of them was a beautiful stairway leading up to two bedrooms on the second floor. An oak banister, ending at the base of the steps, was held in place by two upright square columns, each supporting a four-inch round wooden ball. A long hallway, running the length of the staircase, led to the kitchen. A white cast-iron wood cook stove stood by the outside wall right next to a brand-new icebox. Whitewashed cabinets hung on the interior walls with the base cupboards, covered with gray Formica counter top, directly beneath them. Inside the kitchen, there was enough floor space for a large dining room table. Built into the west wall was a fireplace. A wooden box holding just a few sticks of kindling sat close by. Myrtle thought to herself, *Probably need to split wood 'fore long. Never know when a spring storm might hit.* By the back door was a wooden stand, a perfect place for the ever-present water bucket, washbowl, and soap dish. Above the stand, small porcelain pegs had been fastened to the wall to hold the dipper and a hand towel.

Myrtle and her children couldn't help but marvel over the thought that in comparison to the house on the river, this was a mansion.

While Myrtle and her children were checking out the interior of the house, Lonnie was busy looking over the outbuildings and the lay of the land. The house sat back from the crest of a hill. A few hundred feet from the back door was the smokehouse. It was approximately four foot wide, five foot long, and seven foot high and sat directly on the ground. A small wooden door provided access into the building. The roof was a piece of corrugated metal that lay angling up and into a peak at the top. Layers of mud and straw sealed the gaps between the roof and the walls.

Lonnie's nostrils were assaulted by the stale smell of burnt hickory wood when he opened the door to peer inside. *Well, it may be small, but it sure is tight,* he thought to himself. After his eyes grew accustomed to the dark interior, he noticed that wooden shelves, worn and blackened from years of smoke, lined the entire little room from ceiling to floor. Looking up, he saw rafters that were made from crisscrossing wires. "Well, I'll be. Never seen the likes of that afore." A steel meat hook hung from the wires directly over a rock fire pit. Backing out the doorway, Lonnie closed and latched the door. He was pleased that the door fit snug. This would ensure the smoke couldn't get out and animals couldn't get in.

Across the road and a few hundred yards from the house sat the barn. The building was structurally sound but was in need of some repairs. There were three small stalls, a tack room, and a haymow large enough to store bails of hay. To the side of the barn, a pigpen made from split railing was attached. A corncrib, also built out of split rails, was across the barnyard.

A well, where the family could get its water, had been drilled sixty feet down through rocky soil to the waterbeds far below. In order to protect the well from weather or dirt and debris, a small wooden framed structure with a roof set on top of vertical side beams had been built around it. A long cylinder water bucket was tied to a rope. The rope stretched up to a wide pulley and was wound around a horizontal rod at the top of the frame. When the bucket was not in use, the loose end of the rope was looped around a bracket attached to the wooden side of the frame to hold the bucket in place at the top of the frame house.

A small pond filled with fresh ever-flowing spring water was below the hill. It provided fresh water year round for Lonnie's cows, pigs, mules, and horse. It was also a dandy place to go swimming on hot summer days.

There was an apple orchard with about twenty mature trees scattered haphazardly in the neighboring hillside. Fresh apples in the summer, dried apples in the winter, apple butter and cider all year long. Nothing could be better than that.

The farmland, however, did not fair as well as the house or the outbuildings. "Too many rocks," Lonnie complained.

34

Growing Children ♥

Howard and Lillie, forced to leave the river along with his parents, moved up to Dry Ridge. Howard moved his family into a one-room house called the weaning house. This small house sat across the road and up a little hill behind Lonnie and Myrtle's big house.

"That's a funny name," laughed my granddaughter Chelsea.

"Why'd they call it a weaning house?" asked Anetta, her mom.

"The weaning house," I explained, "was a place where a married child could live until they established a home of their own. Sort of like being 'weaned' away from his parents. In the case of daughters, the weaning house was a place she could live with her new husband until he proved he was not abusive and could take good care of her."

"Too bad they don't have 'weaning houses' today," laughed Anetta, looking at her little girl.

"Oh, Mom," sighed Chelsea.

In this little one-room house, Lillie made a plain but comfortable home for her husband and their young sons. The small woman, very gentle and kind with her words and actions, was an extremely hard worker and very knowledgeable at many household tasks.

One task in particular was sewing and making quilts for her family. Using material from feed sacks, many of which she had swapped her own feed sacks with neighbor ladies until she had all one pattern, Lillie would hand stitch the edges together to make large squares. She would continue to sew squares of feed sacks together until she had a piece of material that would fit a full-sized bed. Using the backing material from an old warn quilt, she would patch or stitch together any worn or torn spot in the fabric. Turning it over so that the inside was now the outside, the material looked brand-new. After pinning cotton batting between the large piece of cotton fabric and the feed-sack squares, Lillie would hook two corners of the material to nails she had hammered into the ceiling, letting the rest of the material hang to the floor. On the end of a piece of string, about six inches long, she'd tie a knot. On the other end of the string, she'd tie a piece of chalk. Then starting in the corner, after pinning the knot to the material, she would take the chalk and draw a fan-shaped line directly on the material, as one would use a protractor. She would move the knot an inch, stretch out the string, and make another chalk mark. She would continue moving the knotted end of the string across the quilt, drawing fan-shaped lines. When she had uniform fans drawn all over the material, she had a pattern to follow as she made small uniform sized stitches. When she wasn't quilting, Lillie took the other two corners of the quilt and fastened them to the remaining nails. The quilt, now hanging from the ceiling, allowed the family to live below it. Within three days, Lillie could produce a beautiful handmade quilt.

Nera and her husband, Henry Ricker, had moved back to their beloved Ozarks from north central Missouri to establish their home north of Macks Creek, in Coffey Holler, where Henry had lived growing up. During his grade school days, Henry acquired the nickname of Sug because he was the courier of love notes between half-grown boys and girls who were smitten with each other. Several times a week, the young lad heard, "Hey, Sugar, take this note to so and so." As he grew older, his nickname of Sugar was shortened to Sug. Throughout his life, Henry was known to most of the town's people as Sug Ricker.

During their life together, the Ricker's operated a small farm before venturing into the retail business.

Because the Great Depression had the United States tightly in its grasp, Ray decided to move north to Booneville, Missouri. There, he was able to find employment working with a crew of men shoring up the banks of the Missouri River. No matter how far the young man ventured away from home, he would always return to his family every three to four weeks for a short visit, and then he would be gone again.

Florence continued teaching until the Moulder School ran out of money and was forced to close. With the lake project complete, workers moved out of the area in search of their next job, taking their families with them. Florence remained living at Sherman Roger's boardinghouse. Throughout her young life, she had never stopped searching for Mr. Right. She finally found him living in Roach, Missouri. His name was Ralph Morgan, an aspiring young businessman. When the Missouri State Highway Department built Highway 54 through Macks Creek bringing the automobile industry into the hills of the Ozarks, Ralph recognized the need that was rising for automobile fuel. He started construction of his first gas station with plans to own many more.

Dick was eighteen years old when the Moulders moved to the house on Dry Ridge. Along with helping her mom care for the younger children and working in the fields beside her dad, Dick had the never-ending chore of sewing on loose buttons, putting patches on knees of trousers and elbows of shirts, and mending torn seams. She had inherited from her mother a talent of making new clothes out of worn garments. Dick could take an old piece of clothing, tear out the seams, turn the collars and cuffs inside out, and replace old buttons with new ones. Before long, a new outfit would evolve. Using the Sears Roebuck catalog to see what the latest fashions were and then using the pictures as a guide, Dick would cut out patterns from old newspapers to aid her in making new clothes for her herself and her family. It wasn't long before Macks Creek recognized Dick's talent with a needle and thread. The young woman received offers to hire out as a seamstress to some of the townspeople. Prior to the family leaving the river, Dick had been dating Leon Ricker, a local schoolteacher. After the move, their courtship continued.

Before the family left the house by the river, Mayme had been attending the Moulder School. During her grade school years, there would sometimes be only one or two students in her class. The school system deemed these extremely small classes, the off-years class. When this occurred, those few students would join the class ahead of them or the class behind them. Myrtle never allowed her daughter to advance to the next higher grade because according to Myrtle, "You could never get too much learnin'."

"Wait a minute," Danielle said, interrupting me. "How did she ever get out of school if she always went backward?"

"Well," I tried to explain. "The way I understand it is that Mayme advanced to the next grade every other year."

"Bummer," scowled my niece.

Mayme was so anxious to learn as much as she possibly could, she never complained about having to repeat a grade. When the family moved to Macks Creek, Mayme attended the eighth grade with her sister Ruby at the Dry Ridge School. At the age of sixteen, Mayme finally received her eighth grade school certificate. She wanted to continue with her education, but Lonnie had already sent two daughters to high school and couldn't afford to send another one. So when school started that fall, Mayme found employment around town doing odd jobs such as light household duties and babysitting.

One day, while Mayme was in Macks Creek visiting her sister Nera, a brand-new Chevrolet came speeding down Main Street. The car stopped in front of the bank. The driver's door opened and out stepped the most handsome man Mayme had even seen. He was wearing a clean white shirt and a pair of pinstriped overalls. A straw pompadour hat was cocked off to one side of his head, resting just above his eyebrow.

"Who's that?" Mayme asked.

"That's Onie Woodall. He lives on a farm out west of town."

"Well," declared Mayme. "Someday I'm gonna marry him."

Ruby was now thirteen years old. In May of 1931, she received her eighth grade school certificate along with Mayme from the Dry Ridge School. Wanting to follow her older sister into the workforce, Ruby asked permission to get a job. Her parents felt she wasn't old enough and said no. When summer was over and the fall school session began, Ruby convinced her parents into letting her attend eighth grade again. With a grin across her face, she told Mayme, "It sure beats pickin' apples." In the spring of 1932, Ruby received her second eighth grade school diploma.

Fern was twelve years old, and Beryl nine years old when they started attending school up on Dry Ridge. The little girls were excited to be able to go to a school that was only a mile from their home. No more walking three miles to and from school each day, and definitely no more rivers to cross!

Six-year-old Thomas was old enough to attend school with his big sisters. Leaving his little sister, June, at home each morning upset the little boy. However, the excitement he felt racing across the hills and up the road toward the one-room schoolhouse soon replaced his feelings of sadness.

Three-year-old June was the youngest of Lonnie and Myrtle's eleven children. It didn't take her long to become her daddy's buddy. She would toddle around after Lonnie whenever she could sneak away from her mom's watchful eye. "C'mon, Pug, lets go to the field," Lonnie told June. "Your never too young to help out around the farm." Pug, being the nickname Lonnie had given his little girl, slid off the kitchen chair and ran to her daddy. "There's rock needin' picked before I can plow." While all of the older children were away from home making a life for them selves or attending Dry Ridge School, June remained home with her parents to pick rocks.

35

Florence Gets Married ♥

    Florence had grown into a beautiful young woman, full of grace and charm. Her voice was as soft as a summer's breeze. Her short brown hair framed her porcelain looking face making her appear to look as fragile as a china doll. When she spoke about her upcoming marriage to Ralph Morgan, her dark hazel eyes sparkled, like stars twinkling in the night.

    In the quiet surrounding of her room at the Rodger's boardinghouse, Florence spent many evenings looking through catalogs for a dress to wear on her wedding day. Montgomery Wards, Sears & Roebuck, and Spiegel's mail-order catalogs had a large selection of beautiful dresses and suits with matching hats from which to choose. But her dress had to be perfect. After days of searching, Florence finally found her wedding dress. Using the hard-earned money she had left over from her paycheck, Florence placed an order to Montgomery Ward and then waited anxiously for the days to pass.

    One day, several weeks later, Florence arrived home and was informed by Mrs. Rodgers that a box had been delivered and was sitting on the table. Racing into the kitchen, the anxious young woman grabbed the box and ran up the steps to the privacy of her room. Holding the package secure with both hands, Florence kicked the door closed with one foot before putting the box on the bed. Holding her breath, she untied the stout string that was holding the brown wrapping paper secure. After gently unfolding pieces of white tissue paper, there in the bottom of the box lay the beautiful blue chiffon dress. Holding the garment, Florence pressed it tightly against her body. Turning around and around in front of the full-length mirror, the pretty young women admired how the pale blue in the material made her cheeks turn a soft shade of pink. She would be the most beautiful bride on her wedding day. Carefully, she hung her new dress from a wire hanger hooked to the window frame.

    Every evening after dinner and the dishes were washed and put away, Florence would retire to her room to gaze at the beautiful wedding dress, while daydreaming about the day she would become Mrs. Ralph Morgan.

Her dress was the first thing she saw each morning and the last thing she would see right before she closed her eyes every night.

One afternoon, Florence returned home to find her beautiful wedding dress gone. *Maybe my dress has fallen to the floor behind the curtains,* she thought. Moving the bottom of the curtains away from the wall, she was disappointed when she didn't see her dress. *Okay, stop and think,* Florence said to herself. *Where could my dress have gotten off to?* Starting to feel sick in the pit of her stomach, she knelt down to look under the bed. Not finding the dress there, she ran to look behind the bedroom door. The dress was simply not in the room. In a panic, Florence ran out of her room and down the stairs. Taking them two at a time, she almost collided with Mrs. Rodgers, who was coming in the front door.

"Oh my," Mrs. Rodgers called out, in a started cry. Seeing the look of panic on the young woman's face, she questioned, "What in the world is wrong?"

With tears streaming down her flushed cheeks, Florence blurted out, "It's gone. My beautiful wedding dress is gone! Have you seen it?"

"Calm down, dear. It should be in your room," the housekeeper said, trying to soothe the distraught girl.

"But it's not. I've looked all over, and I can't find it. It was hanging by the window this morning. Now it's gone!" Florence screamed, almost to the point of hysteria.

"You must calm down. I'll help you look."

Both of the women returned to Florence's room. Sure enough, the dress was gone. After a complete search through the rest of the boardinghouse, the beautiful blue chiffon dress was nowhere to be found. Taking the distressed young woman by the arm, Mrs. Rodger's helped Florence to the kitchen.

After fixing them both a cup of hot tea, Mrs. Rodgers said, "Come now, dear, let's sit down and try to figure out where your dress could be."

Florence sunk into a chair, her head lying down cradled in her arms. Downhearted, her tears fell, making a wet puddle on the smooth service of the table. "What could have happened? Who would do such a thing?" she sobbed. Raising her swollen eyes to look at the woman sitting next to her, Florence screeched, "Who would do such a dreadful thing? Who stole my dress?"

Gently Mrs. Rodgers brushed Florence's dark brown hair back away from her face. Using her forefinger to tilt Florence's chin up, Mrs. Rodgers looked directly into the young woman's red, tear-swollen eyes. Gently, she said, "While you were out this morning, those rough characters that had been renting the rooms next to yours left. They packed up everything. I guess they've headed back to Arkansas."

A startled, dismayed look came across Florence's face. Squaring up her small shoulders, squinting her red eyes as she lowered her eyebrows, her young forehead creased with a deep frown, Florence whispered strongly emphasizing each word, "One of those rascals stole my dress!"

The feeling of sadness Florence felt about her stolen blue chiffon wedding dress slowly faded with each passing day. The feeling of anger and sadness was eventually replaced with happiness and excitement of her upcoming marriage.

March 7, 1931, dawned bright cold and crisp. There wasn't a cloud in the big blue sky. It was a beautiful day for a wedding. Florence was waiting at the window, watching for Ralph to come down the road. *Honk! Honk!* Hearing the distinct sound of the truck's horn, Florence ran out of the front door before Ralph's truck came rolling around the corner, stopping in front of the boardinghouse. Florence waited patiently by the curb for the dashing young man to climb out from behind the steering wheel. With pride, she watched him walk to the passenger side of the truck cab and gallantly open the door. Taking Florence's elbow in his hand, he gently helped his young finance onto the seat of his truck. As the couple drove off, they were oblivious to the dark ominous-looking clouds that were forming overhead.

After a three-hour ride, Ralph and Florence arrived outside the courthouse in Stockton, Missouri, where the young couple was guided into the county clerk's office.

"Sir, that'll be two dollars for a marriage license," the clerk said.

A stunned look crept across Ralph's eyes as he stood there, looking at his checkbook, the color draining from his face.

"What's wrong?" Florence softly asked.

"I don't have any money. I'm going to have to write a hot check," Ralph whispered.

"Don't do that. I have money left over from my teaching job. Here, take it," Florence told Ralph, slipping him two one-dollar bills.

Standing there in front of the justice of the peace, Florence quietly repeated her wedding vows. The thought of her beautiful blue chiffon wedding dress, somewhere in the Arkansas Hills, never crossed her mind. Dressed in a pair of men's blue-striped bib overalls, Florence Moulder became the wife of Mr. Ralph Morgan. Leaving the courthouse hand in hand, the newlyweds were giddy and in high spirits, as they climbed back into the truck for the ride home.

They had traveled only a few miles when the dark gray clouds that had been building earlier that morning were now covering the sky. The sun looked hazy, as clouds filtered its warm bright shine. "Looks like snow. We better hurry," Ralph said. The words were no sooner uttered than small snowflakes started to drift down from the sky. The farther they drove, the bigger the snowflakes became. Then, the wind started to blow. Snow was whipping around the truck with such a vengeance that Ralph could hardly see to drive to the top of the next hill. The falling snow was quickly turning into a spring blizzard, and the temperature was dropping dangerously low. "We're going to have to stop," Ralph told his young bride. "I can't see through this storm."

By the time they reached Buffalo, Missouri, it was impossible to travel any farther. Florence and Ralph were stranded for the night. They rented a room at the local hotel on the town's square. The wind continued to howl around the building as though trying to creep into each and every crevice, under the windowsill and beneath the door. But Florence and Ralph were oblivious of the storm howling outside their window. They were lost in each other's arms, keeping warm with their soft kisses and caressing embraces.

The next morning, it was no longer snowing, and the winds were calm. When the newlyweds stepped out of the warm lodging into the bright glare of the morning's sunlight, they were acutely aware of the dilemma that the storm had left in its wake. Due to drifting snow, all of the roads leading in and out of Buffalo were closed to traffic.

Holding Florence's arm, Ralph helped his bride through the deep snow as they walked up the street to a little corner café. Over a cup of hot coffee and a shared piece of toast, the couple assessed what they were going to do. Ralph's bank account was empty, and Florence had only a few dollars left from her paycheck. The newlyweds were anxious to get back home, so they hired a local man, who owned a tractor, to plow through the snowdrifts on Highway 54. The going was slow, but Ralph and Florence finally made their way back to Roach, Missouri. Florence's dream of marrying her Prince Charming had finally come true.

Florence continued to teach at the Moulder School until the waters running in the Big Niangua and the Little Niangua rivers became too deep for her to cross safely. After her job came to an end, Florence stayed busy working with her church and various community organizations. She was soon recognized as an outstanding citizen and always a supporting companion for her husband. Ralph had a job working with his brother, hauling gravel to newly constructed roads. Eventually, Ralph Morgan owned and operated several standard gas stations in the new town of Camdenton, Missouri.

"That's so romantic," Suzanne commented.

"Did you know that for many years, Aunt Florence kept it a secret that she had been married in a pair of men's overalls?"

"Why?"

"I don't know. Back then women often wore overalls, as you wear blue jeans today. She probably was a trendsetter and didn't even know it. As the years passed, her secret did slipped out though. However, out of respect for Aunt Florence, no one ever admitted to knowing she got married in her overalls."

36

Disobedience Comes to the Moulder Home ♥

As traumatic as leaving the Happy Holler home had been for Lonnie, Myrtle, and their children, their heartache was short-lived. It was the beginning of spring, and there was much to do in order to prepare for the coming winter. There were gardens to plant, fields to plow, crops to sow, buildings to mend, and wood to chop.

Within a few weeks after moving his family into their new home, Lonnie came to the house to join his wife for a cup of morning coffee. After taking a sip from his saucer, Lonnie exclaimed, "My God, woman, this taste like an old warn-out shoe."

"I know," Myrtle softly replied. "But it's the best we got."

"Why? Where's the coffee?"

"I'm out, and we can't afford more 'til the first of the month."

"This gall-darn depression. Ain't it never goin' let up?" barked Lonnie.

"I'm sure someday. But until then, I'm havin' to roast grains of wheat to make coffee."

"Wheat? What in tarnation!"

"If I roast the grains nice and brown and then grind them, I can make something that resembles coffee."

"Woman, I suggest you leave the grain in the bin. God, this taste awful." With that, Lonnie got up from the table and stomped back outside.

A few days later, Lonnie and Myrtle were sitting in their oak rockers, relaxing by the fire, when suddenly Lonnie put down the book he had been reading.

"Butler," he said. "That oak lumber I hauled up here from the river shore did come in handy. I finished siding that old barn today."

"That's nice," replied Myrtle looking up from her mending.

"And I've been a ponderin' what to do with the rest. I do believe there's enough to build you a chicken coop."

Laying her mending down in her lap, Myrtle exclaimed, "I've seen that ole fox snoopin' around the barnyard lately. Having the hens roosting in a henhouse should keep him at bay." After a few moments she continued, "I should be able to get enough eggs out of those hens to feed us, then I can sell the rest in town. Maybe I won't have to wait until the first of the month to get more coffee after all."

"I'll git started first thing after daybreak. I can already smell good black coffee brewin'," Lonnie said, returning to his book *The Texas Ranger*.

Lonnie was true to his word. Within a few days, he and Howard had a small chicken coop built, standing next to the barn.

For several years, Myrtle traded eggs, a couple of old hens, or a container of fresh-churned butter to a traveling salesman for a year's subscription to a newsy little newspaper called the *Capper's Weekly*. The newspapers not only informed Myrtle of new and exciting things that were happening in and around the area, but they were going to help keep drafts from coming in through the plaster and lath walls. Over the years, she had managed to save enough colorful sheets to paper the interior walls of the living room, parlor, and kitchen.

One Saturday morning, while helping their mom clean the house, Dick and Mayme started whispering.

"She will," Mayme said under her breath.

"No, she won't," Dick replied.

"I bet she will. Let's ask," Mayme said.

"Okay. Ask."

"No, you ask. You're older. She'll listen to you."

Noticing that her daughters were doing a lot of whispering behind her back, Myrtle asked, "What are you two up to?"

Cautiously, and with a little encouraging nudge from her sister, Dick approached her little mom. "Mom," she asked. "While we're cleaning, can we move the furniture around?"

"I don't think that would be a good idea. I've told you before, your dad likes it just the way it is," Myrtle tried to explain to her teenage girls.

"Please, Mom!" joined in Mayme. "We promise we'll move it back if Dad doesn't like it. PLEEEASE!"

"Oh, all right." Myrtle said, giving in to her daughters' pleading. "I don't have time for the likes of you two. But mark my words, he won't like it."

Returning to the kitchen, Myrtle left the two girls to the chore of moving furniture around the rooms as they cleaned, swept, and dusted. It took all morning for the girls to accomplish their task, but by dinnertime, they were satisfied with how the house looked and considered it a job well done.

Coming in to the house for his noon meal, Lonnie looked around the living room before setting down at the head of the table. He didn't say a word as he pinched off the crusty corner of the freshly baked corn bread. Slowly, Dick and Mayme exhaled their breath. Looking at each other beneath hooded eyes, they thought, *Good. It must be all right or else he would say something.* Lonnie just sat there slowly chewing his food.

When he finished eating, he looked at his two daughters, belched, and said, "Before you two git ready for town tonight, make sure you plant the corn." Without another word, he rose from the table, leaving the house through the back door.

After the dinner dishes were washed and put away, Dick and Mayme ran out to the barn to get a bag of corn. Racing to the freshly plowed field, they dumped a small pile of kernels at the end of each row of freshly turned dirt. Using the balls of their feet, the young girls quickly smoothed the dirt over the kernels.

"There, that should do it," they remarked.

"That didn't take long," committed Myrtle, as the two girls ran back inside the house and started up the stairs. "Are you sure you planted that whole bag of corn like your dad told you to?" Giggling, the two teenagers said they had indeed. Turning, they ran up the stairs toward their bedroom.

It was Saturday night. Dick and Mayme had plans to double date with Dick's fiancé Leon Ricker and Jack, a friend of Mayme's.

Holding up a blue pinstriped skirt and matching jacket, Dick remarked, "This outfit is going to look just beautiful on me." She had spent many hours separating the seams of one of her brother Ray's old worn-out suits. After pressing the material flat, she cut out pieces for a skirt from the trousers, shortened the hemline of the jacket and the sleeves to just the right length.

"Wait just a minute," Mayme replied. "I was going to wear that." Grabbing the suit from Dick, Mayme turned around and started to walk across the room. She had just taken a step when Dick reached out and grabbed a handful of her sister's hair.

Pulling Mayme backward, Dick screamed, "I don't think so. I made it, and I'm gonna wear it!"

"Ow, let go of me." Twisting from Dick's grasp, Mayme yelled, "Just for that, I am too gonna wear that suit!"

"Oh no, you aren't!" Dick reached out and slapped Mayme across the face just as Mayme grabbed a handful of Dick's hair.

Both girls were bound and determined not to give up the fight; caterwauling, screaming, and crying, they rolled around and around on the hardwood floor. All of a sudden, they heard the bedroom door open. Lying twisted together on the floor, their fist full of dark brown hair and welts from fingernail scratches turning red, the girls stopped wrestling and looked toward the door. There, in the doorway, was their mom. At that moment, Myrtle, who was only four foot ten inches tall, looked like a giant to the girls. Her small body, silhouetted by the setting sun, seemed to take up the whole space of the door opening.

"What's the meaning of this?" she asked in her calm but authoritative voice. Both girls rose from the floor, disheveled from the wrestling matched.

"I was planning to wear the suit," Mayme cried.

"No, I was. Besides, I made it," countered Dick.

Very slowly, Myrtle walked to the middle of the room. Without saying a word, she bent down to retrieved the crumpled suit from the floor. Standing upright, with the suit tightly clutched in her hand, Myrtle turned and silently walked back to the door.

Without turning around, she spoke in a voice just above a whisper, "Your dates will be here soon. Best git ready."

Stunned, Dick and Mayme watched Myrtle walk out of the room, taking the suit with her. After a few seconds, Mayme looked at Dick, and Dick looked back at Mayme. They knew their mother was very sweet tempered, but when she spoke, she meant business. Bursting out with laughter, the girls did as their mom had told them to do. Leon and Jack would be there soon, and they needed to get ready.

That night, after the girls returned home from their dates, Lonnie called out to them.

"Mayme, Dick, git in here."

"Oh, oh," said Mayme.

"Must be in trouble," Dick whispered.

Wondering if their dad was upset because of them fighting earlier or because they had moved the furniture, the girls looked into the living room. Their dad, a big scowl across his face, was seated in his rocking chair by the stove.

"He looks mad," Dick murmured.

Lonnie saw the girls, peering through the doorway. "Git in here, NOW!"

Having trouble meeting their dad eye to eye, the girls stood just inside the living room, looking down at the floor.

"Did you girls plant that seed corn like I told you to?" Lonnie asked.

"Yes, sir, we did," the girls replied, looking up into their dad's stern face.

"What?" he yelled.

"No, sir, we didn't," the girls confessed, lowering their eyes again to stare at the floor.

"What did you say?" he bellowed.

"No, sir, we didn't."

"Before the sun is in mid sky tomorrow mornin', you will have that corn planted. And by God, you better do it right. Do you hear me?" Lonnie's face had turned beet red, as he glared at his two daughters. Lonnie, loud and boisterous when angry, never struck his children. However, the look he would get in his blue eyes, like the look he had at that moment, made the girls shutter with fear.

"Git on up to bed."

Dick and Mayme knew they had defied their dad. Tossing and turning in their beds, it took them several minutes before falling into a fretful sleep. All of a sudden, out in the henhouse, the chickens started raising a ruckus, awakening the family.

Listening from their upstairs bedroom, Mayme and Dick heard their dad quickly jump out of bed. "The fox must have gotten in the chicken coop," he said. Then a loud resounding, "Ouch!" penetrated up through the floor. "What the hell," he screeched. "Where's the table? Hell's bells, Myrtle, where's the lamp?" *Crash!* Hearing the lamp fall to the floor, breaking the glass globe in thousands of tiny pieces, Dick and Mayme crawled deeper beneath their quilts. "Dammit all to hell, who moved the furniture?" Finally, the front door slammed shut. All was quiet once again. Staying safely beneath the quilts, both the girls dreaded when the morning sun would start to rise and they would have to face both their mom and their dad.

It was still dark outside when Dick and Mayme quietly rose from their beds. After getting dressed, they tiptoed down the stairs, through the foyer, and out the front door, softly pulling it closed behind them. Their feet seemed to fly across the yard as they raced to the barn. They each grabbed a bag of corn kernels and ran to the field. By the dim light of the lowering moon, the two girls planted the rows of corn. After the corn was in the ground, they ran back to the barn to hang up the empty sacks and then back to the house. Very easily, they opened the front door. The coal oil lamp in the kitchen was sending a dim glow of light down the hall.

"Oh, oh," Dick whispered to her younger sister when she heard her mom and dad talking.

"It's a good thing those chickens set up a ruckus last night. That fox, snooping around the chicken coop, was up to no good," Lonnie was saying.

"I'm glad you got that chicken coop up, or else he'd have gotten all my good laying hens," Myrtle replied.

"Darn! Mom and Dad are already up," Mayme whispered to her sister.

"Be quiet!" scolded Dick. "They'll hear you."

Depositing their shoes by the front door so they wouldn't make a sound, the girls tiptoed in their stocking feet to their parent's bedroom.

"Pick it up."

"Don't drag it."

"Shh! They'll hear you."

Within a few minutes, the girls had the furniture in their parents bedroom back exactly as it had been in the previous morning. The living room furniture would have to wait until their dad went outside.

Lonnie slurped down the last of the coffee, rose from the table, and left the house by way of the back door.

"All right, girls," Myrtle called out from the kitchen. "Your dad's outside. Best get the rest of the furniture back in place before he comes in for dinner."

Quickly and without much sound, Dick and Mayme did as their mom ordered. Before long, the living room furniture was just the way Lonnie liked it, plain and simple. To the relief of the girls, their parents never mentioned the acts of defiance they had shown that spring.

The summer of 1932, in Bolivar, Missouri, Zilpha May (Dick) and Leon E. Ricker were married. After their wedding at the local justice of the peace, the couple moved into a little house a few miles south of Dry Ridge School where Leon had been hired to teach. Dick continued to take in mending and sewing to help with their meager income.

37

The Tobacco Patch ♥

With most large families, when one child left home, one of the other children would step up to take over his or her responsibilities. The Moulders were no different. Mayme and Ruby took Ray and Howard's place working in the fields beside their dad. Fern took Florence's place helping her mother with the daily chores of milking cows, cooking big hearty meals for the family, washing piles of dirty laundry, and general house cleaning. Beryl was now old enough to take Ferns place with the responsibility of trying to keep Thomas and June from getting underfoot. Thomas was given the chores of feeding the chickens, gathering the eggs, and trying to stay out of mischief while young June, finding a playmate in Thomas, followed him everywhere he went.

That first spring up on Dry Ridge, Lonnie took his mule Molly out to the fields that lay fallow behind the house. He stood on top of the hill looking around at the wide-open space and down into the valley. A feeling of sadness came over him. He shook his head and muttered, "This shore is poor land. I had good sandy soil and plenty of water down on the river. Here, all I got is rocks." Pulling his hat down low on his forehead, Lonnie gave the reins a slight whip across the mule's back. Speaking out loud he said, "No sense in feeling sorry for what no longer is. Git up Molly. We got work to do."

With an occasional gee and a haw, Lonnie guided the mule through the field. The animal slowly trudged through the dirt pulling the plow behind her. The blade on the plow dug deep into the soil, uncovering hundreds of small rocks.

Thomas and June were following their dad in the field picking up rocks when June asked, "Thomas, does Dad grow rocks?"

"No, silly. Rocks don't grow," Thomas scoffed at his little sister.

"Are you sure?" June asked again, a frown creasing her little brow. Picking up yet another small rock and putting it in her metal bucket, she continued, "Thomas, I know we got all these rocks last time. But now there's even more. Are you sure Dad doesn't grow rocks?"

Lonnie turned the soil in an area approximately fifty feet long by twenty feet wide. While he was plowing the field, Ruby and Mayme were in the meadow scooping up fresh cow manure with a shovel and putting it into a wheel barrel. When the barrel was heaping with manure, the girls wheeled it to the plowed field. Using a hoe and the shovel, they mix the manure into the freshly turned soil making a "hot bed." The nitrates in the manure would make the soil turn hot, therefore rendering it useless to any other crop except a tobacco plant. Once the soil and manure had been mixed together, Lonnie took tobacco seeds, left over from the previous year's crop, and planted them in the ground.

With an abundance of warm sunshine during the day and moist cool nights, young tender plants started breaking through the ground, stretching upward. When the plants reached a few inches tall, Ruby walked down the rows, hoeing weeds while Mayme plucked them from the ground close to the base of each plant. Both girls were very careful not to disturb the new growth.

The days continued to be warm and sunny, and the tobacco plants continued to grow. When the plants were about knee high, Ruby and Mayme, after giving the ground a good weeding, would go in search of tobacco worms. These ugly fat green worms would sometimes be as big as the girl's little finger. The worms would attach itself with their spiny little legs to the underneath side of the big leaves. If left unattended, the worms could destroy the whole tobacco crop. Searching one plant at a time, the girls would turn each leaf over looking for a worm. When they found one, she would carefully pluck the slimy, squirmy thing from the leaf and drop it in to a small tin can of kerosene. The worms were usually full of eggs, so they were very careful not to squash it. If she happened to do so, slime would get all over her hand. The girls hated this job. And rightly so!

Tending the tobacco patch spanned out through the summer months and into the fall. By the end of October, the plants had grown to five feet tall. Large dark green tobacco leaves, wrapping around the stalk and then fanning out, resembled small palm trees. Each plant had a great head of seeds sprouting up and out from inside the core. It was evident that Ruby and Mayme had done a fine job.

One cool autumn day, Lonnie carefully cut the seeds from the plants. He took them to the barn, storing them in a cool dark corner. Retrieving his machete from a hook on the wall, Lonnie returned to the tobacco patch. With a big swing to the left and then again to right, he swung the sharp blade at the base of each stalk, falling it to the ground. Ruby followed close behind her dad, picking up the plants. When she had her arms full, she carried them to the barn and gently draped them over a pole that had been placed across the top railing of the stalls. For several days, the breezes blew through the interior of the barn, drying out the big leaves.

Lonnie checked the tobacco leaves daily. When they started to dry, he and Ruby stripped the leaves from the stalks. Taking several of the large leaves and a piece of twine, Lonnie tied the bases together then drape them back across the poles. After a week or so, the tobacco would be dry enough to twist but not so dry as to crumple in his hands. Lonnie would then take a bunch of tobacco, hold it by the twine, and start to twist the leaves together. He would twist and twist and twist until he had a nice tight wad. He would then hang the twists of tobacco by the twine and upside down along the poles until they were good and dry. Lonnie grew only enough tobacco for his own use.

In the evening, after all the chores were done for the day, he would retire to the back porch to enjoy a chaw of good fresh tobacco. While sitting on his toolbox, a wad of tobacco placed securely in his cheek, Lonnie would lay his pointer finger, along with his middle finger, making a V directly under his bottom lip. Puckering up, he would let the brown spit fly. Wow! Better get out of the way or you might get hit.

"I remember Grandpa doing that," Tom commented. "When I was small, there were many times I had to jump to get out of the way of a stream of tobacco juice."

"Ugh, that's so gross!" chimed in his daughter, Tammi.

38

Listen to the Corn Grow ♥

Corn was an essential food item for the Moulders. It was not only needed to help feed the family but was also used to feed the chickens and livestock.

"Mayme," Lonnie called out to his daughter. "Go hitch Molly to the plow. Its time we get the corn in the ground." Mayme hurried to do as she was told. Now that Ray and Howard were grown, she enjoyed being Lonnie's "boy," helping her dad in the field. It took only a few hours for the girl, the animal, and the plow to have the dirt turned over. Lonnie had hitched Jude, the other mule, to the rake. They followed Mayme through the freshly plowed field, harrowing the dirt, making it smooth and level.

To make sure the corn would be planted in nice straight rows, Mayme and her dad strung twine between two wooden stakes that were placed about one hundred feet apart. With a feed sack slung over her shoulder, the young woman took three kernels of corn from the bag, dropping them on the ground below the twine. With the aid of her big toe, she would push a little mound of dirt over the corn. Taking another step, she would drop three more kernels of corn. Another step and more kernels were dropped. When a row of corn was completed, she and Lonnie would move the stakes and twine over about three foot, tap the stakes back into the ground making a guide for yet another row. When the cornfield had been planted, Lonnie told Mayme, "Well, that's done. All that's left to do is pray for rain."

God answered their prayers, and the spring rains came. For several days, Mayme woke in the morning to cool rainy days. Finally, one day the sun broke through the overcast sky, chasing away the clouds. The warmth of the sun soon had the corn sprouting out of the ground. At first, all you could see were small pale green buds breaking through the soil. When the plants were only a few inches high, Mayme walked down each row, looking closely at the base of each corn stalk. When she found two or more plants spouting up, she would pull the weaker ones, giving the stronger plant room to grow.

By the beginning of summer and the days grew warmer, the small plants turned into bright green shoots. One evening, as the sun was lowering in the western sky, Lonnie and Mayme stood on the porch looking out over the cornfield. The dark green plants were growing tall and straight. They could see golden corn silk starting to show above the husks. "Look's like it's gonna be a good crop this year," Lonnie confided in his daughter. "You did a mighty fine job, girl."

One lazy summer evening, Thomas snuck off from the house, June toddling behind him. The two youngsters were headed toward the cornfield. The plants had grown to about four foot tall. They didn't have to go far into the corn until they were out of sight of the house and their mom's watchful eye. Thomas squatted down in the middle of a row. Pulling June by the hand, she plopped down on the ground beside him.

"What we do'in here?" she asked.

"Shhh," Thomas whispered. "Hear it?"

"What?"

"The corn. It's growin'. Hear it?"

June, being very quiet, tilted her small head toward the ground as she replied, "It's crackling."

"See, I told you," Thomas said. "It's growing." Amazed at their discovery, the two children remained hunkered down in the field, listening to the corn grow until they heard their mom calling.

"Thomas, June, better git on in here before the night air makes you come down with the fever." At the sound of their mom's voice, the children jumped up and ran out of the field toward the house, leaving the corn stalks crackling, as the leaves unfolded.

During the hot summer, when the stalks were about five foot tall and the corn was shiny and full of milk, Myrtle took the wagon to the field. When the wagon was loaded down with fresh sweet corn, Myrtle returned to the house where she removed the husk and silk from each ear. After a thorough cleaning, she cut the corn from each cob. Then she loosely packed the plump kernels into quart jars. Pouring salt into the palm of her cupped hand, for an exact measurement, Myrtle added it to each jar full of corn. She then poured hot liquid from a kettle into the jars, covering the corn, but leaving a one-inch head space. After twisting the cap onto the mouth of the jar, Myrtle carefully placed the corn-filled jars inside a pressure cooker, locking down the lid. After about an hour, she slowly released the lock, removing pressure that had built up inside. Taking one jar at a time out of the cooker, she placed them on the table to cool. Then the process started all over again until she had seventy jars of corn. The preserved corn was added to her supply of pickles, beets, green beans, peas, sauerkraut, fruits, and other homegrown produce that would be needed to get the family by until the next year's harvest.

It was an Indian summer. The leaves on the trees surrounding the farm had turned a brilliant color of gold, red, rust, and yellow. The changing of the season was Lonnie's way of knowing it was time to bring in the bounties of the crops he had planted earlier that year.

Lonnie didn't own a corn picker or a combine, so the corn had to be picked by hand. Ruby, Fern, and Beryl joined Mayme and their dad in the field. Sitting on the buckboard, Lonnie called to his mules, urging them to pull the wagon down the rows of corn. Fern and Mayme walked alongside the slow-moving wagon, plucking the dried yellow ears of corn from the stalks and tossing them into the back of the wagon. It was Ruby and Beryl's job to follow the wagon, picking the ears of corn off the stalks that had fallen to the ground.

When the box was full, Lonnie drove the wagon to the corncrib. He unhitched Molly and Jude. The girls scampered from the loaded wagon to the ground where they proceeded to unload the corn. Finding an old tree stump to sit on, Fern and Beryl spent the rest of the day removing the husk and silk from the ears of corn. They would toss the husk off to one side and then throw the ear of corn into the interior of the crib. While the girls were busy shucking corn, Lonnie took Mayme and Ruby back out to the field to cut the stalks. They bunched six to eight stalks together, making a fodder shock. These shocks would come in handy to feed the cattle in late winter.

Before the first freeze of the year, Lonnie would take corn to the mill to be ground. The day before the trip was to take place, he told his daughters to go shuck some of the corn in the crib and fill the gunnysacks. Obeying their dad, the girls climbed into the interior of the crib. Finding a place to sit on top of the dried ears of corn, they placed a wooden bucket between their knees. Holding the ear of corn securely, they rotated their hands in different direction as if they were wringing out a wet towel. The twisting motion caused the dried corn to come off the cob and fall into the bucket.

"C'mon, Pug. Wanna go to the mill?" Lonnie called out to his youngest daughter. Hearing her dad call, June hurried out to the wagon. Scampering up onto the wagon seat, June turned to watch her mom walk toward them. Myrtle was holding three fat hens by their feet. When she reached the back of the wagon, Myrtle swung her arm in an arc, raising the chickens a little above her head. Bringing her arm back down, she plopped the birds on the base of the buckboard. The chicken's lower backs were tightly pressed together, looking in three different directions with their wings fanning out around their fat little bodies, as if they were sitting on a feathery table skirt. The sight of the hens sitting in the back of the wagon made June giggle. When Myrtle released the chickens, they didn't move.

"Are they dead?" asked June.

"No, they're alive," replied her mom.

"Then why aren't they movin'?"

"They can't. Their legs are tied together."

"Oh."

The springs underneath the wagon groaned, as Lonnie lumbered up on the seat next to his daughter.

"Those fat hens should help pay for getting the corn ground," Myrtle told her husband. Lonnie just nodded to his wife as he clicked to the mules. Turning back around to face the front, June felt proud to be riding on the wagon seat, going to the mill with her dad.

"Let's go," she shouted.

Ensuring that his family would have enough corn mill to last through the winter, Lonnie would make a trip to Mill Creek each fall, getting two fifty-pound sacks of corn ground. Sometimes, during a good year, he would sell some of his corn to the mill owner, getting only about fifty cents per bushel.

After the corn had been harvested and the straw had been made into shocks, Lillie, Howard's wife, would help Myrtle to make brooms. They would stack several pieces of straw, which had been left in the field, making a small pile. Then they would place a long piece of baling wire horizontally across the middle of the pile before folding the straws in half, lengthwise. Lillie would weave the ends of the wire, which were protruding out from the sides of the pile of straw, in and out, until the entire length of wire had been woven along the folded edge. Taking a long pole made from oak wood, she would wire it to the broom. Finally, using a sharp knife, she would carefully trim the bottom of the straw broom, nice and straight.

"I just barely remember Aunt Lillie," Phyllis interjected. "Still I do remember Mom saying her sister-in-law could do just about anything. She was versed in ways that could make her hard life more endurable. And Lillie was always ready and willing to share those talents with others."

Donnis, sitting beside Phyllis, nodded with agreement.

39

Making Hay ♥

One midsummer morning, George Hart, the mail carrier, came riding up the hill in his buggy. It was his custom to stop and visit at each resident's home, regardless of whether or not they had a letter. While there, he would share any tidbit of news coming from town.

"Mornin'," George called out to Myrtle. "Got a letter here from Liberty, Missouri. Says it's addressed to Ruby and Mayme. Isn't that where your boy, Ray, is livin'?"

Leaving the shade of the porch, Myrtle walked toward the mail carrier. "Well, I'll be. Wonder what he wants with those two," Myrtle said, taking the letter from the man. "Come in for a cup of coffee."

"Sure, maybe just a cup."

Ruby and Mayme were coming down the stairs just as their mom and George came into the house. "Here girls. A letter from Ray." Tearing the envelope open, Mayme read as Ruby looked over her shoulder. Inside the letter, Ray was bribing his sisters into doing his part of the farm work that summer. In return, he promised each of them a new store-bought winter coat. The girls raced into the kitchen in search of a notepad and pencil. They quickly scribbled a short reply, agreeing to do as their brother asked.

By this time, Myrtle and George had finished their cup of hot coffee. After taking Mayme's letter, the mail carrier bid them all farewell. While George continued his way toward Mill Creek Road, Myrtle returned to the porch. With a sigh, she lowered herself into her rocking chair to resume her task of snapping green beans for supper.

A large meadow full of sweet native grasses lay down the hill behind the house. During the summer, between the times the crops had been planted and the time of harvest, Lonnie took his mules and the mower to the meadow to cut the grass. When all of the grass lay on the ground, Lonnie, with Thomas sitting beside him, coaxed Molly forward, pulling a wide rake behind her. The steel rakes gathered up the fallen grass, making nice even rows. Every other day, Lonnie would return to the meadow to rake the rows of cut grass. First, he would turn it over one way, and the next day he would turn it over the other way. He continued rolling the grass, back and forth, until it was good and dry.

One morning, several weeks after the grass had been cut, Lonnie went outside to join Howard, who had come over the hill to help his dad work the hay. After the early morning dew was gone, Mayme, Ruby, Fern, Beryl, Thomas, Howard, and Lonnie were in the meadow. This time it was Thomas who coaxed Molly to drag the rake. Just as the rake turned over a row of grass, the girls, who were following Thomas, picked up a handful, wrapped the bottom end of the bundle into a knot, making a sheave. Laying the small bundle on the ground, they picked up another handful of grass, working their way across the meadow. About midmorning, they became aware of the hot summer sun beating down on them. Adjusting the brim of their straw hats lower over their foreheads, they noticed small red lines covering their arms, where the sharp ends of the straw was scratching their tender skin. Their small hands were becoming stiff and sore, even though they were wearing rough gloves.

At noon, Myrtle came driving the wagon out to the meadow. In the back was a wicker basket overflowing with food. She had prepared a platter of fried side pork, freshly picked green onions and radishes from her garden, cold biscuits, which had been left over from breakfast, and a jar of plum jelly. A stone crock filled with ice-cold buttermilk sat on the seat beside her. Work came to a stop while the family sat down to eat their dinner in the cool shade of the wagon. After they had eaten their fill, Lonnie's booming voice echoed across the hills. "Time to get movin'!" Everyone rose from the ground and went back to work.

By late afternoon, all of the grass had been tied into sheaves. Mayme, Ruby, Fern, and Beryl now worked in pairs. Gathering up six of the straw sheaves, one of the girls would hold them bunched together while the other girl took a piece of straw and wrapped it tightly around the middle. Howard and Thomas, following behind their sisters, picked up the bundles of grass, standing them on end with the grass pointing up. Using each bundle as a support for the next one, the brothers stacked the straw up against each other, making a round base, until they had a small pile of hay. Moving on to another location in the meadow, the boys made another small pile and then another, until all of the grass in the meadow was now standing on end.

As the sun was starting to sink low in the west, Lonnie leaned backward stretching the tired, sore muscles in his back. With one hand on his hip for support, he used his other hand to remove his sweat-stained hat. Using the sleeve of his shirt to wipe the sweat from his brow, he thought, *It sure has been a long day.* The meadow, where tall grass had swayed in the summer breezes, was now full of small haystacks.

The smell of food filled the kitchen when Lonnie and his family came in to the house for supper. They were so hungry they barely took time to clean up in the washbasin by the back door. In the center of the kitchen table sat a large platter of crisp fried chicken. Bowls of mashed potatoes, creamy white gravy, stewed cabbage that was still steaming, a bowl of wilted lettuce, and a huge pan of golden corn bread made their mouths water.

Interrupting me, my daughter Anetta spoke up, "Wait a minute. Why would Grandma feed her family wilted lettuce? Wouldn't that make them sick?"

Phyllis, who had been standing in the kitchen, walked back into the dining room just as Anetta spoke. "I remember when we went to visit, Grandma would fix us wilted lettuce. It was one of Mom's favorite dishes," she explained. "Grandma would mix fresh lettuce leaves and chopped green onions she had picked from her garden before stirring in a few pieces of crumbled-up, crisp fried bacon. To make the dressing, she would add a little apple cider vinegar and a pinch of sugar to the leftover hot bacon grease. After dribbling the hot mixture over the lettuce, onions, and bacon, Grandma would set a plate on top the bowl, trapping in the steam. This would make the lettuce wilt."

"That's disgusting," Anetta laughed.

"Oh, but it was one of the family's favorites," Phyllis replied.

I picked up the story where I had left off.

The family was famished after a hard day's work in the field. However, it didn't take long before their hunger was satisfied and exhaustion to set end. The girls could barely keep their eyes open as they gulped down a glass of cold milk before heading to bed.

The next day, after the morning chores were done, the family finished a hearty breakfast consisting of fried corn mush, fried eggs, and bacon before returning to the field to finish stacking the hay. Mayme fastened a travois to Molly. The travois had two long poles extending down the sides and behind the animal. Riding astraddle, Mayme guided the animal to where one of the small stacks of hay stood. Gently, she coaxed Molly and the poles backward to where one of the other girls was waiting to guide the travois under the small stack. Once the poles were completely underneath the hay, a rope was tossed over the mound, as if a lasso had been thrown. After making sure the rope was tightly secured, Mayme would ride the mule forward, pulling the small stack of hay behind her. The poles would act as a sled holding the hay up off the ground as it slid across the field.

The girls learned this technique of moving stacks around the field at an early age. They were very careful in doing it right because if they turned a stack over, they had to face the wrath of their irate dad.

Mayme moved the stack to where Lonnie and Howard were waiting to toss it onto another small stack of hay. Mayme would continue bringing her dad and brother more piles of hay until the stack was so large Howard could no longer heave the shock up to the top. Enabling them to go just a little higher, Lonnie would get his wooden ladder, lean it against the growing haystack before adding more hay.

Making haystacks was too strenuous for seven-year-old Thomas. He wasn't strong enough to help make shocks with his sisters, and he wasn't tall enough to help his dad and Howard toss the bundled shocks up on the haystack. So like kids are prone to do when they are bored, Thomas struck out across the field to find a new adventure. His dad, older brother, and sisters were so engrossed in what they were doing they didn't pay any attention to the little boy.

Thomas was on the other side of the field when he happened to look down. There, on the ground, lay a rolled-up cigarette. Looking over his shoulder to see where his family was, and to make sure they were too busy to pay him much mind, Thomas picked up the cigarette and ran to the barn. There, on his dad's workbench was a matchstick. Looking around to make sure no one was watching, Thomas grabbed the match and ran back outside to the far end of the field.

Thomas hunched down, so as not to be seen, hiding behind one of the finished haystacks. Casually, he struck the match across the back of his denim-covered thigh. The boy took a long drag on the loosely packed cigarette. His eyes immediately filled with water. Tears overflowed, running down his dirty little cheeks. His throat felt as if it were on fire. Try as he might, he could not breathe. Deep coughs rose from his chest.

Finally, after several seconds, Thomas stopped coughing long enough to catch his breath. He wiped tears from his wet cheeks. His eyes had stopped tearing, and the back of his throat wasn't burning quite so much. Feeling better, Thomas leaned back into the haystack to enjoy his first real smoke.

The young boy was unaware that, while he was having a coughing fit, some of the ashes from the cigarette had fallen onto loose pieces of straw. The straw started to smoke, drifting up to Thomas's nose. Startled, he looked down. Seeing the smoldering straw at his feet, Thomas immediately started stomping the ground in a frantic frenzy. It didn't take long for him to build up a hot sweat as he tried to squelch each small spark of embers. He knew if he got caught smoking, his dad would take the leather strap to his backside, for sure.

On the other side of the field, Lonnie happened to be standing back, looking up at a finished haystack, when he notice a faint trail of smoke rising from the back of one of the haystacks. He knew, that if some of the grass was still green when it was stacked, a chemical reaction could cause the straw to become hot enough to burn. So coming on a run, Lonnie sprinted across the field to the smoking stack where he found Thomas jumping up and down.

Noticing the burnt straw lying all around Thomas's feet, Lonnie yelled, "What's the meaning of this?"

Thomas looked up at his dad, tears streaming down his cheeks as he admitted, "I was smoking, and the straw caught on fire."

Lonnie, not at all affected by his son's tears, grabbed him by the ear. Thomas's short legs had trouble keeping up with Lonnie's wide angry strides, as they made their way back to the barn. After a few quick thrashes with a razor strap, the young boy learned a harsh but very valuable lesson. He learned that without that hay, the cows would go hungry when the winter snows covered the ground.

That fall, Ray came home from Liberty, Missouri, to visit his family. True to his word, he brought with him two of the most beautiful store-bought coats Mayme and Ruby had ever seen. "Here ya go," he said to his sisters. "Thanks again for doing my share of the farmin' this year." The two girls didn't even hear their brother's remarks of appreciation. They were too busy trying on and admiring their new coats.

40

A Night to Remember ♥

Harvest season had just ended. Myrtle had seventy quarts of each type of homegrown vegetables and all kinds of berries safely stored away in the root cellar. On the side of a nearby hill, she had located a good place to bury the cabbage, carrots, potatoes, and apples. Lonnie had tobacco drying in the barn, corn in the crib, and tall haystacks were scattered across the meadow. It had been a good season for crops. The Moulders were ready for winter.

"I heard from my friend in town that the vaudeville is in Macks Creek," Mayme remarked one Saturday morning. "They're performing at the Odd Fellow Hall. Can Ruby and I go?"

"As long as you get your work done," replied Lonnie.

"Okay," shouted the girls, running off to complete their daily chores.

After supper, Mayme and Ruby rushed upstairs to get ready for the evening. Both of them were giddy with excitement. They looked forward to a night of socializing with their good friends who lived in town. Before long, the two sisters bounded back down the stairs wearing their Sunday dresses and the brand-new store-bought coats Ray had given them.

Myrtle was waiting for them on the landing. "You girls be careful," she said. "There's gonna be a bunch of strangers in town tonight."

"We will," her daughters promised.

As the young teenage girls walked down the road, Mayme's good friend, Sarah[*], who lived over the next hill, joined them. Before the girls realized it, they had reached the end of County Road O, where it intersected with Highway 54. Mayme bent down to tie her shoelaces.

Looking up at Sarah, she said, "Go on ahead. We'll be along directly."

"Okay, I'll save you a seat."

As soon as Sarah was across the highway, Mayme and Ruby jumped in to the road ditch and removed their old and worn everyday shoes. Quickly, they put on their Sunday shoes that had been cleverly concealed in the

---

[*] Sarah is a fictitious name.

pockets of their coats before setting their old shoes just inside the opening of a culvert that ran underneath the road. Climbing out of the ditch back onto the road, Mayme and Ruby now looked their very best from head to toe as they hurried across the highway and headed up Main Street.

Main Street took a turn to the north, ran over a rock slab and continued up a hill. At the top, on the corner of Main and Baptist streets, set the Odd Fellow Hall. There were already several people lingering outside the large building. Mayme and Ruby made their way through the crowd, up the steps, and walked inside. After a few minutes they located Sarah.

The Moulder girls had just settled into their seats when a good-looking young man, dressed in a white shirt and blue-striped overalls, walked through the side door. He stopped, removed his pompadour hat that had been tilted to one side of his forehead, and looked around the room. His eyes settled on Mayme, who was sitting with her sister and best friend.

The man meandered over to the young woman. With his hat in hand, he asked, "Is this seat taken?" Mayme couldn't take her eyes off him.

Shaking her head, she whispered, "No, it isn't."

"Then can I sit there?"

Still not being able to find her voice, Mayme just nodded. The man sat down in the seat next to her. She couldn't believe that the good-looking young man she had seen driving a brand-new Chevrolet down the street in Macks Creek several months earlier was now sitting beside her at the Odd Fellow Hall.

"Hello, I'm Onie Woodall."

The following year on March 12, 1932, Ila Mayme Moulder became the wife of Onie Woodall. The couple made their home on a farm west of Macks Creek, Missouri.

41

School on the Ridge ♥

Standing at the foot of the stairs, Myrtle called up to her daughters, "Girls, git on down here. Fern, the cows are waitin' to be milked. Beryl, it's your turn to git the eggs. Be careful mind you and don't go breakin' any. I'm plannin' on takin' some to sell in town. Hurry up now. Your dad and Thomas are about done with their chores. You kids don't want to be late for school." Before Myrtle could turn away from the staircase, she saw June running down the steps. Coming to a stop in front of her mom, the little girl twirled around and around. "Okay now, let's see how you look." Reaching down to straighten the collar of her daughter's dress, Myrtle remarked, "My, don't you look pretty."

Myrtle had removed the lining from one of Lonnie's old coats, washed, and pressed it just right. Using a newspaper pattern to cut out pieces of the material, and after spending several evening hours skillfully sewing the pieces together, she had finally made June a brand-new dress. Small narrow pleats, held fast against the bodice by tiny little stitches, ran vertically down the front yoke making the dress flow gently down June's body. The little girl was so proud that morning. She was wearing a beautiful new dress with delicate smocking her mom had so lovingly made. And she was going to school with her older sisters and brother.

Myrtle stood at the door watching her children leave. Bare feet stirred up a cloud of dust as they walked along the dirt road leading to the schoolhouse. Tears silently slid down her cheek. Her little ones were growing up. Fern was now in the eighth grade. Beryl was eleven years old and attending the fifth grade. Her little boy, Thomas, was in the third grade and her youngest child, June, was starting school. Turning away from the door, Myrtle was acutely aware of the silence that surrounded her. After years of having children underfoot, the house seemed so empty, as quietness settled over the farmhouse.

Dry Ridge School, a small one-room schoolhouse, set in a clearing surrounded by tall cedar trees. The building stood just a few yards north and east from the intersection of county roads O and Mill Creek. As with most rural schools throughout the area, the potbellied stove was the only source of heat. The student's desks were lined up in straight rows on the hardwood floor. A large picture of Harry S. Truman, the current United States president, hung on the wall behind the teacher's desk. Along the top of the adjoining two walls were pictures of the preceding thirty-one presidents. A wooden flagpole, holding the American flag, stood on the floor between a long black chalkboard and a large map of the United States.

Standing on the hard-packed dirt behind the school was a seesaw with a long wooden plank lying across a big round tree log. One end of the plank was up in the air. The other end was sitting on the ground. There were two rope swings hanging from limbs of a nearby oak tree. The baseball diamond, well worn from years of children running and playing ball, was in a large open field across Mill Creek Road to the south. The boy and girl's outdoor toilets stood a good distance from the back door. Between the schoolhouse and the road was a pump jack. The well underneath the pump was deep and filled with ice-cold water.

"I've been there," shouted Chelsea. "That's where Mema took us one time. But all I saw was a metal pipe going into the ground."

Donnis, interrupting my granddaughter, replied, "That's right, Chelsea. Just an old rusty pipe is all that's left of the pump jack. Except for memories." Looking around the living room at the rest of us sitting there, my sister asked, "Do you remember when Mom took us to the well? How we would, just to be silly, bend over the hole where the pipe ran deep into the ground? 'Hello, Well. I'm June Moulder's daughter. Remember her?' we would yell. After everyone had their chance to yell down the well, we would stand on the cement slab, where the pump jack had once stood, listening, as Mom told stories about when she attended this little country school and drew water from this very spot."

I wiped tears from my eyes as memories of those precious times flooded my mind. I took a moment to look at my children, my brothers, and sisters along with our nieces, nephews, and grandchildren. All had tears of laughter rolling down their cheeks. Yes, indeed, we all remembered yelling down that hole.

"Tell us more," begged Chelsea.

"Okay. Want me to finish this story?" Donnis asked.

I just nodded.

Late days of summer turned into early fall. Every morning, as the Moulder children walked down the road toward the little schoolhouse, their friends would come running up the hill and out of the woods to join them. There were the Johnson's, the Wheeler's, the Varner's, and the Minnas's boys. Meeting there in the middle of the dirt road, they would laugh and joke with each other as they continued on their way. Friendly fights would sometimes erupt, only to be squelched before coming in view of the school. June, spotting her best friend Joy would run to greet her. Thomas, always full of energy, joined his friends, running down the road while his older sisters walked slowly behind. Fern, now being the oldest Moulder child at home, had the responsibility of seeing Beryl, Thomas, and June safely to school.

One particular morning, as the Moulder children were walking to school with their friends, June and Joy started to whisper and giggle, sharing some sort of secret. When they came to where Mill Creek and O roads crossed, the two little girls stopped, turned around looking back down the road.

"Come on, we're gonna be late," scolded Fern.

"You just go on," June said.

"Whatcha lookin' for?" ask Beryl.

"Nothin," giggled the little girls.

Just then, Beryl saw two older boys Pete* and his rowdy brother Charley* coming up the hill. "I bet you're smitten with that boy Pete," teased Beryl.

"I am not," June yelled back.

"Betcha are."

"Better not be late," cautioned Fern, as the two sisters skipped off into the schoolyard.

"We won't." After her sisters disappeared through the doorway of the schoolhouse, June turned back around and shouted in a very loud voice, "Sty, sty, git off my eye. Git on the next one who happens by!" Grabbing Joy by the hand, the two little girls ran as fast as they could to the school steps. Thinking she had put a hoax on her two schoolmates, June told Joy, "That'll pay those boys back for being so mean."

Holding hands, the little girls came skipping through the front door where they noticed the rest of the children were already in their assigned seats. "Uh-oh," whispered June. "We're late." The girls stopped immediately when they spied their teacher, Mr. Leon Ricker, standing in front of his desk.

"That name sounds familiar," commented Samantha.

"That's because Leon Ricker was the man Aunt Dick married," Donnis told her.

"You mean Mema's brother-in-law was her teacher?"

"That's right."

A stern look of disapproval glared out of Mr. Ricker's dark eyes. A deep crease was engraved in his forehead. His long straight nose reached

---

* Pete and Charley are fictitious names.

downward, almost touching the frown that stretched across his narrow lips. He was slapping a wooden ruler across the palm of his hand.

June had trouble keeping a straight face as she watched dark red splotches pop out around his throat, trailing down his neck underneath his skinny black necktie. "What's the meaning of this?" he shouted. June swallowed a giggle. He was so puffed up with anger she thought he was going to explode. "Ms. Johnson, Ms. Moulder come here," he ordered. The girls immediately walked to the front of the room. They stood holding each other's hands, their heads hanging low. Mr. Ricker turned to face the blackboard. Taking a piece of chalk from the tray, he drew two little circles. Turning back to the girls, he said in a stern voice, "Young ladies. Put your nose in those circles. Stay there until you can settle down and can act like young ladies." Embarrassed, the two youngsters did as they were told.

"Wow. I bet Mema hated that," Samantha said.

"And rightly so," Donnis commented. "For the rest of the school year, Mom remained fearfully respectful of her brother-in-law. She was relieved when school started the next fall. Uncle Leon had been offered a job in another school."

The months passed quickly. Red, orange, and yellow leaves that had recently been on the trees a few days before were now covering the ground. Cold nights and cool days signaled that winter was approaching fast. That fall, Ray, Lonnie and Myrtle's second oldest son, had come back to live in the Ozarks. On November 25, 1933, he married Florence Ricker, a young woman from Macks Creek. Together, they purchased a farmhouse in Rag Holler, several miles northeast of Macks Creek. Along with farming a few acres of land, Ray found a job working for a man by the name of Green, who owned and operated a grain mill on the Little Niangua River.

After Thanksgiving, the attention of the youngsters turned to the preparations for the school's Christmas program. Each child was given a small poem to recite in front of his parents. They practiced them daily, trying to make the piece as near perfect as they could. A week before the program, Mr. Ricker pinned notes to the children's wool coats asking their mothers to bring cookies for refreshments.

Excitement was in the air when the day of the program finally arrived. Early that morning, once all the children had arrived, Mr. Ricker wrapped the wooden yardstick across the edge of his desk. The short, snapping sound gained the children's attention. "All right, students. Settle down. We have a lot to do today. You need to finish your studies this morning so we can have the entire afternoon to get ready for tonight's program."

"Yahoo!" shouted the kids in unison.

"I said quiet. You have work to do," scolded Mr. Ricker.

Shortly after lunch and the children were seated in their assigned desks, Mr. Ricker said, "Well, children. You did very well this morning. You have completed all your studies for the day. Now we can get ready for tonight."

"Yea!" shouted the room full of children.

"Quiet down now," he ordered. "First of all we need a tree." Looking across the room, he focused in on Pete and Charley. "You two will do," he said to the brothers. "Now, don't go fooling around out there and forget time. Get the tree and get back in here." Eager to be outside, the boys hurriedly put on their coats, hats, and gloves and raced out into the outer rim of the woods.

While they were gone, Mr. Ricker instructed the other children with what types of decorations needed to be made. Fern and her best friend helped June and Joy cut red and green construction paper into strips. June insisted she was big enough to squeeze the bottle of Elmer's glue, putting white sticky stuff on each end of the strips.

"Okay, but be careful. Don't get glue all over," cautioned her big sister.

Before long, the girls had made a pretty red and green garland. Beryl, Thomas, and the rest of the younger children bundled up in their coats, mittens, and hats to go outside to collect berries. Mr. Ricker stood at the stove popping corn in a large heavy cast-iron skillet. Fern and her friends sat close to the stove tying little bows out of pieces of red ribbon. They waited patiently for the younger children to return. Outside, light snow was just starting to fall. Beryl and her friends hurried to fill their bucket with berries while Thomas and the other boys ran and jumped, trying to catch snowflakes on the tips of their tongues. The bucket was soon filled.

"Come on," Beryl called out to her young brother. "It's time to go back in."

The smell of the freshly popped corn greeted the youngster when the front door swung open. The cold draft reached inside the hot core of the potbellied stove, making the fire blaze higher sending sparks flying upward. Beryl was the first of the children to come in. She was carrying the heavy-laden bucket full of ripe red berries. Thomas, not wanting to come back inside, slowly walked through the doorway, slamming the door behind him. Beryl sat the bucket down next to a big bowl of popcorn. Sitting down in an empty chair that was next to the stove, she helped her friends thread popcorn and berries on long lengths of quilting thread. By now, Pete and Charley had returned with the Christmas tree. It was a tall skinny cedar, but the boughs were full of pointy green needles. Dragging the tree by the trunk to the corner of the room, the boys stood it up in a bucket filled with small rocks. After the tree had been decorated with the red and green paper garland, red berries, popcorn, and small red bows, Mr. Ricker carefully tied small wax candles to some of the branches.

Just before school was dismissed for the day, the student's desks were slid to one side of the room. With the help of Mr. Ricker, two of the tallest boys stretched a wire across the front of the classroom. An old-patched sheet was tossed over it, making a makeshift curtain. By the end of the afternoon, the small one-room schoolhouse was transformed into a grand theater.

That evening, when friends and families gathered at the schoolhouse, a fire burned low in the potbelly stove making the small room nice and warm. The pleasant smell of nutmeg, cinnamon, and spices mingling with the tangy odor of cedar brought a festive mood to the room. Small flames flickered from wax candles burning low on the boughs of the Christmas tree. Lonnie remained outside in the schoolyard laughing and joking with the men while Myrtle joined the other moms inside the schoolhouse. It was always a joy during the Christmas season to take time away from the daily grind of work to socialize with the neighbors.

The children, sitting up nice and straight on wooden benches in the front of the classroom, knew better than to wiggle and squirm around. They sat perfectly still, with their eyes looking straight ahead, hands folded in their laps, and feet planted firmly on the floor. Mr. Ricker, standing off to one side of the room, kept a close eye on his charges, especially Pete and Charley. Chuckling to himself, he hardly recognized the two brothers. For once, their faces were clean, black hair slicked back, and their plaid flannel shirts were tucked neatly into the waist of their trousers.

When it looked as though everyone had arrived, Mr. Ricker removed a watch from his pocket, flipping open the lid. Straight up 6:00 p.m. He opened the front door and asked the men, who were still lingering in the yard, to come in and find their seats.

A hushed quiet descended over the room when Thomas came out from behind the sheet curtain. He firmly held his little hat in his chubby hand.

Standing tall and proud he said, "Christmas is coming, the old goose is fat. Could you drop a dollar in a poor man's hat? If you cannot drop a dollar, a penny will do. If you cannot drop a penny, God bless you."

Taking a deep bow, Thomas stepped back behind the curtain before returning to his assigned seat. One by one, the rest of the children stood in front of the sheet to recite their Christmas poem.

When all of the students had performed for their parents, the crowd of spectators gave them a loud round of applause. After the program ended, the adults joined the youngsters eating fresh-baked gingersnap cookies and drinking hot apple cider. Thomas, bundled in his hat and coat, chased past the teacher's desk, grabbed a cookie, and ran outside to join his friends playing in the fresh-fallen snow.

The cold winter passed, and spring was ushered in with warm balmy sunshine and gentle rains. Green sprouts of grass could be seen everywhere. Buds on tree limbs burst open revealing pale green leaves. The pungent smell of freshly turned dirt assaulted the children's noses as their dads worked in the nearby fields getting the ground ready for planting their yearly crops.

Every day the little country school was filled with noisy children anxious to go outside and play in the warm sunshine. They found it extremely difficult to concentrate on their studies. No matter how many times Mr. Ricker rapped the yardstick across the edge of his desk making a loud popping noise, it never curtailed his students' high spirits. Everyone was anticipating the end of the school year. Mr. Ricker had planned a field trip for his students and their parents to Jefferson City, Missouri's state capital. The highlight of the day was going to be the tour of the capitol building.

42

The Field Trip ♥

 The last day of the school year arrived. The sun was warming the night chill out of the air. A few wispy clouds high in the clear blue sky drifted along on the current of a slight breeze. It was promising to be a grand day.

 Fern, Beryl, Thomas, and June could hardly contain their excitement the morning of the field trip. During breakfast, they wiggled, giggled, squealed, and laughed. Lonnie, joining the fun, egged his children on with teasing jesters and remarks, while Myrtle tried to coax her family into settling down long enough to eat. "You're gonna git mighty hungry," she scolded.

 Thomas, anxious to be on his way, gobbled down his corn mush and swallowed a glass of warm milk in one long gulp before jumping up from the table. Myrtle called after him, "Don't slam the do—" Bang went the screen door. In his rush to get to the wagon, Thomas leaped over Ole Slim lying sprawled out in the shade of the front porch roof. The only movement coming from the old coonhound was an occasional switch of his long tail at some bothersome deer flies buzzing around him.

 "C'mon, Pug," Lonnie said, rising from the table. "I need help hookin' Molly and Jude to the wagon." Fern and Beryl started clearing the table.

 "You two better hurry and get ready," Myrtle said, taking a stack of dishes from Fern. "We need to git going." After Myrtle had finished clearing the breakfast things from the table, she handed Fern a small wooden crate. Inside was a quart jar filled with pickled pig's feet, several pieces of strong-tasting longhorn cheese, soda crackers, carefully wrapped so they wouldn't crumble, and a freshly baked cherry pie. She handed Beryl a stone crock full of sweet apple cider.

 Grabbing the quilt that was lying on a chair by the back door, Myrtle and her girls hurried outside to join Thomas, June, and Lonnie, who were impatiently waiting in the wagon.

 "Hurry up, slow pokes!" June shouted, when she saw her mom and sisters coming out of the house.

 "Climb on up here, you two," Lonnie called out. "Better hurry or we're gonna git left behind."

Beryl and Fern joined Thomas in the back of the wagon. Myrtle sat on the seat next to Lonnie, sandwiching June in between them. Everybody was in a festive mood as they drove off down O road toward the school.

When the wagon carrying the Moulder family arrived at the schoolhouse, there was an old cattle truck parked on the side of the road. They heard Mr. Ricker call out, "The Moulders are here. It's time to get started." The children came running. "Climb on in and sit down. You little ones, make sure you get in the middle. I don't want you bouncing out."

After unhitching the mules from the wagon and making sure they were hobbled, Lonnie went to help the smallest children. They were too little to climb up the sides, so he picked them up and placed them safely in the back of the truck. After making sure no one was being left behind, Lonnie and the man who owned the truck picked up the wooden tailgate, securing it to the back fenders. Lonnie lumbered into the cab of the truck to ride shotgun. As he stepped on the running board, the truck leaned to one side, the springs groaning under his weight. The children in the back of the truck giggled. Fern glared at them all.

As the truck started to roll, a cry was heard coming from the direction of the woods. "Wait for me!" Thomas yelled. Hearing the youngster calling, the driver stopped the truck, just as Thomas came running out of the outhouse. Taking a flying leap, the youngster scampered up the wooden side railing, jumping down into the crowded truck bed.

The truck pulled out onto Highway 54, headed east. The children, full of jubilance, started to sing, "Skip, skip, skip to my Lou. Skip, skip, skip to my Lou. Skip, skip, skip to my Lou, skip to my Lou my darlin'." With each passing mile, their excitement built.

By midmorning, the sun had climbed high in the bright blue sky. After they traveled several miles, Myrtle reached into her purse, retrieving her headscarf. She tied it snug about her head, trying to keep dust that was swirling around in the bottom of the truck bed out of her hair. The children were oblivious to the dirt as they continued to sing, keeping beat with the thump, thump, thump of rubber tires hitting the pavement.

At best, the top speed of the old cattle truck was thirty miles per hour. So the sixty-mile trip to the capital city took all morning. For most of the people in the truck, this was the farthest they had ever ventured from home.

The clock in the old courthouse tower was just striking noon when the truck driver stopped at a pleasant-looking park. "Okay, everybody out!" he called, as he and Lonnie removed the back gate. Resembling cattle that had been brought to market, everyone exited the truck.

"My, that sure was a long way," commented one of the women.

"It sure was," Myrtle agreed. "And it sure is good to be out of that dusty old truck and into fresh air again."

The two women walked side by side to a pump jack that was close by. Using hankies that had been tucked up under the sleeves of their dresses, they washed the dust from their face, neck, and arms. After rinsing the hankies in the stream of ice-cold water, they stood by, waiting patiently.

The children ran, jumped, and started to play a game of Keep Away. When, by chance, a child got too close to the pump jack, one of the women would reach out and grab him. She would have to hold on tight to the squirming child with one hand while she tried to clean their dirty face with the other.

Thomas and one of his little friends scurried to a nearby oak tree. Its branches were high and wide and very inviting. It didn't take long for the two boys to climb high inside its branches.

After letting the children run off some of their pent-up energy, Myrtle called out, "Time to eat!" Her children hurried to where two large quilts had been spread out under the branches of the big oak tree.

When Beryl and Fern arrived at the makeshift table, Fern looked around for her brother. "Where's Thomas?" she asked her dad.

"I don't rightly know where that kids got off to," he replied, lowering him self to the ground.

Fern looked up. "There they are!" she shouted, pointing. Away up in the canopy of leaves were two sets of small feet dangling in the air.

"Okay, you boys, git on down here," called Lonnie.

"Thomas, if you don't hurry up, all this good food is gonna be gone," Myrtle threatened.

Hearing that, Thomas and his little friend hurriedly climbed down, jumping from the last low-hanging branch.

The group of people was enjoying the picnic lunch when Myrtle noticed one of the other mom's was sitting by herself. Rising from her place beside her family, Myrtle ventured over to join the woman. When she crossed the yard, Myrtle overheard several other women talking softly and snickering about a piece of material found in a pie.

"That pie of yours sure looks good. May I have a piece?" Myrtle said, sitting down. The woman, not making eye contact, shrugged, "I suppose, if you want." When Myrtle looked down at the pie, she saw what the other women had been laughing about. There, in the bottom of the pie pan was a piece of gingham-checked material. Not wanting to make the woman feel uncomfortable, Myrtle ignored the material and cut herself a large piece of minced meat pie. As she ate, the two women struck up a conversation.

"Why was there material in the pie?" questioned my niece Tammi.

"Grandma knew that her friend was having a difficult time making ends meet." I explained. "There was absolutely no extra money for the woman to purchase a new pie pan. So when a hole was worn in the bottom of her old one, she simply placed a thin piece of material over the hole before baking her pie."

Giving his students and the adult's ample time to eat their packed lunch, Mr. Ricker finally called out, "It's time to get started. You children find a partner and line up behind me. You parents can bring up the end of the line. Now pay attention to what you're doing. And by all means, don't touch anything."

The building of Missouri's state capitol stood on a high bluff overlooking the Missouri River. Parents and children alike were in awe of its magnificence. Fern and her classmates, standing on the beautiful manicured lawn, studied the grand architectural lines of the building that covered almost three full acres. The building was two hundred feet wide and four hundred thirty-seven feet long. Reaching two hundred sixty feet into the cloudless sky was a large bronze dome.

"What's that?" Fern asked her teacher, when she noticed something unusual on top of the dome.

"That's Ceres"

"Who or what is Ceres?" asked the curious young girl.

"Ceres is the goddess of grain. This particular goddess was chosen to symbolize Missouri's great agricultural heritage."[1]

"Oh."

Once everyone was safely across the street, they walked around the grounds admiring the statues. The first statue they came to was the Fountain of the Centaurs. This granite fountain represented "the wild untamed life of the vast forest primeval which covered these hills and spread over these plains in the long ages before the 'white man came'."[2] A reproduction of the Liberty Bell was located next to the Fountain of the Centaurs. The next statue was one of Robert Livingston, James Monroe, and Francis Barbe-Marbois signing the Louisiana Purchase document. However, the best statue of all was a thirteen-foot bronze statue of Thomas Jefferson, standing at the entrance of the capitol building.

When everyone had finished admiring the statues, Mr. Ricker instructed the grown-ups and his students to move to the south lawn. There, they stood together, staring up at a grand thirty-foot wide stairway, extending all the way up to the third floor. With baited breath, the group of people climbed clear to the top, coming to a stop between two tall stone columns. Eight forty-eight-foot columns lined the south side of the portico. More columns, lining the entire veranda, made the visitors feel very small by comparison. The children followed close behind Mr. Ricker as they walked

---

[1.] www.sos.mo.gov/archives/history/capitol.asp
[2.] www.visitjeffersoncity.com/attractions_capitol_grounds.html

past the statue of Thomas Jefferson. They stopped in front of a thirteen-by-eighteen-foot bronze door. Mr. Ricker pulled open the heavy door and ushered the group through the grand doorway. The first thing they realized was the limestone marble floor was so shiny they could almost see their reflections. Looking around, they noticed all the woodwork in the room shining, like it was made of glass.

Walking forward, and with their mouths agape, they found themselves standing in the center of the state capitol's rotunda. The area measured sixty-eight feet in diameter. "Look at that," Lonnie whispered, pointing to the ceiling. All eyes turned upward. A huge bronze chandelier hung from the center of the dome, one hundred seventy-one feet above them. Big beautiful murals depicting scenes of the history of Missouri, its people, and landscapes decorated the walls of the dome.

"Can we go all the way to the top?" Fern asked.

"Sure we can," answered her dad. "But first, let's check out what's on the first floor."

Climbing down a curved stairway, they saw pictures, telling about events in Missouri's history, hanging on the walls behind elaborate frames. Portraits of Missouri's famous people hung on the walls, lining the long hallways and wings of the building. The most impressive artwork was the huge murals in the House Lounge. The artist of these murals was Thomas Hart Benton, Missouri's own son.

Climbing a stairway to the second floor, the students were cautioned once again by Mr. Ricker. "When we go into the museum," he said, "make sure to keep your hands in your pockets. Don't touch anything," he warned. Thousand of artifacts and objects from all aspects of Missouri's history were encased in glass cases. On display were over one hundred twenty-five Missouri Civil War battle flags.

Leaving the museum, Mr. Ricker led his students through a wooden door leading to the third floor. On that floor, they were able to see the huge rooms where the house and the senate assembled.

"Okay, come along," Mr. Ricker called out to his students. "Find your partner and line up behind me." Walking in single file, the group of spectators went through a small doorway where they found the stairway leading to the top of the rotunda. Around and around it went along the interior wall of the dome. As they started to climb, each step took them higher and higher. The closer they got to the top of the dome, the narrower the steps became. They hadn't climbed very far up the stairs when Lonnie started to huff and puff. "Are you okay?" Myrtle asked. "Yea, I'm fine. Just a little winded. You go on ahead," he told her. "I'll meet you all at the top."

Following their teacher, the children continued to ascend the stairs. When they were about halfway to the top, the steps became so narrow they were forced to walk single file. Without warning, Mr. Ricker stopped. Fern, who was about in the middle of the line, leaned over the railing to see what was holding them up. When she was finally able to look around the line of people in front of her, she saw a huge woman talking to her teacher. The woman's body was so large she took up almost the whole space between the railing and the wall. *Oh, my goodness*, she commented to herself. June and the rest of the children followed Fern's lead. They too leaned over the railing, glancing up.

"Uh-oh," June squealed, when she saw the woman. "How's she going to get past us?"

"Forget about us, how's she gonna past Mr. Moulder?" laughed Charley.

"Oh, hush up," Fern scolded the boy. Looking around for her dad, she finally saw him below her, cautiously taking one step at a time, making his way upward. She could tell that his breathing was labored. Not only was she concerned for the safety of her dad she also couldn't help being embarrassed about his large size. She looked back up the stairs and saw the woman still standing on the step just above Mr. Ricker. He had turned around, telling the children to move over against the wall. "Let this nice woman pass," he was saying.

Not wanting to be squashed, the children did as they were told. When it was time for the woman to pass June, the little girl held her breath, squinted her eyes shut, and pushed back as tight as she could against the wall. June felt the woman's large soft body brush against her. June tried to squeeze just a littler tighter up against the hard wall. When the woman passed, the youngster opened her eyes and let out a long deep sigh. Looking at her friend Joy, she whispered, "Boy, that was close. I got almost squished."

"Me too," giggled Joy.

The two little girls turned to watch the retreating back of the woman as she slowly descended down the steps.

"What's going to happen when she meets Mr. Moulder?" they heard Charley whisper.

"Hush, he'll hear you," Fern, once again, scolded Charley.

By now, Lonnie was just a few steps behind the children. Resting one foot on the next higher step, he looked up. There, directly in front of him was one of the largest women he had ever seen. She was so large he couldn't see around her. Slowly, Lonnie moved to the right as the woman moved to the left. *Nope, that ain't gonna work*, he muttered to himself. Next, he moved to the left as the woman moved to the right.

"Well, sir, that isn't going to work either," she remarked.

Leaning over the railing, Lonnie looked up. Then he turned his head to look back down the steps. Scratching his chin hairs, he remarked, "Well, lady, looks like we got a problem. The way I have it figured, somebody's gonna have to back up." Once again, Lonnie leaned over the steps, looked up, and saw Mr. Ricker and the children looking down at him. Then he looked back down the steps. Looking once again at the fat woman in front of him, he stated, "Seems to me there's a lot less of a problem below us than above us. So if you give me a minute, I'll back down these steps. Then you can follow." With that, Lonnie took one cautious step backward and then another, the woman following close behind, until they were both standing on the floor.

The older boy, who had made fun of Lonnie earlier, whispered to his friend, "See, I told you they couldn't pass each other. They're both too fat."

On the verge of anger and embarrassed tears, Fern retorted to the two boys, "Oh shut up, or I'm gonna poke you in the nose."

Mr. Ricker and his students, along with the parents, finally made it to the top of the rotunda. Fern soon forgot about being embarrassed, as she stood beside her big strong daddy, looking out the windows that encircled the dome. The view was spectacular. She could see clean across the town on one side and on the other the Missouri River away down below.

Soon, it was time to leave this great city. Mr. Ricker, Lonnie, and the other two chaperones guided the tired children back to where they had left the truck. The driver was already there, patiently waiting for them. Lonnie, once again helped the youngest children into the bed of the truck. "Sit down now," he said. "We'll be on our way soon."

While the children sat quietly in the back of the truck, Fern and her schoolmates started to reminisce about the day, discussing all the great things they had seen and done. Before long, the tires hitting the pavement lulled the youngest children to sleep.

The moon was just rising when the students of Dry Ridge School arrived safely back at the schoolhouse. Lonnie carried sleepy little June in his arms back to the wagon while Myrtle and the rest of their children followed. It didn't take long for him to hitch up the waiting mules for the short ride home. It had been a very grand day indeed.

43

Ruby ♥

Early one morning, the family was finishing their morning meal when Ruby mustered up the nerve to ask her dad a question that had been lying heavily on her mind for quite some time. "Dad," she said, "now that I'm older, and have two eighth-grade school certificates, can I get a job in town?"

Lonnie, taking the time to slurp down the last swig of coffee, replied, "Well, I don't rightly know if that's a good idea. It seems like with you bein' gone, there'll just be Fern, Beryl, and Thomas here to help with the chores and the farmin'."

June, sitting quietly at the table beside her dad, spoke up, "What about me?"

"Ah, you're just a little kid," Thomas joked, poking his younger sister in the ribs with his finger.

"Leave me be. And I'm not a little kid. I'm getting bigger every day. Ain't I, Mom?"

"You two yahoos stop fighting," Myrtle scolded. "Okay, kids. Best git started on your chores. C'mon, leave your dad and Ruby be."

Ruby waited until she and her dad were alone before she spoke up again, this time with determination. "Well?" she asked.

"Well what?"

"Can I get a job in town? I can still do my chores before and after work. And I figure, with some of the money I'm gonna be making, I can help you pay for stuff around here."

"Let me think on it," replied Lonnie. "Now quit botherin' me. Git! You have chores to do."

Ruby rose from her chair. She slowly walked down the long hallway leading to the front of the house. Feeling a little defeated, she turned to look back at her dad. He was still sitting at the table, looking straight into nothingness. Ruby knew better than to bring the subject up again. She would just have to wait until he made up his mind.

One day, a few months later, Ruby and Lonnie were in the field planting corn. In a hushed voice, Lonnie said, "I reckon it wouldn't hurt none for you to git yourself a job. We could use the extra money anyhow."

Surprised, Ruby dropped the cloth pouch she had been carrying, spilling corn on the ground. Rushing over to her dad, she gave him a big hug. "Oh, Dad, thank you," she cried.

"Hurrump. Git back to work. This corn ain't gonna plant itself."

Ruby was up bright and early the next morning. She hurried through breakfast, made the beds, and helped Fern milk the cows and Beryl feed the chickens. After that was done, she helped Thomas gather the eggs. Ruby stopped at the washbasin just long enough to clean her hands and face before bounding up the stairs to her bedroom. She put on her best dress and shoes. Looking at her reflection in the mirror, she carefully combed her short brown hair. Finally, she was ready to go out into the world in search of a job.

Ruby was in such high hopes of finding a job she skipped and ran all the way to Macks Creek. *There's lots of businesses in town*, she told herself. *I bet I won't have any trouble getting a job.* Full of confidence, she entered the locally owned mercantile. "I'm looking for a job," she told the owner. "I'm a hard worker and can do most anything."

"Sorry, young lady. But I can't afford to hire any help," she was told. Again and again, at the grocery stores, the candy factory, the hotel, and the variety stores, Ruby was greeted with, "Sorry, but we're not hiring." Late that afternoon, Ruby returned home downhearted. During supper, she was exceptionally quiet.

"Any luck?" Lonnie asked his daughter.

"No, sir. No one's hiring."

"Well, that don't surprise me. Nobody has much money anyways," Lonnie replied, trying to sooth his young daughter's feelings.

That evening, after Ruby had gone upstairs to bed, Myrtle quietly came up the steps, where she found her daughter sitting on the side of her bed, twisting a rumpled hankie in her hands. Myrtle sat down drawing Ruby close.

"This darn old Depression. When's it gonna be over?" she asked her mom.

"Nobody knows," Myrtle said soothingly. After a few minutes passed, Myrtle asked, "Ruby, have you thought about asking your grandma if she needs help at the café?"

Ruby raised her head and looked deep into her mom's fawn-colored eyes. "No, ma'am," she whispered.

"Well, I don't rightly know if she's willin' to take on any help, but it won't hurt to ask. Now dry your tears and git to bed. You don't want to be all puffy tomorrow when you go to town."

The next morning, right after the chores were done, Ruby went into Macks Creek to see Grandma Mat. "Dad said I can get a job," the young woman told the older woman. "Do you have work I can do?"

"Well, I can't pay much," Mat told her granddaughter. "But I know you're a hard worker, so I'd be willin' to pay you fifty cents a day if you're up to it."

Mat told Ruby her duties would include waiting on customers, helping with cooking, and washing the dishes. After the café closed in the evening, she was to sweep and mop the floors. It was a lot of work and long hours, but Ruby, feeling very fortunate to have a job, never complained.

Waiting on customers was Ruby's favorite part of her job. She enjoyed visiting with the town's people when they came in the café from time to time, just to sit and visit over a cup of coffee. When a motorist, traveling along Highway 54, walked through the front door, looking for a good hot meal, Ruby found it most fascinating to be able to listen to them talk about where they had come from and where they were headed. She never failed to ask what their business was in Macks Creek. Were they staying long or just passing through? The more she heard the travelers talk about faraway places, the more she dreamed of being able to pack her things in a suitcase and go with them. She didn't really care where they were going; it was just the thought of being able to go. But reality always set in with the young woman. Making just fifty cents a day, and then sharing the money with her family, it was always just a dream.

One morning, a young man with sandy blond hair came strolling in to the café. Ruby couldn't help noticing how tall he was, standing there in the doorway. But of course, with her being just five feet tall herself, everyone seemed tall. It was almost closing time. The young man looked around the café. Only a few people were left sitting at a table in the corner of the room. They were finishing their evening meal, quietly talking. He sauntered up to an empty stool at the end of the counter.

Over the past few years, since Ruby's family had move to Macks Creek, she had been dating a young man whose family lived on Mill Creek Road. But this tall stranger defiantly caught her eye. Ruby placed a glass of cold water in front of him. "What can I git ya?" she asked.

"Just some coffee," he replied.

Finding her self becoming smitten with this tall man, Ruby tried to strike up a conversation. "I don't recall seein' you around here. Travelin' through?" she inquired.

"Nope. Just got back."

The young woman's interest peaked. "Back from where?"

"Oh, no place in particular. I just finished a job putting in a new bridge up on North 5."

Ruby realized he was not a traveler, probably just a local man from over by the lake. But still there was something about him that intrigued her. Wanting to continue their conversation, Ruby asked, "Got family around here?"

"Yea, some," was his short reply.

Just then, Ruby heard the front screen door shut. A man and woman came in, sitting down at one of the empty tables. Turning her back on the blond-haired man, Ruby came out from behind the counter. "What can I get you?" she asked the couple.

"Menu please," was their reply.

Ruby hurriedly served the couple their meal. When she returned to the counter, the handsome young man was gone. She had been so busy waiting on the man and his wife she had failed to notice that the stranger had left. Ruby went back to work, angry with her self for not asking his name.

A few days later, Ruby was in the kitchen, helping her grandmother with kneading dough to make fresh bread, when she heard the front screen door open. Wiping white flour off her hands onto her bibbed apron, Ruby walked through the swinging doors to the front of the café. Sitting on the same stool he had sat on a few days earlier was the tall blond man. As she approached him, her heart flip-flopped in her chest. "Coffee?" she asked.

"Sure. And I'll take a piece of that cherry pie while you're at it."

Anxious to have another chance to visit with this stranger, Ruby said, "I see you're still here."

"Yeah, I found a job down at the saw mill. So I'll probably be around for a while."

The young woman, not wanting this stranger to slip away again, quickly asked, "Got a name?"

"Sure. George Kincaid."

George and Ruby's relationship progressed outside the Macks Creek café. They spent hours talking about a common dream, the dream of being able to leave the Ozark Hills, striking out across the country just to see what's there. The couple dated a year before George asked Ruby to marry him. She said yes.

Ruby worked at the café, saving all the money she could. When she wasn't working, she went shopping at Osborn's general store where she found a lovely piece of blue eyelet material, perfect for a wedding dress. Using a dollar of her hard-earned money, Ruby purchased a dress length. With her mom's assistances, they made a pretty little wedding dress with a matching cape. Then splurging, Ruby spent another dollar on a pair of brand-new white slippers.

On July 20, 1935, Ruby Edith Moulder and George Kincaid stood in front of the justice of the peace to say their wedding vows. Their first home in Macks Creek was a single room on the second floor of Dr. Myers building.

The couple eventually found gainful employment as faraway as California and Oregon. However, as much as Ruby thought she wanted to leave Missouri, the love of her family always beckoned her back home. Time and again, they discussed returning, until Ruby convinced George they needed to go back to the hills of the Ozarks. George and Ruby eventually bought a farm south of Macks Creek. In addition to farming, they worked at several different jobs while raising their children.

44

Harvest of the Grains ♥

Lonnie had relied heavily on his children to help with the farming. Now, with seven of them married, he had to ask his friends for help. Lonnie joined forces with his neighbors, first harvesting one man's crops before moving on to another man's fields. The men would continue moving through the area until all the farmer's crops were harvested.

The winter snows had melted. The ground was warm once again. It was time for Lonnie to get his crops in the ground. That piece of low flat land that lay over the hill behind the house was a perfect spot to plant a wheat crop.

One morning, Lonnie went out to the barn. "Well, old boy," he said, stroking the gray-streaked hair on Jude's neck. "Are you up for another year of plowin'? And how about you, Molly? Got it in you for one more time?" Still talking to the old mules, Lonnie continued, "Maybe, with the help of those two young mules I bought this past winter, it won't be so hard on you two." After hooking the harnesses to the four mules, Lonnie led them out to the field to where the plow stood idle. The plow had three wheels and a foot pedal, that when pushed, raised and lowered the blade. Two handles made it easy to adjust the depth of the plow. And best of all, there was a seat for him to sit on. The plow was so big it took four animals to pull it through the field.

After Lonnie was seated on the iron seat, he snapped the reins across the mule's rump. "Git up," he called out. Jude, lowering his head toward the ground, started to walk. The other mules followed his lead. The mules, taking slow steady steps, pulled the plow behind them, breaking up the sod. Jude stumbled, righted his gait, and then continued on down the field. Lonnie, remembering the past, thought, *I've relied on this mule for nigh on thirty years. Guess I'm gonna have to put him out to pasture.* Then talking out loud, he said, "Just give me one more year, boy, just one more year."

While Lonnie rode on the plow, June and Thomas led the way, picking up small rocks. By now, June was certain rocks grew in the field, no matter what her older brother, Thomas, said. By the end of the day, the field had been plowed and most of the small rocks removed.

The next morning, Lonnie hitched Jude to the harrow (a large rake with rows of teeth). Dragging the harrow through the field, the rake broke up lumps, smoothing the dirt. After dinner, Lonnie and Thomas went back out to the field, each with a canvas bag slug over their shoulders. Thomas watched his dad closely as they walked up and down the plowed field. Lonnie was tossing the seed out away from his body in a fan-shaped motion.

"Why are you throwing seed that way?" the young boy asked.

"So I can plant it thin."

"Why do you want it thin?"

"Because the ground here is dry most of the year. And the drier the ground, the lighter you want it seeded," Lonnie explained.

"Why?" Thomas asked again.

With great patience, Lonnie told his son that if the wheat came up thick, the crop would quickly sap up all the available moisture in the ground. Without the needed moisture, the crop would be poor.

At the end of another long day, all the seed had been planted. Lonnie stood side by side with his son, looking out over the field. Removing his sweat-stained hat, Lonnie and Thomas bowed their head. "Lord," Lonnie prayed. "Protect and bless this land so's I can harvest a good crop." Before his death, Lonnie said that he planted and harvested crops for some fifty-five years and had only lost one crop. That was to a flooding river.

After the planting was done, Lonnie kept his promise to his faithful mules by turning Molly and Jude out to pasture. Every few days, he walked along the boarders of his property, looking for his good friends. And every few days, Lonnie would find both mules standing close by each other, watching him approach with big brown eyes. One day, Lonnie was walking up the hill on the far side of the meadow when he saw Molly standing alone, her head hanging low. Jude was nowhere in sight. Sensing something amiss, Lonnie hurried his pace until he was at the mule's side. There on the ground was Jude's body, Molly guarding over her lifelong friend. Lonnie suspected Jude had died sometime during the night. Several minutes later, Lonnie led Molly back to the barnyard.

The next morning, Lonnie went outside to check on his mules. Finding Molly gone, Lonnie returned to where Jude's body lay. There, he found her, once again, standing guard over her friend. "Come on, old girl," Lonnie said gently, coaxing Molly back to the barnyard.

The very next morning, finding Molly gone again, Lonnie went to retrieve her from Jude's side. When he got to the top of the hill, he saw

Molly, lying on the ground beside Jude. She was dead. Lonnie fell to his knees and wept.

Within a few weeks, the days turned warmer with the coming of summer. Gentle spring rains covered the countryside. Before long, small tender shoots of wheat stretched up toward the big blue sky. The field looked as though it had been planted with dark green grass.

Heat from the summer sun followed the spring rains. By summer's end, the wheat was waist high and had turned golden brown. From now on, Lonnie would need to keep a close eye on his crop. He knew he had to be careful and not wait too long after the wheat dried to get it harvested. Late summer in south central Missouri was unpredictable. Dark clouds could appear in the skies in a matter of a few hours, bringing with them heavy rain, strong winds, and sometimes hail. A late-summer storm could destroy his entire crop.

Lonnie finally determined the wheat was ready to harvest. After a good hearty breakfast, which consisted of a bowl of fried corn mush, poached eggs, side pork, a glass of warm clabbered milk (milk that is just on the verge of spoiling), and a cup of coffee, Lonnie called to his children, "Time to get started."

A puzzled look came over my great-nephew's face. "Papa," Chris said, looking at Dad. "Did Grandpa own a combine?"

"No," Dad replied. After noticing his grandchildren and great-grandchildren looking directly at him, he explained, "Mema's dad didn't own a combine or even a tractor for that matter. All his farming was done behind the back end of a mule."

"Then how did he harvest the wheat?" Chris asked.

"When it was time to cut his crop, Grandpa would walk down the field, swinging a cradle scythe."

"What was he swinging?" my inquisitive nephew asked.

"A cradle scythe. It's a long narrow blade attached to the end of a curved wooden handle. A wooden framework grid, attached to the side of the blade, and the lower end of the handle provided a 'cradle' for the wheat stalks to fall onto. When it was full of stalks, Grandpa would empty the cradle. His kids would follow him through the field, picking up the stalks from the ground, bundling them into sheaves. Several bunch of sheaves stood together to make a shock."

"Then what?" my nephew Lonnie asked. I could tell from the look on his face, as well as the rest of my family's, it was difficult to comprehend harvesting a wheat crop without all the modern-day implements. After all, we had been raised in Kansas, a state where thousands of acres of wheat were harvested each year. So trying to imagine doing such work, without a combine or a truck, was almost impossible to imagine.

Dad continued.

The exact time of threshing the wheat was determined by two factors: the dryness of the grain and the availability of a big machine called a thresher. The threshing machine was used to separate the wheat from the straw. Will Varner, who lived up on Hack Ridge, just a few miles east of Macks Creek, owned the only thresher for miles around.

Lonnie got word to Varner that his wheat had been cut and was standing in the field. Early in the morning on the day Will planned to thresh Lonnie's wheat, he came up the hill from Hack Ridge, dragging the thresher behind his team of horses. Will was parking the thresher in the field just as Myrtle called her family to breakfast.

After breakfast and the chores were done, Wil Varner had the steam engine fired up, creating enough steam to last the day. Lonnie's neighbors started to arrive with teams and wagons. Out in the field, the wagon drivers would halt his team next to a shock of wheat. Some of the older children were waiting there to throw the sheaves up onto the wagon racks before the driver moved on to the next shock. When the wagon was fully loaded, the driver clucked at the horses and drove to where Will and his threshing machine were waiting.

The wagon driver drove up beside the thresher, tying the reins securely to a front ladder, thus hindering the mule's movement. The driver and Will would unload the sheaves directly into the maw of the machine. The steam engine sputtered and coughed, causing the conveyor belt that stretched between the steam engine and the thresher to turn. The threshing machine clanked and whirred. After the wheat was separated from the straw, the small wheat grains went up a spout and poured out of the thresher in a golden stream into bushel baskets, the straw emptying out onto the ground below. When each basket was filled, some of the bigger boys carried them to the grain bin and dumped the golden brown wheat into the granary. Others were standing close by the thresher, hoe in hand, and ready to pull the loose straw from beneath the machine, piling it in a stack.

Harvest always took place during the end of summer when the air was hot and dry. Nary a breeze would blow to help cool things off. Myrtle dreaded this time of the year. However, she never complained. She knew the work was necessary for her family's welfare.

For several days before harvest, Myrtle would stay busy baking cakes, pies, and cookies. She saved the sweet cream, from her best cows, in order to have enough to churn fresh butter. On harvest day, it was Myrtle and the other wives' responsibility to furnish a full-scale meal for the entire threshing crew.

Shortly after the sun was up but before her neighbors started arriving, Myrtle went to the henhouse to get five fat hens. Holding each one by neck, she swung them around wringing its necks before tossing it to the ground to bleed out. June hated when her mother did this because she was sure the headless chickens, flopping around on the ground, somehow knew she was close by and would take off chasing her. Myrtle would retrieve the dead chicken from the ground, hold it by the legs, and submerge it into a large kettle full of boiling water. Steam would rise from the kettle with the smell of hot wet feathers, making June turn up her little pug nose. Carefully, Myrtle plucked the feathers from the chickens before gutting them. After putting the chickens to soak in a dishpan full of cold clear water, Myrtle cleaned the vegetables she had picked from her garden that morning.

After breakfast was over, the neighbor women started to arrive. With them they brought hams, pork ribs, fresh vegetables, stewed tomatoes, boiled turnip greens, sauerkraut, and baked white bread and pans brimming full of warm golden corn bread. When added to Myrtle's fried chicken, mashed potatoes, gravy, fresh vegetable, jars of canned fruit, and fresh-baked biscuits, it was a quite a sight to behold.

Myrtle stepped out on the porch. There wasn't a breath of air anywhere. The hot sun was burning down from a cloudless blue sky. Grabbing a moment for herself, Myrtle leaned against the wooden corner post of the porch, took the hem of her apron, and wiped away sweat running down her face. Even with all the windows in the house opened wide, it seemed as if her kitchen had been turned into an inferno. Slowly, Myrtle reached up, took hold of a short rope, and with a might tug, she rang the dinner bell.

When the men and children in the fields heard the clanking sound of the bell echo through the hills, they immediately stopped what they were doing. The work that morning had been long, hot, and tiring. Everyone was famished and ready to eat.

The hungry men were ushered into the dining room first, while the woman stood by, watching them fill their plates. When the last man was seated at the table, a heaping plate of food in front of him, Myrtle called to the children, who were standing close to the back door. The mouthwatering smell of food being prepared had been drifting outdoors all morning, and they were anxiously waiting for their chance to dive in. "Come and git it!" Myrtle called.

The aroma of the cooking food not only attracted the kids, it also attracted every fly in the county. Myrtle stationed Fern, with a peach tree switch held firmly in her hand, to stand beside the open door swishing flies away from the table.

Myrtle and her friends waited patiently for their families to eat. When a platter or bowl was emptied, they were there to refill it. After the satisfying meal was over, the men found whatever cool place they could to stretch out and rest for a while. Even the small children, who were usually rambunctious and full of energy, didn't argue with their dads when told to go lie down. It was only then that the women had the opportunity to fill their own plates with whatever food was left over.

Threshing day continued until dusk when all work stopped. Before the neighbors loaded up their wagons and headed for their own homes, they once again came into the house to eat their fill of what was left of the noon meal.

When harvest was complete and all of the wheat was in the grain bin, Lonnie would take all of the cloth sacks Myrtle could find and fill them with grain. He would take a wagonload of grain to Mill Creek and have it ground into enough flour that would last the family through winter.

"Gosh, that was a lot of work," commented Torrie, Phyllis's youngest son. "But, boy, could they ever eat," chimed in Rusty.

I finished the story for dad.

The joy of harvest, the odor of new wheat, the dusty gray appearance of men and children coming in from out of the fields, the noise, the hustle and bustle was an experience that a child fondly remembers. One of Mom's fondest memories was curling up at the end of a long day, the feel and smell of a big straw tick mattress, stuffed full of new straw, layered with a feather bed, upon which to sleep.

45

Hauling Water ♥

Marla had been sitting quietly in Mom's big overstuffed chair, listening to the stories. All of sudden she spoke, "I remember Mom telling about a time when she was out in the fields and got caught in a rain shower."
"Would you like to share that story with the rest of us?" I asked.
"Sure, I'd be glad to."
By the time June was old enough to work alongside the rest of the family in the fields, Fern, Beryl, and Thomas were teenagers. The older children took the heavy-duty jobs, while June helped with some of the lighter chores. One summer day, when June was about nine, she pitched in to do her duty to help with the farm work. On this particularly bright and sunny day, her job was to haul water from the well out to the workers in the fields.
June was so little and lightweight, a bucket full of water weighed almost as much as she did. When she went to draw water from the well, it was impossible for her to haul the bucket up out of the well, hand over fist, while holding on to the rope. To resolve this problem, she would jump up as high as she could, grab hold of the rope, and let her entire weight pull the bucket a little way up from the depths of the well. She would put her foot on the rope and, as fast as lightning, jump up again, grab a little higher on the rope, and let her weight bring the bucket a little higher up through the cylinder well. Time after time, she would repeat this process until she was finally able to get the bucket to the top. It was a lot of heavy work for such a little girl!
Lonnie kept one-gallon glass jugs, wrapped in tow sacks, for hauling drinking water. The sacks were made from insulating rough-hewn jute. He wrapped the tow sack around the glass jugs, tied a stick into the neck of the sack, connecting the two jugs. After the glass jugs were filled, June let the rest of the water from the bucket run onto the sacks. The wet cover helped keep the water cool, until she got it to the field. If the workers were in the field right below the house, she would get there pretty quick. If they happened to be in the field, way up toward Willis's place, she had a long walk.

On this hot summer day, on the long journey through the valley and over the hill, the sky darkened and rain started to fall. It was only a quick summer shower, over almost before it began, but it lasted long enough to get the young girl sopping wet. After the rain stopped, June ran on up the hill carrying both jugs on the stick across her shoulders. She found the men working on the far side of the hill. They were hot and thirsty and eagerly awaiting her arrival. Taking the jugs, they quickly gulped down all the water.

Taking the now-empty jars from the men, June turned around and ran back down the hill, heading to the well to draw more water. When she entered the plush green valley, she stopped. Wanting to take a few minutes for herself, June retrieved the book *Little Women* from her pocket and sat down on a nice cushiony section of green grass to read.

The young girl had just opened her book when she realized she was sitting exactly at the end of a rainbow. Awestruck, she jumped up, watching as lights reflected through the raindrops, glistening with a kaleidoscope of colors on the trees and grass around her. As far as she could see the darkness of the sky was pierced only by the bright colorful rainbow. The air was only a hushed whisper, and she felt so very small and so alone. But she wasn't scared. She had a peaceful, uncomplicated feeling and envisioned that she could almost reach out and caress the face of God. It was a time of wonderment for her and awe inspiring! In the stillness of the afternoon, she spread her arms straight out from her little lithe body and gleefully danced, gracefully leaping and bowing and pirouetting like a ballerina, lost in her own whimsical movements. As she danced, the rich hues of the rainbow turned her worn, simple dress into a glistening gown, glimmering with raindrops and resembling a princess's evening dress adorned with sparkling rubies, diamonds, and pearls.

Lonnie, unaware of his little daughter's quiet rendezvous in the tranquil, motionless air, hollered his familiar refrain, "Wattttereerrrr Jack, you ought to a been here and halfway back!"

Jolted from her once-in-a-lifetime dance at the end of a rainbow, June quickly picked up her book and the stick holding the empty jars, rushed up to the well beside the house, drew up two jugs of water before hurrying back down the hill, across the valley, and up the long hill to her waiting father and the thirsty farmhands.

46

Everything but the Oink ♥

In addition to farming, Lonnie raised hogs. The Moulder family enjoyed choice cuts of ham, pork shoulder, bacon, sausage, pork chop, back strap, pork roast, and ribs. Myrtle would occasionally barter with her neighbors some of the cured pork for canned or dried fruits and vegetables. Food swapping between friends added a large variety of flavor to their everyday meals.

Lonnie's hogs were free to roam the woods surrounding the house. They scrounged on apples that lay rotting on the ground and old corncobs that had been tossed out. During June's younger years, Lonnie cautioned his daughter about venturing too far away from the house. "Girl, you be leery bout wanderin' off out there," he told her. "Don't go traipsin' too far into those woods." He was afraid the wild hogs would attack his little girl. Especially if that hog had just given birth. Sows were known to attack and possibly kill anyone or anything she felt was threatening her young.

After the shoats (baby pigs) had been weaned from their mother, Lonnie took six or seven of the small boars and put them in a pen by the barn. During the next few months, they would be fed extra food, getting them good and fat. These hogs would be butchered in the fall, providing the Moulders with ample meat for the winter months. Lonnie left the rest of the wild hogs and baby shoats in the woods. There was plenty of food for them to feed on until he could get the biggest ones to market.

When June was nine years old, it became her responsibility to feed the young pigs out in the pigpen. Early in the morning, she would carry ears of dried corn out to the hungry pigs. Leery of these animals, she stood as far away from the fence as she could and still be able to toss the corn over the railing. Then again after supper, she carried more ears of corn to the pigs while she also carried the slop bucket.

"What's a slop bucket?" interrupted my grandson, Cody. "Remember," his mom, Suzanne, explained, "almost everything was used and reused around the Moulder household."

"That's right," I agreed.

So when mealtime was over, all food scraps, peelings, eggshells, vegetables, and fruit cores were put in a bucket. Even the unusable fat from the frying pan was poured in."

Holding his nose, my grandson commented, "Yuk, that would stink!"

"It sure did," I laughed. "That's why Grandma kept the slop bucket next to the back door."

June, a little slip of a girl, hated this job. It was very difficult for her to lug the slop bucket from the house to the pigpen. No matter how carefully she walked the hundred feet between the house and the barn, the slop would slosh over the top of the bucket onto her little short legs.

Down at the pens, the growing pigs eagerly awaited June's arrival. Their terrific appetites for the stinking garbage made the young girl even more frightened of them. When they saw her coming, the pigs crowded the trough to get first dibs at what June was bringing. In doing so, their big brown bodies would bump and scrape the fence, threatening to knock it to the ground. So first, to draw the hog's attention away from her, she would throw the ears of corn as far as she could over the fence. When the pigs became preoccupied with the corn, June cautiously approached the railings. Scrunching up her face, she held her breath as she poured the family's garbage through the fence rails, splashing it into the trough. When the bucket was empty, June quickly backed up. She stood and watched the pigs, no longer interested in the ears of corn, go wild as they rutted in the trough for his share of the meal. In a frenzy, the snorting and grunting pigs scrambled around, knocking each other out of the way, trying to make sure their snout was first to be submerged deep down into the trough filled with smelly rotting garbage. The pigs quickly gained huge amounts of weight from this daily feast. By early fall, they were so big and fat they found it difficult to even stand up. Lying in the mud, they would lull their big ole heads to the side, dip their snout into the trough, and suck in the food.

In early December, after Lonnie had chosen a day to butcher his hogs, he checked the wood stacked alongside the house. He knew he would need a lot of wood, not only for keeping the fires burning all day on butchering day but also to make sure there was enough wood to burn in the potbellied stove through the cold winter months. Seeing the stack was low, he decided that before butchering day arrived, he would need to go into the woods for more firewood.

Inside the barn, Lonnie had an emerald grinding stone he used to sharpen the blades of his saws, axes, and hatchets. The stone, eighteen inches in diameter, was approximately three inches thick. A six-inch-long cast-iron rod ran through the center of the stone. Each end of the rod was bolted to a wooden frame.

Thomas, now eleven years old, joined his dad in the barn. It was the young boy's job to turn the handle attached to the frame, making the stone spin around and around. One by one, Lonnie held his axe, hatchet, and crosscut saw against the spinning stone, sharpening the blade. The crosscut saw is a flat piece of metal, five feet long. Wooden handles are attached to each end, and sharp pointy teeth fill up one edge of the metal.

When the tools were sharp, Lonnie and Thomas went to hook the mules to the wagon. Just as they were finishing, a neighbor man came walking across the yard. He was dressed in a heavy red and black flannel shirt, brown wool trousers, and a plaid felt hat. Earflaps that could be lowered in cold weather were fastened with silver snaps across the caps crown. His worn leather boots were caked with mud and manure. In his hand, he carried his own ax.

"Howdy, neighbor," Lonnie called out.

"Howdy," the man replied. "I see you're gettin' ready to cut wood."

"Sure am."

"Mind if I join ya? I'm gonna need some myself 'fore winter sets in."

"Sure, I can use the help. Git in. Thomas, git in the house and tell your sisters to get out here. We gotta be goin'." After everyone had climbed into the wagon, Lonnie clicked his tongue, calling out to his mules, "Git up, old gals. We got work to do."

Coming to a stop in the midst of the tall elm, sycamore, hickory, and walnut trees, Lonnie and his children, along with the neighbor man, climbed down to the ground. Lonnie stood studying the trees around him. Finally, he chose a tall hickory to start with. Taking his ax and standing with his legs apart, he swung the ax high above his head, as one would swing a baseball bat. Then he brought the ax forward with such force the blade bit into the side of the tree trunk, sending small wood chips flying. Again and again, Lonnie chopped at the trunk until he had a cut a deep V in the wood. He then grabbed hold of the handle on the crosscut saw. When the neighbor man joined him, on the other end, the two men started pulling the blade back and forth across the truck.

Before the first tree fell, Lonnie's two sons, Howard and Ray, along with Howard's two young boys, Earl and Donald, came riding into the woods in Ray's old truck.

"Mighty glad you could join us," Lonnie called out to his sons.

"Wouldn't wanna miss this fine day in the woods," teased Ray, climbing out of the cab.

Crash! The tree fell to the ground. Lonnie and his neighbor went to the next tree and starting chopping. Howard and Ray used their saws and axes to cut the limbs off the fallen tree. When the trunk was void of all the limbs, Howard used his saw to cut the trunk in to blocks while Ray, using a steel spike and a sledgehammer, split the blocks into firewood. Beryl and Thomas along with Earl, Donald, and June loaded the small logs onto the wagon and in the back of Ray's truck. While the children were waiting for the next tree to be cut, they cleaned the area of wood chips and small kindling, putting them into a wooden bucket.

After a day of working in the woods, Lonnie remarked, "Well now, I suppose that's gonna do it."

"That's a plenty for me," replied the neighbor.

"Yep, that ought to do it for us too," echoed Howard and Ray.

"See ya in a few days," Lonnie called to his two sons, as they drove off down the road. "Climb on, kids. We need to git home 'fore it gits dark."

When they arrived back in the barnyard, Lonnie told his neighbor he would see to it that he got his wood. "I'd be obliged," the man called back over his shoulder. Lonnie watched his neighbor walk back across the field before he disappeared over the hill. It had been a long hard day. But at least now, there was a huge stack of wood standing by the side of the barn.

A few days before hog butchering day, almost everyone in the Moulder family pitched in to help. Shortly after sunup, Howard with his wife, Lillie, came from their home down in Lower Prairie Holler. Ray and his wife, Florence, came up from Rag Holler while George and Ruby arrived from Macks Creek.

Howard and Ray dug a pit in a pre-designated area behind the barn. The pit was two feet wide, two feet deep, and about eight feet long. Over the pit was placed a sturdy iron grate. A fifty-gallon steel barrel called a scalding box was brought from the barn and placed on top of the grate. Earl, Donald, and Thomas carried buckets of water from the pond to dump in the scalding box, while Ruby and Beryl drew water from the well.

Another smaller fire pit was dug closer to the back door of the house. Standing over the pit was a tripod from which Lonnie hung a big heavy black cast-iron kettle. George made several long tables from planks of wood and sawhorses, standing them around the yard.

Inside the house, Myrtle, Lillie, and Florence were busy sterilizing glass quart jars before sitting them upside down on the kitchen counters. The galvanized washtubs, buckets, pails, and big black iron kettles were washed with hot lye soap. Every cotton dishtowel Myrtle owned was bleached with liquid bluing and hung by the kitchen stove to dry.

After a hearty evening meal, Lillie, Florence, and Ruby bundled up their young children in warm coats and blankets for the ride home. Beryl, Thomas, and June were so tired they could hardly stay awake long enough to say goodbye. The older children were barely out of the yard when Lonnie and Myrtle retired to their beds, satisfied with the knowledge that all the preparations needed to butcher their hogs were complete.

The following Friday, Myrtle rose from her bed long before daybreak. In her head was a mental list of last-minute things she needed to do. Barely taking time for her morning coffee, she soon had loaves of freshly made bread rising on the shelf above the cook stove. She needed to dig potatoes from her garden and retrieve apples and cabbage from the hole in the hillside. There were pies to be baked using berries she had canned the previous summer. She needed to make an apple cake, gingersnap cookies, and churn cream into butter. All of this was in addition to her daily chores.

The very next morning, while the sky was still gray black in color, Lonnie was up and out of bed. Quietly, he dressed by the glow of the full moon streaming in through the bedroom window. By the back door, he pulled on his over boots, heavy wool coat, and fur-lined hat before going out into the cold morning air. Looking up at millions of twinkling stars in the clear sky, he determined it was going to be a good day for hog butchering. By 4:00 a.m., he had a roaring fire built in the long pit, sending a smoky haze through the valley. The smell of burning wood drifted inside the house waking his family.

Just as the sun was creeping into the eastern sky, Myrtle and Lonnie's sons Howard and Ray, their wives, and children started arriving at the farm. Ruby and George once again came out from town. Several of their neighbors also came over the hill to help. Butchering hogs was a huge undertaking. Lonnie and Myrtle welcomed any help they could get from neighbors, family, and friends.

Myrtle was excited about hog-butchering day. She knew that even though the day would be long and the work hard, it was one of only about three times a year she could get together with the other women, enjoying their company. While they worked, each woman would try to outdo the other with their cooking techniques and recipes, while chatting about everyday life. On this day, the women were in "their hay."

June, relinquishing her babysitting duties with her young nieces and nephews to Beryl, was anxiously waiting outside for Earl and Donald to arrive. June didn't have to wait long before Howard's wagon came lumbering up the road. When the boys saw June, they jumped from the moving wagon and came racing up the hill toward their young aunt. June ran out to meet them. Then off they scurried to the barnyard. The youngsters knew this was going to be a busy day, full of all kinds of activity and lots of good things to eat.

Myrtle greeted her two daughters-in-law at the kitchen door, ushering them inside to join the other women, who were already sitting around the kitchen table. She had just poured them a cup of coffee when she happened to glance out the window. Seeing Lonnie come from behind the barn holding his shotgun, her eyes quickly darted around the yard searching for June, Earl, and Donald. "Oh my gracious," she exclaimed when she saw the three youngsters standing on the wood railing fence surrounding the pigpen.

Opening the back door, Myrtle yelled, "Lonnie, git those kids in here. They have no business bein' out there."

"Oh, Mom, why not?" begged June.

"Better do as your ma says, Pug," Lonnie told his little girl.

"Why can't we watch?"

"Cause your ma says no. Now, git on in the house like you was told."

The three children hopped down to the ground and ran into the house. "C'mon," June whispered, chasing past Myrtle, who was still standing at the door. Without missing a step, they ran down the hallway, grabbed hold of the wooden banister, and darted up the stairs. Jumping onto the center of the bed, June pulled open the curtains that were covering her window. From there, the three children had a bird's eye view of what was taking place in the barnyard.

Bang! The children jumped when they heard the sound of Lonnie's shotgun. Startled, June ducked down into the cornhusk mattress, quickly covering her head with the pillow. Before the repercussion of the shotgun stopped echoing through the hills, a second shot was fired. A couple of minutes passed. Hearing no more shots, June, coaxed by her nephews, slowly raised her head. The three children look out again into the barnyard.

They saw two strong neighbor men dragging the dead hog to a nearby tree. After securing a chain around the hog's hind ankles, the men tossed the other end of the chain over a stout limb. It took both men, pulling on the chain with all their might, their muscles straining underneath the sleeves of their flannel shirts, to slowly hoist the huge animal up until its head was barely hanging above the ground. June watched as her dad picked up a long-bladed knife from a nearby table. Quick as a wink, he slit the dead hog's throat. Bright red blood, flowing into a large washtub, gushed out of the animal. Howard picked up the tub of blood and carried it to the back door where Myrtle was waiting. She took the tub from her son and walked to the stove, where a large black kettle was sitting. After pouring the blood into the kettle, Myrtle adjusted the heat and set the blood to simmering.

"What in the world is she cooking the blood for?" asked Diane, my nephew Lonnie's wife.

"I'll tell you later," I replied.

The young children, still watching from the upstairs window, saw Lonnie once again take the razor-sharp knife and slowly slit the hog's soft underbelly. Suddenly, June's mouth filled with bile as her stomach did flip-flops. She was afraid she was going to be sick. Quickly, she covered her eyes with both hands.

"Ugh!" she heard Earl exclaim. And then, she heard Donald say, "Look at that!" as the hog's guts poured out into another large washtub. Not wanting to miss what was causing such a stir with the boys, June peeked through her fingers. Lowering her hands, she pointed toward the steam rising from the barrel. "Look!" she squealed. "They started the guts on fire!"

"No, they didn't, silly," Earl said, feeling very proud of himself for knowing more than his aunt. "The guts are warm from being inside the hog. When they hit the cold air, it makes steam."

"Oh," commented June, screwing up her face. She wasn't quite sure she understood all that.

The children watched Ray carry the tub full of entrails to the big black iron kettle hanging from the tripod. From their vantage point, they could see the hot soapy suds in the kettle turn red as Ray dumped the entrails into the water. Florence, his wife, came outside, rolled up her sleeves, and submerged her hands deep into the red sudsy water. As if she was washing clothes, Florence cleaned the long rope of intestines, inside and out, before placing them in yet another washtub filled with clear cold water.

The hog was taken down from the limb. One end of the chain was still secure around the hog's hind legs while the other end of the chain was drawn through a pulley, attached to another limb high above the scalding box. The hog was once again hoisted up. Two strong men, one on each side, pulled and pushed the animal until it was directly above the boiling water. Slowly, the hog was lowered. Even though the temperature outside was just above freezing, beads of sweat popped out on the men's foreheads, as steam spewed out of the barrel. After a few minutes, they raised the hog out of the scalding water, rolling it onto stout wooden planks, lying lengthwise across three sawhorses. Using a sharp razor, the men scraped the hog's hide to remove its hair.

After removing the strong chains from the hog's hind legs, it was carried to a gaming pole—a tree where strong metal hooks had been pounded into the wood. The animal was hung upside down, its hind legs hooked on the metal hooks. The hog's head was removed and taken inside the house. Lonnie took a sharp knife and cut the skin from around the hog's ankles. With Howard's help, they gently pulled the skin down, cutting the sinew that connected the skin to the meat. When the hide had been removed, Howard laid it across one of the tables, where it would be scraped clean of all blood vessels and any remaining paper-thin membranes.

The carcass of the animal was taken down from the gaming pole and carried to another table that had been set up in the yard. Ruby's husband,

George, used a large meat cleaver to chop the meat into large sections. This would make it easier to cut the meat into choice pieces.

The process of slaughtering the hogs was repeated until all of the animals had been killed, gutted, skinned, and the meat was lying in large chucks on the table just outside the back door.

June, Earl, and Donald became bored with watching the activity that was going on outside so they decided to head downstairs to see what was going on there. As they walked down the long hallway leading into the kitchen, the lip-smacking smell of food cooking drifted out to meet them. Entering the kitchen, the three children could tell that their moms had spent the morning preparing a noon meal fit for a king. There were platters filled with pork liver and slabs of back strap sitting in the middle of the kitchen table along with steaming bowls of fried apples, sauerkraut, mashed potatoes, and creamy gravy. A breadbasket was overflowing with fresh-baked bread. A sideboard sat along the back wall and was heavily laden with pies, cakes, and cookies. "You kids, git!" Lillie scolded, when she saw them grab a couple of gingersnap cookies. "Ah, Ma," cried Earl. "Nobody's gonna miss these with all this other stuff here."

The children walked into the kitchen just as Myrtle stepped out on the back porch to ring the big iron dinner bell. At the sound of the clanging bell, the men stopped what they were doing and headed to the pump jack where they took turns washing their hands, arms, faces, and necks in the cold water. Try as they might, they couldn't remove the smell of burnt hair, blood, and guts from their nostrils. However, when the back door of the house opened, the smell of fried pork liver had their mouths watering.

The women stood by watching the hungry men fill their plates before calling to the children. "Time to eat!" June didn't have to be told twice. While the other moms helped the little children with their plates, June piled her plate high with liver and sauerkraut smothered in pork gravy. When their husbands and children were taken care of, the women had the opportunity to fill their own plates.

After dinner, the men returned to their duties outside. The meat of each hog lay in large chucks on long wooden tables. Ray and Howard cut the meat into choice cuts of ham, pork shoulder, pork chop, back strap, pork roast, ribs, and slabs of bacon. Big thick slices of pork were placed in a wooden barrel, filled with salt brine, for making salt pork.

Lonnie salted each piece of meat before carrying it to the smokehouse, where a small fire had been built in the center of the dirt floor. The sweet smell of smoldering hickory rose into the air every time he opened the small door. He hung the hams from the rafters and laid the rest of the meat on shelves.

Lonnie would tend the fire inside the small smokehouse for several days. Then Myrtle would wrap the meat in brown paper, secured with a piece of twine, before hanging it in the root cellar. The smoked pork would remain good throughout the year.

While the men were busy outside, chopping, cutting, slicing, pickling, salting, and smoking the fresh cut-up pork, Myrtle and the women were busy inside making blood bread, headcheese, lard, and sausage.

Large chucks of pork fat had been removed from the poorer cuts of meat and put in a large kettle to make lard. Ruby slowly stirred the milky white liquid with a long-handled wooden paddle. As the fat chucks floated to the top, she would scoop them up with a spoon, put them on a plate, and smash them with a potato masher before retuning them to the kettle. This would ensure that the lard would be nice, smooth, and thick. Brown cracklings that came to the surface while the fat was simmering were skimmed off and saved. Some of the cracklings would be mixed with pork broth and canned in quart jars. Some would be used later for a delicacy treat or flavoring over vegetables. June, Earl, and Donald stood close by the stove to receive whatever cracklings might be left over. After cooking all day in the iron kettle, the fat was strained through a thin dishcloth into a washtub. Then it was poured into jars. As it cooled, the lard would thicken.

The excess fat was also trimmed from the choicest pieces of meat. These trimmings were pushed through a meat grinder before adding the right amount of spices to make mild and hot sausage, liver sausage, and sage sausage. Some of the meat was fried until it was nearly done before putting it into glass jars, covering it with hot lard. After several hours, the hot lard would harden, making a nice seal over the meat. The rest of the meat was stuffed into clean hog entrails and tied for link sausage.

The hog's blood had been simmering in a large black kettle all morning and was now ready for Lillie to make blood bread. In a large bowl, she mixed together graham flour and boiling water until the mixture was smooth. Then using a wooden paddle, she stirred in melted lard, salt, cloves, allspice, and some yeast. When all of this was well mixed, Lillie stirred in the blood, some rye, and white flour, continuing to stir until the mixture no longer stuck to the paddle. Then she set the bowl filled with dough on the shelf above the stove. After a few hours, the dough had doubled in size. Lillie stirred the dough down, spooned it into bread pans, and placed it back on the shelf above the stove to rise once more. When it had again doubled in size, she put the pans in the hot oven to bake.

The head of the hog was placed in a large kettle filled with water. As it slowly simmered, the meat would come off the bone. With a slotted spoon, the meat would be dipped from the hot water, placed in a bowl, and spices added. This mixture was put into cleaned pork stomachs and submerged back in the kettle of hot water, where over a low fire it would simmer for hours. When thoroughly cooked, the headcheese was shaped into balls before being wrapped in cheesecloth, a very thin mesh, for storing.

The meat off the tail was a favorite among the children. June, Earl, and Donald watched closely as Myrtle placed each of the tails on a hot griddle. When the tails started to sizzle and pop, their mouths would water. Before long, Myrtle removed the tails from the stove, handing them over to the waiting children. "Careful, they're still hot," she cautioned. The children would toss the tail slightly into the air from hand to hand, cooling it before eating the meat off the bone.

The meat from the hog's feet was cleaned, boiled, and placed into brine. The fermented feet provided the family with a nice sour side dish.

The only thing left to process was the skin. Myrtle cut the skin into small strips. Carefully cleaned once more, she put each strip into a frying pan filled with hot melted lard. The frying skin swelled up, popped, and snapped. When it was fully cooked, Myrtle removed the rind from the pan, laying it on a clean gunnysack. After it was salted down, the rind became a crunchy, crispy treat to be munched on as a snack.

The women could find a way to use every inch of the hog. Everything that is except for the oink!

One night after butchering, Lonnie and Myrtle, satisfied that there would be enough pork to help feed their growing family in the coming year, put their tired children to bed; and exhausted them selves, they also retired to their own bed. During the night, a light snow fell. The next morning, Lonnie went out to the smokehouse to check the fire and noticed a man's footprints. They lead up to the smokehouse, around the barn, and then continued down through the field and up the hill to a neighbor's house. Lonnie tracked him. When he returned home, he told Myrtle where the tracks had led.

"What are you going to do?" Myrtle asked.

"Nothing," Lonnie replied. "You know he's lazy and likes to steal better than work. But he has a house full of kids and probably nothing to feed them, so let him have whatever he took."

"So you aren't gonna say anything?" Myrtle asked.

"Nope."

47

Entertainment ♥

Phyllis's grandson spoke up. "Grandma," Chris said. "Did Mema's family ever do anything just for the fun of it?

"Yeah, did they ever go out to eat or to a movie?" inquired Samantha, Chris's sister.

"Not very often," Phyllis told her grandchildren. "The Great Depression was still affecting everyone. If there was any money, it was seldom spent on things like going out to eat at a restaurant or going to a show."

"Then what did they do for fun?" the curious young man asked.

"Mom's family had to rely on their own means of distraction from the difficulties of everyday living. So the Moulders would occasionally enjoy outings with their friends. They would attend box suppers, picnics on warm summer days, and they would go to the closing-of-school programs. Neighborhood gatherings were a great way for everyone to get away from the daily grind of everyday living.

"One of the family's favorite outings was when they had the chance to meet their friends at the schoolhouse for a neighborhood gathering. After all of the necessary chores were completed, Lonnie would hook up the mules to the wagon while the kids anxiously piled in the back. 'C'mon, Butler,' he would call out to his little wife. 'Else we're gonna be late.' Myrtle carefully pulled herself up onto the wagon seat while holding on to some sort of homemade dessert. The warm fresh smell drifted up and out from the folds of a clean linen dishcloth she held in her lap.

"Everyone would be in high spirits as they traveled over the hills. When they arrived at the schoolhouse, their friends would already be gathering. After a warm greeting, Myrtle would join her friends inside where they were unpacking refreshments. There were always homemade pies, cakes, plenty of fresh-baked cookies, and several glass jars of sparkling clear apple cider. It wasn't until after the children had been shooed away from the table and were outside that the women could enjoy gossiping about what was happening in and around their neighborhoods. The children never minded being chased away from the food, especially if they had been successful at snatching a small sweet tidbit first. It wouldn't be long before the kids were entertaining themselves with a rowdy game of tag or hide-and-seek. The men folk gathered outside and away from the women. They enjoyed discussing market prices of crops and livestock, swapping off-colored stories while guzzling homemade whiskey from a gallon crock.

"The Moulders were comfortable doing so much with so little," Phyllis explained. "Everyone who lived around them, on farms and in small towns, had been living the same way. It wasn't until years later that Mom and her family realized just how hard things had been."

"Wow," Chris remarked.

Phyllis continued, "The Moulder girls were fast becoming teenagers. So Lonnie started allowing them the privilege of going to town to be with their friends."

"Cool," commented the young teenagers who were sitting in Dad's living room.

One Saturday morning, when Fern was about sixteen years old, she begged permission to go to town. "Some of my friends are meeting at Pleasant Grove Church tonight," she explained to her dad. "Can I go with them?"

Looking up from his book, Lonnie replied, "Just make sure you go directly to the church and nowhere else."

"Yes, sir, I will." After supper that evening, Fern put on her good dress, combed her hair, and bid her parents goodnight. Her friends, who were also walking toward town, soon joined her on the road. When the girls came in view of Highway 54, Fern started to lag behind. Reaching the highway after her friends had already crossed the road, she jumped into the ditch and removed her everyday shoes. Quickly she replaced them with her good shoes that had been hidden in the pockets of her dress and was soon back on the road.

Fern and her friends arrived at the church where they discovered the original plans had changed. Instead of staying at the church, it had been decided to go to a neighboring town several miles away to take in a movie. Giving in to her misgivings about disobeying her dad, Fern climbed into a 1927 Ford with her two girlfriends and two boys. Five young teenagers were soon headed down Highway 54 toward Warsaw, Missouri. They had traveled several miles when Fern realized just how far she was from home. She reasoned that unless she convinced everyone to return to Macks Creek, there was no way she could get back home before her dad woke up, finding her still gone. She also reasoned that without causing a scene, there was nothing she could do about it now. So in spite of her concern, she relaxed and thoroughly enjoyed the night out with her friends.

Early the next morning, when Fern came outside, Lonnie was sitting on the back porch. "Where do you think you're off to?" he asked.

Fern, not wanting to shun him, slowly turned to face her dad. "I'm going to milk the cows, sir," she replied.

In a gruff tone, Lonnie spoke again, "Young lady, where were you last night?"

Fern had never lied to her dad and not for anything in the world would she start now. "The plans at church fell through," she said. "A bunch of us kids decided to go to Warsaw to the show."

Rising from an old wooden toolbox he had been sitting on, Lonnie said, "Well now, young lady. I believe you need a good whippin' for disobeying me. Do you agree?" The tone of his voice was eerily hushed.

"Yes, sir, I guess I do."

Lonnie took out his pocketknife and handed it to Fern. "Git on down there and cut me a switch," he ordered.

Fern hurried across the road to the orchard, looking for a big branch. She knew if she got a little limb, her dad would end up getting the switch he wanted and then she would really get it. Finally, she spotted one that would do. Using Lonnie's knife, she cut down a peach tree branch and quickly returned to the porch. Standing in front of Lonnie, Fern closed the knife and handed it back to him. Then she handed him the switch. Taking the knife and the switch from his daughter, he whispered in a hushed tone, "Young lady, you'd better get on down to the barn. Your mom needs help."

"Is that all she got?" asked Chris.

"Yes, it sure is," replied Phyllis. "Lonnie never had to resort to physically striking his children. He had raised them to recognize and respect his authority. When he spoke, they knew to listen."

"What else did they do for fun?" Chris inquired.

Every summer, fliers advertising a weeklong church revival would start showing up on building fronts and taped to store windows. Everyone grew excited when the revival was coming to town. Not only was it a time to worship, it also was another reason for the locals to get out and socialize among their neighbors.

The day before the revival was scheduled to begin, a large canvas tent would be erected in a nearby field just outside of town. Some of the local men would gather to set up wooden folding chairs in front of a large wooden platform. During the evenings of the revival, it was common for people from all around the county to show up underneath the tent. They were prepared for an evening of good old down-home singing of great country gospels. Once the traveling preacher started to talk, you could hear him preach hell and damnation for miles around. He was looking for lost souls in the crowd to step up and accept Christ into their hearts. As the people listened to the word of God being delivered, a feeling of jubilance filled their souls so full they had to let it out with a robust, "Amen!" On the last day of the revival, the whole congregation would leave the tent, following the preacher to the banks of Macks Creek. Standing beside the water, they would be a witness to their new brothers and sisters in Christ being submerged in the cold clear water over the words, "I baptize you in the name of the Father, the Son, and the Holy Ghost."

The summer Fern accepted Christ as her savior the revival was held at the Dry Ridge School. Lillie had generously offered to take Fern, Beryl, and June, along with her own children, to listen to the preacher. Fern became mesmerized with each word he spoke. It was a powerful message. That night, Fern couldn't stop thinking about the sermon she had heard. After retiring to her room, she lay tossing and turning, falling into a fretful sleep. The next morning when Myrtle saw her daughter's puffy and bloodshot eyes, she asked, "Are you feeling okay?"

"I'm all right. I just didn't sleep good."

Early the next evening, Lillie and her children returned to the Moulder house. Hearing about Fern's restless night, Lillie whispered to her mother-in-law. "I think I know what Fern's frettin' about. I'll pray for her."

That evening, at the end of another powerful sermon, the preacher once again offered an invitation to anyone wanting to accept Christ as his or her Savior. Fern rose from her seat and walked to the front of the small room. She didn't notice the other people in the congregation. All she saw was the preacher standing in the front, his arms outstretched, ready to receive her as a new lamb into the flock of believers. It must have been a beautiful thing. The following Sunday morning, Fern followed the Baptist preacher to the waters of Macks Creek where she was baptized in cool clear waters.

One day, a few years later, while Fern was conducting business in the Macks Creek bank, she met Eldon Clemmons. Eldon, a native from Lead Mine, Missouri, a little town southwest of Macks Creek, was employed as a teller. The couple courted for a year before they were united in marriage on January 18, 1937. Eldon and Fern resided in Macks Creek, where Eldon, an auditor for the Missouri Farmers Association (MFA), became a prominent figure in the banking business. Fern spent her life as a faithful wife, while raising their children.

48

First Date ♥

"Beryl Moulder," Donnis said with a sigh. "This is a woman who steals everyone's heart as soon as they meet her. When in her presence, your insides feel good as if you are sitting on the banks of a stream, your bare feet dangling in the water, and minnows are nibbling at your toes. Old people, young people, and those in between marvel at the way this one woman can bring a smile to your lips just by mentioning her name. Everyone loves Aunt Beryl."

One afternoon, Beryl was enjoying the early spring day with her best friend Betty, whose family had recently moved from Dry Ridge into Macks Creek. Deciding to share a Coca-Cola at the Macks Creek café, Beryl and Betty were busy discussing the upcoming dance scheduled for the following weekend.

"I hope a lot of boys come to the dance Saturday night," Beryl confided in her friend.

"Don't be silly. You know there will be. And as pretty as you are, you aren't going to have any trouble catching the eye of one of them, even though you already have your pick of all the boys on Dry Ridge."

"Oh, how you go on," Beryl said, her face turning a soft shade of pink.

"Beryl, you're always the life of the party, and you know it. Some boy will surely notice you right off the bat."

"We'll see about that."

The young teenage girls were finishing their Coca-Cola when into the café walked a handsome tall man. Beryl had noticed him around town before, but this particular day, for some unknown reason, this young man struck a chord in the young girl. Trying to seem nonchalant, Beryl continued to observe the young man from under her dark eyelashes while she finished sipping her soda.

The man stopped just inside the doorway, looked around the interior of the café, and then boldly approached the girls. Looking directly at Beryl, he asked, "Would you like to go to the Spring Dance with me?"

"You're mighty brazen," Beryl replied. "I don't even know you!"

"Well, let's fix that. I'm Ethridge Rash. I live with my family on a farm west of here, and I would like for you to go to the dance with me."

"I can't go with you," Beryl responded flippantly.

"Why not?"

"You don't even know my name, and besides we just met." Then lowering her voice, Beryl whispered, "My dad won't let me."

"Okay. I suppose that's reason enough." With a shrug, the young man turned and started to walk away.

"My name is Beryl Moulder, and I still can't go with you, but I can meet you there."

So a date was made for the following Saturday night. Beryl knew that her dad, Lonnie, would be attending the festivities, and she figured he wouldn't mind if she tagged along.

The festival, sort of a founder's day celebration combined with the rites of spring, was a yearly event in Macks Creek. Most of the town's people and residents from the surrounding areas including Dry Ridge, Hack Ridge, and Tick Ridge would be there. There would be a box supper and then dancing until midnight. After the long cold winter months, it was going to be a pleasant break from everyone's day-to-day living.

The festivities were scheduled to take place on a grassy hillside just outside of town. Light bulbs, covered with colored globes dangled from electrical lines, had been strung around the outskirts of the park, emitting a soft glow. After dark, there would be dancing at a wooden pavilion that had been built especially for the occasion.

The activities of the evening were just getting started when Beryl whispered to Betty, "See you later," and darted away. Beryl had noticed Ethridge driving up the road. When he arrived, there was a line of cars sloping down the winding drive to the park. Ethridge smiled when he saw Beryl racing toward him. Even from a distance, he could see the sparkle in her brown eyes.

"I'm surprised you found me so quick with all these people," he remarked.

With excitement in her voice, Beryl explained, "Oh, there are people here from all over. They came from as faraway as Branch and Lebanon."

"Well, let's go join them." Taking her elbow gently in his hand, Ethridge guided the young woman toward the crowd of people. The sun was just beginning to set. "There's going to be a full moon tonight," he whispered. Looking down at the pretty young woman at his side, he thought, *I wonder if the town planned it that way or if I just had a streak of luck.* Taking Beryl's hand in his, he began to walk with her to the crest of the hill. On impulse, he leaned over and kissed her on the cheek.

Feeling butterflies skydiving in her stomach, Beryl turned to look up at Ethridge. "What's that for?" she asked.

"Nothing special. Just wanted to." Standing there on top of the hill, the sunset glowing brilliant shades of choral, pink, and lavender behind them, the young couple soon became lost in each other's eyes.

All of a sudden, a loud bang shattered the silence. The music had started. "It's fabulous!" Beryl exclaimed, drawing away. "Absolutely fabulous. Hurry! I have to get close to see." Beryl grabbed Ethridge's hand and raced back down the hill. Already gathered on the dance floor was a maze of people. Some of the women wore skirts, their petticoats flashing as they dipped, swayed, or spun. On their feet, they wore shoes that looked like oriental slippers with a single strap across the instep. Some of the men were dressed in plaid cotton shirts tucked into the waist of brown khaki trousers, and on their feet were black leather shoes. To Beryl, it didn't matter what was worn. She just saw that everyone was having a grand time moving around the dance floor. The dancers were in lines, six, no, eight, Beryl realized after a quick count. There was a line of men facing a line of women until they simply ran out of room. They were moving to the music in a system that looked both confusing and fluid.

Beryl saw her older sisters Mayme and Dick among the dancers. Bobby Jackson stood at the edge of a small wooden stage in front of the band and belted out instructions in a singsong voice. Beryl might not have understood most of the words, but she understood rhythm. Already, she was itching to get out onto the dance floor. Ethridge placed his arm around Beryl's waist. She was so giddy and full of happiness, her laughter carried across the fields, as that of the toll of the church bell on a clear, crisp Sunday morning.

As darkness settled in the park, the lights, strung overhead, spilled over the dancers. The floor vibrated under Beryl's feet, as she kept beat with the music. With Ethridge's arm around her, she watched with the pure fascination of discovering something new and exciting. She felt as if she were already dancing. She recognized the postmaster, a rather severe-looking, middle-aged man spinning by and flirting like a young man. Flirtation was part of it, Beryl realized, as she began to watch faces instead of feet and bodies. Eye contact was essential, as were the saucy smiles, she noted, and the quick head tosses. It was, as perhaps dances had always been, a kind of mating ritual. That was probably why Lonnie was so protective in letting his young girls attend dances with the boys.

When the next dance started, Ethridge guided Beryl out onto the dance floor. She thrilled in the sense of confusion when they joined the dancers. Young boys danced with grandmothers. Grandfathers danced with their granddaughters. Ladies in frilly dresses swirled around with men in overalls. Women danced with women. Obviously, anyone was welcome to line up and dance. Beryl noticed that women picked men for partners just as often as men picked women. It was free for all, and the rules were loose. The first few dances were a blur of color, sound, and music. Beryl let herself go. She had never had as much simple fun as she was having now following the caller and the fiddle.

After a few dances, Beryl and Ethridge wandered over to some tables where the food and beverages had been set out. The couple piled their plates high, though the light was so dim, and it was impossible to tell what they were eating until it was tasted. They sat on the grass under a tree and chatted easily to the people who passed by. She hoped Ethridge was having as much fun as she was.

The young woman never tired, even after the moon was high in the sky. The music and the movement gave her the release she needed for all of her pent-up energy. Some dancers faded; others became only livelier as the night grew late. As the evening wore on, the generators that were supplying electricity to the lighten globes begin to dim. Ethridge, along with some of the other men who owned cars, pulled their vehicles up, shining the headlights on the dance floor. All the while, the music never stopped.

Beryl noticed her dad moving toward the shadows with other men who were sipping homemade brew from a gallon crock. *They'll be gone for a while*, she mused to herself, allowing Ethridge to fold her deeper in his arms. Standing near the floor of dancers and swaying to the music, he could feel life vibrating from her—strong and exciting. *Once she stops for the night*, he thought, *she's gonna sleep for hours*. Beryl moved closer, snuggling up against Ethridge. She wondered if he could feel her heartbeat racing in her chest. She tilted her head back and smiled. Ethridge was stunned and speechless, as he looked deep into those dark brown eyes. She smelled so good and felt so soft. While she stood there looking up at him with those big eyes, he vowed someday he would make this little beauty his wife.

The spring turned into summer and then summer into fall. Beryl and Ethridge continued to see each other as often as time would permit. In September, Ethridge asked Beryl to accompany him to Sedalia, where the Missouri State Fair was taking place. "You bet I'll go," she squealed, jumping up and throwing her arms around his neck.

The following weekend, Beryl and Ethridge set out for Sedalia. The weather was perfect for a road trip. The big blue sky was cloudless; the summer sun beamed down on the road. A cool breeze was blowing from the north. However, Beryl was oblivious to the nice weather as she sat beside the man she had fallen hopelessly, head over heels, in love with. He was everything she had ever dreamed of. He was tall, good-looking, has dark brown hair and brown eyes that danced when he laughed. And she admired the fact that he laughed often. The young couple was so in love.

On a whim, they decided at the last minute to get married. Not sometime in the near future. Right now. Today. So before they left Sedalia, the couple found a justice of the peace and eloped. Late that afternoon, before heading back to Macks Creek, Letha Beryl Moulder became the wife of Ethridge Rash. Wanting to keep their marriage secret until Beryl could figure out a way to tell her parents, Ethridge gave her a pretty little wristwatch in place of a wedding band.

The closer the newly weds came to Macks Creek, the more upset Beryl became. It wasn't because she had gotten married. She would never regret that. It was just that with each passing mile, Beryl wonder how in the world she was going to tell her parents. By the time they drove the car into the yard of the Moulder's place, Beryl had convinced Ethridge to wait before telling her parents they were married. They would have to live separate, seeing each other whenever possible.

The newlyweds had been married only a few months when Beryl tearfully came to her husband. "I'm pregnant," she sobbed. There was no more waiting. She had to tell Lonnie.

"We're going to tell your parents tomorrow," Ethridge told his young bride. "Now, wipe those tears away. It's going to be all right."

"But Dad's gonna be so upset," Beryl said, as new tears welled up in her eyes.

"Well, that can't be helped now." Engulfing his bride into his strong loving arms, Ethridge tried to calm her fears.

The next day, Beryl rose early from her bed already dreading the encounter she knew would take place that evening. All during the day, she tried to be as inconspicuous as possible while attending to her chores.

"Child," Myrtle said, when she noticed how unusually quiet her daughter was. "Are you all right?"

"Yes, ma'am. My stomach's just a little bit queasy is all."

"You've been spending a lot of time with that young man Ethridge. Are you sure you're okay?"

Realizing that her mom knew her secret, Beryl whispered, "I'm okay, really."

That evening, the Moulder family was sitting in the living room listening to the *Amos and Andy* show on the radio when Lonnie saw headlights of a car coming up the road. "Is that young man coming to see you again?" he asked.

"Yes, sir." A few moments later, Ethridge was knocking on the front door.

"Guess you better let him in." Beryl jumped up from her chair and raced down the hall. She quickly swung open the door for her husband. When she saw him standing there on the porch so tall and strong, Beryl finally was able to calm her nerves that had been stretched taught all day. "Come on in."

Ethridge leaned down and gave his young bride a quick kiss of encouragement before handing her his coat. "It's going to be all right," he assured her, before they turned to walk down the hall, arm in arm, into the living room where Lonnie, Myrtle, Thomas, and June were still sitting.

"How you doin'?" Lonnie asked the young man.

"I'm fine, sir, just fine."

During the last few weeks, Myrtle had suspected something was going on with these two. *Maybe tonight I'll find out what it is*, she thought to herself. Then speaking out loud, she asked, "You two, young'uns, goin' out again tonight?"

"Yes, ma'am, we are." All of a sudden, Beryl blurted out, "I'm married!"

Startled by his daughter's outburst, Lonnie shouted, "You're what!" as he came up out of his rocking chair.

"Now, Lonnie, calm down," Myrtle said, coming to the rescue of her young daughter. "Beryl, I think you better explain yourself."

Try as she might, Beryl was unable to find her voice and sat very still in her chair, wringing her hands together. Ethridge spoke up to explain, "Sir, ma'am, I love your daughter. I have loved her from the first time I laid eyes on her last spring at the spring dance in Macks Creek. When we went to the fair last summer, we decided to get married."

"You've been married all this time, and you're just now telling us?" bellowed Lonnie.

Beryl saw the crease draw deeper across her dad's forehead. *Oh my, he's getting really mad*, she thought to herself. *I best speak up now before it gets worse.* Taking a deep breath she whispered, "I'm going to have a baby."

"What? If you have something to say, girl, speak up!"

"I'm going to have a baby," the frightened young girl repeated. Lonnie's cheeks turned a deep crimson shade of red as he shouted, "Well, if that don't beat all!"

Thomas and June, who had been witnessing this outpour of confessions by their older sister, sank deeper in their chairs. At any moment, they expected a full-blown explosion from their dad.

"I intend to take good care of your daughter, sir," Ethridge said, trying to assure the man now standing in front of him.

"Well, I should hope so now that you got her in the family way." Before stomping out of the house, Lonnie turned to his wife. "You take care of this."

"Boy, I don't think I have ever seen Dad so mad," June whispered to Thomas.

"Me neither."

"You two, git on upstairs to bed," Myrtle ordered her two youngest children.

As soon as the youngsters were in their rooms upstairs, Myrtle sat back down in her own rocking chair.

"Dad's really upset, isn't he?"

"Well, what's done is done," Myrtle told the young couple. "You best git on upstairs and collect your things. You can't take proper care of your husband with you living here and him over on his parents place."

"But what about Dad?"

"Leave your Dad be for now. He'll be all right."

"But, Mom, I don't ever recall seeing him so upset with me."

"Dear, all your dad has ever wanted for you is to be happy and taken care of." Looking directly at Ethridge, Myrtle continued, "I guess that's your responsibility now, young man."

Out of respect for his mother-in-law, Ethridge stood up. "Yes, ma'am," he stated strong and bold. "I intend to do just that."

Myrtle rose from her chair, crossed the living room floor, coming to stand in front of her young daughter. Beryl slowly rose. Tears were swimming in both mother and daughter's eyes. "You take care of yourself." After placing a soft kiss on her daughter's wet cheek, Myrtle turned and walked into the kitchen.

"Did Grandpa get over being mad?" asked Suzanne.

"Of course, he did. Aunt Beryl was his little girl, and he loved her very much. He was concerned for her welfare just as he had always been for all his children. However, it didn't take long for him to accept Ethridge as another son into his large family."

In her young naïve way, Aunt Beryl didn't realize what she had gotten herself into by marrying so young, first a wife and then a mother. However, no matter how hard she worked beside her husband in the fields stacking hay or milking dairy cows, every morning and again at night, Aunt Beryl never regretted getting married at the young age of sixteen, and she could always find fun in everything she did. Ethridge and Beryl laughed and played and grew to love each other more with each passing year.

49

Easter Tradition ♥

Spring was having trouble making its full arrival in the Ozarks. Even though the days were getting warmer, there was still morning crispness to the air. Jack Frost would often make his nightly show, by painting mystical pictures on the windows of the house and barn before swooping down the hill to place a thin layer of ice on the pond.

The Saturday night before Easter, Thomas, a young teenager, invited two of his friends Billy* and Charley* to spend the night. "I suppose it'll be all right," Myrtle replied. "But mind you, there's still chores to do. Don't think havin' company will get you out of helpin' your dad."

"I won't," promised the young boy.

That evening, after everyone had settled down for the night, the three boys lay awake in their bed.

"Sure we should," Thomas whispered to his friends. "Besides, we have to. It's spring."

"It doesn't feel like spring. It's colder than a well digger's butt out there," Billy said, a little apprehension in his voice.

"What, you're goin' be a sissy?" chided Charley.

"No, it's just that it's gonna be cold."

"Of course, it is. That's the point, goofball. Besides, it's tradition," Thomas laughed.

"I'm with you, Thomas," Charley agreed. "We can leave this little sissy back here in his nice warm bed."

"You boys, it's late. Stop talkin' and get to sleep," Myrtle called up the stairs.

"Okay, Ma." When Thomas heard his mom return to her bedroom, he continued with his plan. "Okay, it's a deal. Tomorrow morning, right after sunup."

"Thomas!" Myrtle once again yelled up the stairs.

"Yes, ma'am."

---

*   Billy and Charley are fictitious names.

Early the next morning, just as Thomas and his friends came into the kitchen for breakfast, Myrtle, who was standing at the cook stove, commented, "You boys are up mighty early this mornin'."

"Yes, ma'am. We got early plans," Thomas replied.

"Well, I surly hope those plans are for after you finish your chores. Now eat."

After Thomas and his friends finished breakfast, they left the house heading toward the barn. Myrtle, thinking something was up, stood watching as the boys hurried through the yard.

"Hey, what's up?" called Lonnie, who was just coming out of the barn. "I've never seen you in such a hurry to get about your chores."

"Yes, sir," Thomas yelled back over his shoulder as he passed his dad in the barnyard.

The boys, who were unaware Myrtle was still watching from the kitchen window, rounded the corner of the barn before taking off on a dead run toward the pond. Knowing now what Thomas, Charley, and Billy were up to, Myrtle opened up the back door and yelled, "Boys, stay away from that pond! Git on back here!"

The boys couldn't hear Myrtle calling because they were already across the barnyard and disappearing below the crest of hill. Shouting at the top of their voices, Thomas led his friends, half running and half sliding, down the embankment of the hill. When the pond came into view, they started shedding their clothes. First to come off were their coats and then their shirts. Still running, they had to resort to hopping on one foot and then the other in order to remove their shoes. Next came, their trousers and finally their long scratchy underwear. Running buck naked, the boys leaped into the pond, breaking through a thin layer of ice. No sooner had their bodies hit the icy water than their heads bobbed to the surface. Gasping for breath, Thomas couldn't talk because his jaw was violently shivering. "My God, it's cold," he screamed.

"Of course, it is, you idiot," yelled Billy. "I tried to warn you it would be."

"Knock it off, Billy," Charley scolded.

"Okay, guys, both of you knock it off. Let's have some fun."

The boys were having such a grand time, splashing around, spraying cold water on each other that none of them noticed Myrtle sneaking down the hillside, picking up their clothes as she went. When she arrived at the pond, Myrtle shouted to the three boys, "You boys wanted to go swimming?" she called out. "Well, now you can just stay there!"

Thomas and his friends had been caught. Flabbergasted, they saw their clothes lying in a pile at Myrtle's feet. Thomas didn't know whether to stay in the water and freeze to death or to apologize to his mom for disobeying her. Finally, he decided on the latter. "I'm sorry, Ma," he said. "Can we have our clothes back?"

"What, so soon?" Myrtle chuckled.

"C'mon, Ma. Give us our clothes back. It's cold out here," Thomas sputtered.

"It is? Well, I'll be," she laughed. Finally, when she noticed Thomas and the other boy's lips turning blue with cold and little ice crystals forming in their hair and on their eyelashes, Myrtle relented. "You boys, git on out of there. Hurry up now. Git on back to the house before you catch your death of cold. Thomas, after you get into some dry clothes, you git to your chores like you was told."

Myrtle had just turned to head back up the hill to the house when Thomas, Billy, and Charley came scampering out of the water. Standing there, dripping wet and shivering so hard they had trouble putting their clothes back on, it no longer mattered that they had been caught. Thomas had proudly managed to keep the tradition of an early Easter morning swim alive. Pounding each other on their backs in congratulations, Thomas shouted, "We did it. Tradition lives on!"

"Hey, Tommy," my brother Tom said to his son. "You're about the same age Uncle Thomas was that morning. There are still several frozen ponds in Illinois on Easter. How about you reviving his yearly tradition."

"Thanks anyway," Tommy laughed. "I think I'll pass."

50

Legs ♥

    The 1940s arrived, bringing with it many changes, not only to the Moulder family but also for the entire world. Thomas and June were the last two children of Lonnie and Myrtle still living at home. They shared in the task of helping their dad in the fields, while young June also helped her mom with the gardening and the household chores.

    During the winter of 1940, Ruby and George returned to Macks Creek from Kansas City, where George had been employed at a meat packing company. The couple moved into the little weaning house behind Lonnie and Myrtle. While George went to work, Ruby remained home to care for their little boy, while waiting for the birth of their second child.

    In the middle of February 1941, Ruby gave birth to another son. When the baby was a few weeks old, she became deathly ill with kidney poisoning. Needing more care than Myrtle was able to give, Ruby had to be hospitalized, leaving the care of her newborn son in her mother's loving and capable hands. With the responsibility of taking care of a newborn, Myrtle had to devise a way of feeding him with a supply of much-needed milk.

    Nearly every home had at least one dairy cow for the family's milk supply. Shortly after Lonnie moved his family to Dry Ridge, he discovered the land was poor for crops, so he started raising cattle to help supplement their income. Beef and dairy cows grazed in the woods behind the house until the fall of the year when he would load them up in a neighbor's cattle truck, taking them to market in Springfield, Missouri.

    After some considerable thought Myrtle called out to her daughter, "June," she said. "We need to separate out one of those cows. If we put her in the barn and feed her nothing but corn, her milk should be okay for the baby."

    "What about Legs?" June asked. "She's a good cow, and there's lots of rich cream in her milk."

    Myrtle agreed. "You're right. Legs does give off good milk. Better go call her in from the woods."

"C'mon, Tippy," June called out. Hearing his young mistress's voice, a little black-and-white pup came bounding around the side of the house. "C'mon, boy. Mom wants us to call in Legs. She has an important job to do."

Climbing to the top railing of the fence surrounding Myrtle's vegetable garden, June cupped her hands around her mouth and yelled, "Here, Legs. C'mon, girl!" Quietly, she listened. Then she yelled again, her small but powerful voice echoing across the hills. "Legs, where are you!" Before long, June heard the distinct tinkling of a cowbell. When she saw the dairy cow coming up the hill, she called out, "That's a good girl, c'mon."

Following right behind Legs was the rest of the dairy cows. Removing a bell that was around Legs' neck, June fastened it around the neck of one of the other old cows. Then she yelled, as she waved her hands above her head, "Go back. It's not time for the rest of you. I just need Legs." When the other cows had turned around and were headed back into the woods, June opened the gate. With Legs following, June walked into the barn and tied the cow to the wooden railing of the stall. It was going to be her responsibility to make sure Legs was fed nothing but corn.

For the next several days, about every four hours around the clock, when it came time to feed the baby, Myrtle would go out to the barn to milk Legs. Returning to the house with the warm milk inside of a small pail, she would strain the milk through a clean dishtowel into a stone crock before filling the baby's bottle.

After a couple of weeks, Ruby was able to return home. To her amazement, her baby boy had gained several pounds under Myrtle and June's loving care. The baby had thrived on the warm milk, straight from the cow.

51

California ♥

    Sunday evening, December 7, 1941, Lonnie and Myrtle, along with their son Thomas and daughter June, sat in the living room of their home, listening to the battery-operated radio. No one said a word as President Franklin D. Roosevelt spoke, "This day shall live in infamy." Those words would reverberate across the world for decades to come. The bombing of a large navel base at Pearl Harbor forced the United States to enter the fighting forces of World War II. Huge changes around the world were occurring. The Missouri Ozarks, even though far removed from the Hawaiian Islands and far shores across the oceans, felt the misery of war just as acutely.
    The Great Depression came to an end due to the jobs created to help with the war production. Taking the place of men who left their homes to fight in the war, women and teenage children joined the workforce. Postage stamps, gasoline, sugar, canned food, meats, shoes, and clothing were rationed and could only be purchased with coupons. Scrap drives were held across the country, giving the people of the United States a means of helping to support the war effort as they donated tin, paper, steel, and rubber.
    One spring evening, after the family finished the evening meal, June joined her dad on the porch. She found him sitting on the old wooden toolbox, looking out over his land. "Well now, Pug," he said looking at his daughter. "You seem kinda in the dumps lately. Wanna talk about it?"
    "Oh, Dad, everything's wrong," June cried.
    Lonnie invited his daughter to join him on the toolbox. After releasing a stream of brown tobacco juice from his mouth, he asked, "What could be so bad it takes the smile from my Little Pug?"
    June remained silent for a few moments. Then with a sigh, she asked, "Dad, why does there have to be war?"
    Placing his arm around her small shoulders, Lonnie tried to provide his daughter with an answer. "Now, that's a tough one," he said, "I suppose it's a lot like the Hatfield's and McCoy's feudin'. Somebody wants more than is rightly theirs. And then, somebody's got to step in and stop them from takin' it."

Looking up at her dad, June said, "I still don't understand."

"Pug, I think a lot of people don't understand."

Just then, the smell of smoke filtered up to them. Looking around to make sure neither the house nor the barn was on fire, Lonnie commented, "Well, I'll be. Would you look at that?" A huge orange glow filled the dark eastern sky.

Jumping up from her perch on the toolbox, June asked, "What's burning?"

"Looks like the castle over at Ha Ha Tonka* has caught fire. Wonder what started it?" was all Lonnie said.

The two of them resumed their seats on the old toolbox. Watching Ha Ha Tonka burn, father and daughter were lost in their own thoughts. *Why did we have to go to war?* June wondered. *Why does somebody, out of every family I know, have to go away? And would they come back dead?*

Lonnie knew he didn't have the answers June was wanting. Sitting on his own back porch, watching the flames of the burning castle leap higher and higher over the far hills, Lonnie didn't realize his thoughts were mirroring those of young June's.

A few days after the Moulders buried Grandpa Fred Gerhardt, who had passed away on March 11, 1942, Onie and Mayme joined her parents out on the farm for dinner. While the women were clearing away the remains of the meal, the men went outside. Lonnie sat down at his usual place on top the toolbox, while Onie, leaning on the corner post of the porch, waited patently for his father-in-law to put a chaw of tobacco securely in his cheek.

"Mayme and me's going to California," Onie said. Lonnie sat quietly, with no reaction to the bold statement, as if he hadn't heard his son-in-law. Cautiously, Onie continued, "I got a letter from my cousin Dillard Cobb out in California. There's jobs out there. He says in his letter, the government's setting up war-related industries all up and down the West Coast."

"What do you know about industry work? You're a farmer," Lonnie questioned.

"The government's teaching a trade to everybody who's willing to work."

A few minutes passed before Lonnie looked up. His voice, filled with emotion, questioned the young man. "Why's Mayme and your boy goin'? She ain't no man, and he's too young to work."

---

* Ha Ha Tonka was a European-style castle, built in the early 1900s by a wealthy Kansas City businessman. In 1942, the castle burnt when sparks from one of the fireplaces ignited the roof, leaving the building in ruins. Ha Ha Tonka is now one of Missouri's beautiful state parks.

Trying to reason with his father-in-law, Onie explained, "Mayme's gonna baby sit the other worker's kids."

Hoping for a way to keep his daughter in Missouri, Lonnie asked, "You looking for permission to take Mayme away?"

"No, sir, I'm just letting you know."

The first of April 1942, Onie and Mayme bid farewell to their parents and friends. When the Onie Woodall family left the Ozark Hills, heading west to California, their Model A Ford was loaded down with suitcases, filled with all their bedding and clothes, and cardboard boxes overflowing with canned meats, bread, crackers, cheese, and cookies to eat along the way.

This was Mayme's first time traveling outside her home state and she marveled at everything she saw. Traveling through Kansas, along Highway 54, she was surprised at how many wheat fields they passed. In southwestern Kansas and the panhandle of Oklahoma, she commented to Onie about how flat the land was and how far she could see. After three days on the road, they entered Texas. A hundred miles more, they crossed over into New Mexico.

When evening came, if the family happened to be near a town, they rented a room at one of the roadside inns. But if darkness found them between towns, Onie parked the car in an open field, throwing a quilt on the ground for their bed. When their food supply ran short, they stopped at a small grocery store along the way to buy more.

About halfway through New Mexico, in the town of Tucumcari, Onie turned the car westward again, onto Route 66. Here, they left the familiar Highway 54 behind, saying goodbye to the way back to Missouri.

People from all over the Midwestern States were moving to California in hopes of finding jobs. Traveling west through Arizona, along Route 66, Mayme and Onie met several families traveling in caravans.

After a week of riding in the car, sleeping on the ground, and eating cold food out of a box, Mayme and Onie entered Barstow, California. The beauty of green grass growing in yards and palm trees swaying in the cool breeze was a stark comparison to the hot, dry Mojave Desert they had just left. Leaving the now familiar Route 66 behind, Onie turned the car north, onto Highway 395, heading to Oakland, California.

Traveling north, Mayme soon determined California was indeed a beautiful state. However, it was a far cry from Missouri. The familiar hills back home, covered with tall sycamore, maple, and walnut trees, sporting brilliant colors of emerald and Kelly green, were replaced with hard black paved roads. *Oh my gracious,* Mayme thought, looking out the car window. *Just look at those automobiles and hundreds and hundreds of people rushing from one place to another. For* just a moment, she yearned to see the deer, squirrels, and rabbits that lived in the woods behind her home back in Missouri. With a deep sigh, she said out loud, "Well, I'm here now. And with God's help, we'll be just fine."

Onie and Mayme finally arrived at his cousin's home in Oakland, California. To the dismay of the tired young family, Dillard was offering his garage as a place to stay. "We shouldn't complain," Mayme, always the optimist, told her family. "Dillard has given us the use of a bed, a table to eat at, and chairs to sit on. Here's a hot plate I can use to cook and an icebox. It's clean, and we finally have a roof over our head."

The lodging in the garage lasted only a couple of weeks, until Onie could move his family into government housing in the neighboring town of Richland. The complexes had been built in anticipation of thousand of people who would migrate to California in search of employment. The government housing consisted of several buildings. Each building housed sixteen separate units, eight units on the ground level with eight units on the upper level.

Onie quickly found a job at one of the shipyards down at the wharf, while as planned, Mayme stayed home to care for their young son and the other children living in the complex with their parents.

The day after the Woodall family arrived in Richland, California, they had to report to the government office's downtown here they were issued metal tags. In bold letters, their names were stamped across the face of them. They were instructed to wear the tags at all times. In case of an enemy attack, the tags would aid the authorities in identifying them.

Back in Macks Creek, after school was dismissed for the summer, Mayme's two sisters Dick and Ruby, along with their families, left Missouri, also heading west. For a second consecutive year, they had been hired to work with a harvest crew, picking cherries and apples. Their route was to start in upstate Washington, travel down the Western Coast of the United States, ending up in Richland, California.

Early one morning, to Mayme and Onie's surprise, standing there outside their little apartment was family. Tears of joy overflowed. Mayme, Rudy, and Dick laughed and cried as they hugged each other, while Onie, George, and Leon shook hands and slapped each other on the back. In talking with her sisters, Mayme hadn't realized how just how lonesome she had become. It was a thrilling day for everyone.

Mayme was soon saddened when she learned that Dick and Leon could only stay just a few days. Having a teaching position back in Missouri, Leon needed to return before school started the first of September. However, her sadness turned to joy when she was told George and Ruby had decided to stay in California. Before long, the Kincaids were living in the same government-housing complex as the Woodalls.

A letter arrived for the Moulder girls. It was from their mom. Myrtle was informing her daughters that their brother Ray and his wife, Florence, were living in a place called San Diego. It was by the ocean, and Ray was building ships. She said she didn't know for sure where San Diego was, but if it was close, maybe they could get together for Sunday dinner. She finished her letter with a prayer for their safety.

Periodically, day or night, sirens blared. The sound terrified the Moulder girls. All lights around the city were immediately distinguished. Radios and televisions were turned off. No one moved outside in the yards or in the streets. Everything came to a halt. After what seemed to be hours, the all-clear signal sounded. Every time the sirens sounded, no one knew if this was another drill or, if in fact, the enemy was attacking our shores. Mayme and Ruby had never felt such fear.

The Woodalls remained in California until 1944. At that time, it was a mutual decision between Onie and Mayme that their help with war issues could be used just as well in their home state of Missouri.

Onie, not confident the old model A would make another trip back across the United States, bought his family one-way tickets on a passenger train headed east. After boarding the train, Onie and his family were guided to wooden benches that had been fastened to the floor of one of the empty cars. When he inquired about why his family couldn't sit in the passenger cars, he was told those seats were reserved for soldiers being transferred from one military base to another. After several days, the train pulled into Union Station in Kansas City, Missouri. Having decided to stay in the city, Onie located a job at Pratt & Whitney, a large manufacturing company that makes aircraft engines.

Ruby and George remained in California for the duration of the war. Both had landed jobs in the shipyards. They started work on the bottom of the ships, working their way up, until it was launched into Frisco Bay. George worked as a ship fitter, a person who positions the structural pieces of a ship for riveting and welding. Ruby, joining the ranks of Rosie the Riveter, a name given to thousands of women now working in the shipyards and aircraft factories, found herself spending her days welding in the belly of huge ships. Her small size allowed her to squeeze into places most men were too large to fit.

One day, while working on a ship floating in the bay, Ruby was called into her boss's office. She was told she needed to fix a spot on the side of the ship where the weld had broken. Assuming the side of the ship was the inside she promised, "I'll git right to it." When her superior led her topside, Ruby was dumbfounded when she realized the side of the ship needing repair was the outside. But a promise is a promise.

Looking around her, she saw a wooden four-by-four piece of scaffolding dangling from two pieces of rope. It reminded her of the swings she used to play on when she was a child. The "swing" was brought over the side of the ship. Ruby climbed on and sat down. As she held on tight to her welding torch with one hand and a rope with the other, two burly men slowly lowered her over the side of the ship. Suspended several feet above the water, she went to work.

When she had finished welding the weaken area, Ruby called up to the two men. No answer. She called out again, this time louder. Still she did not see the two men who had lowered her over the side of the ship. Finally, after yelling several more times, a man, looking over the side of the ship, hollered back. "That you making all that ruckus?" he questioned.

"You bet it is," replied Ruby. Relieved she was finally able to get someone's attention, she called out, "Pull me up, will ya?" When Ruby was topside, she couldn't wait to find out what had happened to the two burly men.

Come to find out, they were a couple of winos, prone to drinking on the job. Once they had Ruby lowered into position, they fastened the end of the ropes onto handholds embedded in the side of the ship before taking off in search of their next bottle of cheap wine.

In May of 1945, Eldon Clemmons, Fern's husband, received his draft notice, calling him into active duty. After Eldon joined the financial section of United States Air Corp, he was shipped out to the Philippines where he proudly served his country.

52

1943 ♥

One morning, June and her mom had just finished breakfast when June asked, "Mom, can I get a job?"

"No."

"Why not?"

"Because I said so. You know how I feel about a good education."

"But, Mom, most of my friends have jobs. And besides, all the teachers in school are either deaf or blind," June retorted.

"Why in the world would you say something like that?" her mom scolded.

"Because they are. If they weren't, they'd be off fighting the war."

Myrtle stood firm, even with the knowledge her young daughter was probably right. "June, you're gonna finish high school. Florence and Nera have been good enough to pay the tuition, and you aren't gonna throw it away. Now, I've heard just about enough out of you. Stop pouting and go on about your chores."

Fourteen-year-old June was having difficulty understanding all the changes coming into her young life. In her mind, she couldn't comprehend what was happening. All she knew was that, in some way, almost everyone she came in contact with was involved with the war. Mayme and Ruby and her brother Ray were far away in California building warships. Almost every family in Macks Creek had said goodbye to a son or daughter when they left home to join the service. Then the whole town would mourn when one of them would return in a flag-covered pine box.

Some of June's schoolmates were even anxiously waiting their eighteenth birthday so they too could go off and join the war. Even some of her girlfriends, after dropping out of school, found jobs to help out with the war effort.

Times were also unsettling for her dad. Unnerved by all the changes that had come into his world, Lonnie felt compelled to tighten down the rules when it came to June's privileges. Dances in town on Saturday evenings were no longer safe places for a young girl and her friends to go.

His reasoning, "All the 'good' men are away fighting the war." Pool halls (bars) were opening up in almost every town throughout the area. In no way would a proper girl be seen in one of them. With so many familiar families leaving, being replaced by strangers, even Macks Creek, once the sun went down, was turning into an unruly town. No matter how much June pleaded and begged, her dad remained firm.

One evening, after Thomas left on a date with one of the local girls, June asked, "Why does Thomas get to do things and I don't?"

Looking up from the book he had been reading, Lonnie replied, "That's different. He's a man."

"He's only three years older than me," June cried.

Becoming perturbed at his daughter's insistences, Lonnie laid down his book. "Young lady, you better hush that kinda talk."

"It's not fair!" June cried, stomping off to her room.

"Better watch that temper of yours too!" Lonnie called out to his retreating daughter.

Looking out the big bay window, Lonnie sighed. He knew it wasn't fair being so strict on June. Nevertheless, he reasoned, she's so young and impressionable. With everything happening around his once-safe domain, Lonnie just didn't feel comfortable in letting his daughter go.

June's source of entertainment was mostly limited to after-school events, as long as she was home before dark; Friday night sleepovers with her girlfriends, provided their parents would be home; and weekly trips into town with her mom. Like it or not, her dad had laid down the law. June didn't have a choice. She had to be content with her new boundaries.

One evening, during the week, after the supper things had been put away, Lonnie and his family would gather around the battery-operated radio tuning into President Roosevelt's "fireside chats." This weekly program was designed to inform as well as calm the American population during a time of great despair. Other times, after her chores were done, June would stretch out on the divan, listening to country music, coming into her living room, live from the *Grand Ole Opry*. Ernest Tubb, the Carter Family and Minnie Pearl, along with other artists would entertain the young teenage girl for an hour or so before her family joined her to listen to the funny antics of *Amos and Andy* or the scary radio soap opera *The Shadow*.

Early one Saturday afternoon, Thomas asked permission to drive his dad's 1929 Ford Sedan into town. Lonnie had purchased the car from his son-in-law, Ethridge.

"Is your work done?" Lonnie questioned.

"Yes, sir, it sure is."

"Then I suppose you can go."

June, who had been sitting in the bay window, working on some light mending, jumped up when she overheard the word "town." "My work's done. Can I go too? Please!" she begged.

"I suppose, I don't care. Make sure you stay with Thomas though."

Just then, Myrtle walked into the living room. Holding out a scrap of paper to her daughter, she remarked, "I'm needing some things from Osborn's. As long as you're going, it'll save me a trip." Handing her daughter the grocery list, Myrtle continued, "And don't forget to pick up the mail."

Thomas, recognizing the fact his younger sister was yearning for some outside entertainment, consented into letting her tag along. "Okay, c'mon, kid. Let's go." June didn't have to be told twice. She raced upstairs, put on a clean pair of trousers, a pretty printed blouse, and grabbed her cardigan sweater before racing back downstairs. Thomas barely had a chance to start the old car before June came bounding down the porch steps.

With a rattle and a bang, a chug and a clang, brother and sister started down the road. It was such a beautiful April day. The sun, a big yellow ball in the bright blue sky, shone brightly down on brother and sister as they road into town. Thomas, noticing his little sister's eyes dance, laughed out loud when she let out a wild, "Yahoo! I'm finally free!"

By the time Thomas and June arrived in town, Main Street was crowded with people. Taking time out from their weekly errands, they called to each other.

"Sure is a beautiful day, isn't it?"

"Think the crappie's biting yet?"

"Come on over and see my new bull. He's a beaut."

"Heard from that son of yours yet?"

On this warm spring day, everyone in Macks Creek seemed to be in good spirits.

It didn't take long before Thomas found a group of his friends gathered outside the Macks Creek café. Pulling up to a stop, Thomas overheard someone call out, "Hey, look at that! Thomas, when did you get the car?"

June, looking up at her big brother, grinned from ear to ear when she heard a sweet voice coming out of the crowd. "I don't know and don't care. He's good-looking, single, and hasn't gone off to war."

Thomas's face turned a bright apple red. "Don't you go squealin' to Ma, or this will be the last time you come with me," he cautioned.

"Hey, how about taking us for a ride," a boy shouted.

"Okay, I'm game. Pile in."

Eight friends, three joining Thomas in the front seat, five in the backseat, stepped into the car and sat down, forcing June out of the car altogether. However, she wasn't about to be left behind. Jumping onto the running boards, June hung on tight to the fenders, as Thomas put the car in gear. As the young crowd of people went riding out of town, June heard some old man shout. "Those gall-darn kids. There gonna end up killin' somebody." June, laughter escaping from her pretty little mouth, just waved back at the old codger. Thomas was heading to Green's Mill, a favorite teenage hang out.

My niece, Mandi, was just returning from the kitchen, balancing a turkey sandwich and some raw carrots in one hand while carrying a glass of water in the other. Sitting down beside Marla, she asked, "Mom, is that the bridge at Green's Mill campground?"

"It sure is."

Dad took this moment to interrupt. "Wait a minute. I better explain something here. When your mom was in high school and played on that bridge, there was no campground. It wasn't until a few years later, sometime during the early 1950s, before it became a campground."

"Oh," replied Mandi.

Marla, with a far off look in her eyes as if remembering something, continued, "When we were little, my brothers, sisters, and I would spend our summer vacations at Green's Mill campground. Mom would take us up the road to where the old metal bridge was suspended high above the Little Niangua River."

Just then, Mandi spoke, her voice seeming to bring Marla back to the present. "I remember that bridge well. When we were standing on it, a car passed by, shaking the whole bridge. I was so scared it would break and we would fall in the river."

"It was scary for us too," Marla continued. "Mom would take our hand in hers to help us over the open grids. Standing in the middle of the bridge, we would look far down to the river below. Our fears were soon calmed as we stood listening to Mom telling us about when she and her friends would spend Saturday afternoon playing on that very bridge."

Marla looked at me, sitting there at Dad's dining room table. I had just taken a bite of Phyllis's homemade goulash. "Care to continue?" she asked. With my mouth full, I just nodded.

Making a last-minute decision to take the back roads to Green's Mill, Thomas turned on to Upper Prairie Holler, a small winding road. The car rolled easily around the curves, but when it came to climbing the hills, it chugged and clanged, making Thomas think they would all have to get out and push. But then, the hill was mastered. June, fearing no harm by riding outside of the car on the running boards, laughed along with the rest of them, as the car went speeding down the other side of the hill. Gaining momentum, at the great speed of 25 mph, the car was able to make it up the next hill with very little effort.

Thomas stopped the car before pulling out on to the well-traveled J road. "Okay, kid," he said to June. "Climb on in and sit down." The adventurous young people traveled a few more miles, around curves, up and down hills, passing the little country school at Rag Holler, before finally coming to a stop in the middle of Green's Mill Bridge.

"Everybody out!" Thomas yelled. June quickly ran to the metal railing at the side of bridge. "Hey, kid, you be careful."

"I will," promised June. While young people stood around the car laughing and joking, the young sweethearts in the group wandered off into the nearby woods, sneaking kisses and hugs with each other.

Thomas and June were having the time of their life. The worries of young people were chased away, as they enjoyed this beautiful spring day. June, ignoring her brother and his friends, stood at the bridge railings, looking down at the dark green river flowing by. All of a sudden, a big yellow carp rolled over on its side, splashing water, before it disappeared. When she heard a gentle breeze murmuring through the treetops, she glanced up before it gently brushed her cheek. Behind her, a soft-flapping noise drew June's attention to the bright blue sky. A big gray turkey buzzard, wings spread wide, was circling an open field. Lower and lower he came, diving into the tall grass, capturing a small brown rabbit in its claws.

Before anyone realized it, the sun was dipping down in the western sky. "Hey, we better get back to town before the store closes," Thomas called to his sister. Then to his friends, "C'mon, guys, get in. We gotta go."

Knowing he must hurry, Thomas took J road back to Highway 54. After turning west on the highway, the friends soon arrived back in Macks Creek.

"Thanks for a great afternoon," Thomas's friends called out.

"Oh, Thomas," came this syrupy sweet voice out of the crowd. "Don't forget to call me sometime."

"Who's that?" laughed June.

"Nobody special."

"Wait a minute." June, not wanting to miss an opportunity to rib her brother, ran after him. "From the way she sounded, I doubt she thinks she's *nobody special.*" Dodging Thomas's outstretched arm, June ran down the street.

"Get back here, you little tease," Thomas yelled, chasing his little sister into the safety of Osborn's grocery store. Slightly out of breath, he called after June, "I'll meet you back at the car. I'm going to the post office to see if there's any mail."

Mrs. Osborn was standing behind the counter when June entered the store. Handing the woman her mom's list, June said, "I think we have coupons for this stuff."

Thomas was already seated behind the steering wheel when June returned to the car. After putting the bag of groceries in the backseat, she looked at her brother. He was holding a letter in his hands, a strange look on his face. Sensing something was bothering him, June asked, "Who's the letter from?"

"The United States government."

"The government? What do they want?" June was getting nervous.

"You know I turned eighteen last week."

"Yea, so what?" Looking at his little sister, sitting in the front seat beside him, he softly said, "This is my draft notice. I gotta go to Kansas City to take a physical. If I pass, I'm going into the service." Stunned, June sat remaining silent all the way home. Thomas was now of age to be drafted into the war.

The following Monday morning, the Moulder family sat at the breakfast table, lost in their own thoughts. June's old fears returned. The war was now knocking at her back door. She had to keep swallowing the bitter bile rising from the pit of her stomach. She felt sick and was afraid she was going to throw up. Myrtle was unusually quiet, sitting in her rocking chair as she prayed. Lonnie knew that if his son passed his physical, he would have to leave immediately for boot camp. Thomas could feel his family's anxiety and felt bad, but on the other hand, most of his friends were already off fighting the war, and he wanted to join them.

Thomas placed a small leather suitcase in the backseat of the car before turning around to kiss his mom goodbye. "Don't worry," he said. "I'll be back before you know it," he promised. Then taking the big familiar hand in his own, Thomas pulled his dad to him.

"Take care of yourself," Lonnie whispered, before pulling away.

"Hey, kid. Don't give the folks a hard time when I'm gone," he called out to June. Climbing into the old car, Thomas didn't see the tears rolling down his little sister's cheeks, as he turned the Ford sedan out onto the road, heading for Kansas City.

The next evening, just as night was descending over Dry Ridge, two yellow headlights came up the road proceeding the familiar rattle, bang, chug, and clang. June jumped up from her place on the divan, running outside. Lonnie and Myrtle weren't far behind their daughter. The old Ford was just pulling into the yard.

"You're back," June cried, jumping into her brother's arms, almost knocking him down. Myrtle stood on the porch, wiping tears from her eyes with the hem of her apron. Her son was home, at least for now.

Walking up to the car, Lonnie asked, "What brings you back here so soon?"

"I didn't pass my physical."

"Why not?" Myrtle asked, walking toward her son.

"The doctor says I'm anemic."

"What's that?" June asked, pulling the suitcase from the backseat.

"Don't know. They just told me to go home and eat more of Ma's good-home cookin'. They'll be notifying me again sometime next year."

"Well, glory be," shouted Lonnie.

Myrtle suddenly had a terrible sinking feeling in the pit of her stomach. Not knowing the full meaning of the word "anemic," but with her limited medical skills, she knew this could turn out to be something bad.

53

June Helps Out ♥

While the war was raging in Europe and the South Pacific, spring of 1943 slipped past in to summer, then autumn into winter.

It was now spring of 1944. Every evening, Lonnie, Myrtle, Thomas, and June gathered in the living room, listening to the latest news about the war while during the day, with spring just around the corner, there were daily chores to contend with. Thomas helped his dad in the fields, while June stayed busy helping Myrtle with household chores, planting and hoeing the garden, tending the chickens, and milking the cows.

The fear of overnight frost was gone; it was time to plant the gardens and get the crops in the ground. Lonnie and Myrtle surmised that with only four people gathering around the kitchen table, the need for large crops and gardens were no longer needed. So that year, Myrtle downsized her vegetable garden. Lonnie, while still planting tobacco for his own personal use, planted only a small crop of corn and wheat. There were enough cows grazing in the woods to supply them with plenty of milk and cream. Lonnie reckoned his family would get by just fine.

For Myrtle, it had been a worrisome year. Her father, Fred Gerhardt, had died during the spring 1943, and her mother's health was failing. Three of her children, Ray, Mayme, and Ruby, along with their families, were still in California, thousands of miles away.

One night, after they had gone to bed, Myrtle lay tossing and turning. She just couldn't relax. "Are you sick or something?" asked Lonnie.

Not wanting to worry her husband, she replied, "No, just kinda blue."

"Well, git over it. We gotta get some sleep. We got work to do in the morning."

A couple of months later, the sun was just peeking over the hill when June came bounding down the stairs. It was the beginning of summer, and she was glad to finally be out of school for a few weeks. *Just one more year and I can graduate,* June was thinking when she noticed Thomas sitting at the table, his head cradled in his hand. "What's wrong with you?"

"Just a nosebleed," he replied.

"Oh." Looking around the kitchen, she noticed her mom wasn't standing beside the stove. "Where's Mom?"

"Don't know. She wasn't here when I came in from doing chores."

"That's strange. She's always in the kitchen this time of morning. I wonder if something's wrong."

Interrupting me, Chandi asked, "Was something wrong with Grandma?"

"Yes, there was," I replied. "That year, Grandma had come down with dropsy.

"Drop what?" her brother, Lonnie, asked.

"Dropsy. It's a condition that causes extreme swelling in your face, hands, and ankles. Some days, the swelling in your ankles is so sever you can't stand. And because of the swelling in your hands, you have trouble grabbing things, let alone hanging on to them."

"I get it," cried Lonnie. "You 'dropsy' it."

I, along with everyone else in the room, broke out with uncontrollable laughter. Before long, everyone was holding their stomachs, letting tears streamed down their face. For the past three days, since Mom had died, we as a family had been under such stress it felt so good to be able to laugh again.

Finally, I was able to get control of myself. "Okay, guys," I called out across the room. "Do you want to hear the rest of this or not?"

"Of course, we do," Chandi said. Chastising her brother, she grinned, telling him to straighten up and act right.

"For several weeks, Grandma had been noticing a slight swelling in her hands, face, and ankles. The longer she stood doing chores, the more swollen they became. By the time she went to bed at night, she was in quite a bit of discomfort. I believe doctors now refer to this condition as congestive heart failure."

"Will she be all right?" asked Chandi.

"Yes, but only if she takes it easy."

June left the kitchen in search of her mom. Finding her still in bed and hardly recognizing her, the young girl cried out, "Mom, what's wrong?" Myrtle's eyelids were just small swollen slits caused by the puffiness of her face. Her small hands, lying on top of the quilt, looked as if they were about to burst. June started to cry.

"Now, dear, don't fret." Trying to calm her young daughter down, Myrtle continued, "It's not as bad as it probably looks."

"But what's wrong?"

"Oh, I just imagine I've come down with dropsy. Better get your dad to call Lillie. You three's gonna need some help for a while."

"Can't I do it?"

"I don't know. There's so much with the house and the chores. And soon, the garden will need to be picked and canned. I just don't think you can handle all of it."

"I can try, can't I," insisted June. "And besides, with Thomas's help, we can probably do it all."

"Thomas is helping your dad in the fields. He won't be much help."

"Well, then we'll just have to work together while you take it easy," June assured her mom. "Now, let me help you get dressed. You can sit in the kitchen while I fix breakfast."

June, only sixteen years old, took charge. After helping her mom get dressed, the young girl took her arm, helping her walk to the kitchen. Myrtle had just sat down at the table when Lonnie came walking into the house.

"Where's breakfast?" he bellowed.

"It'll be just a minute," June promised, pouring him a cup of coffee. Turning to face the stove, June rolled up her sleeves and started to work.

Fixing biscuits and gravy, along with a side dish of fried side pork, June was determined she could do this. After all, Beryl got married at sixteen, and she did just fine. After the hearty breakfast was over, June in an authoritative voice said, "Okay, until Mom gets to feeling better, I'm in charge. Thomas, you help Dad with the crops while I tend to the house. Then after dinner, we'll both go out to the garden, bringing in what's ripe. Mom, you can help me from your chair, by telling me how to put up the tomatoes, green beans, beets, and peas. Thomas, you can dig potatoes, pick the cabbage, and pull the onions. Dad will help you bury them. Before long, the apples will be ready." A frown suddenly creased June's forehead. *But I'll think about that later*, she thought to herself.

While June was doing all the talking, Lonnie and Thomas were sitting at the table with their mouths wide open. "Who does she think she is bossing me around like that?" Thomas argued.

Beaming with pride at his daughter's can-do attitude, Lonnie told his son, "Hush your mouth, unless you want to do all the work yourself."

After handing out orders, June, talking to Thomas, said, "I'll call the cows in from the woods if you'll help me get them in the barn?"

"Sure, let's go."

When Thomas and June were outside, Myrtle asked Lonnie to keep an eye on their daughter and that if she needed help, he should call Lillie.

Trying to reassure his wife, Lonnie replied, "Oh, I think little Pug can handle it. Besides, she has me and Thomas to help her."

"I know, but for once, would you just do as I asked?"

"Okay, Butler, I'll do it."

Standing on the split rail fence that encircled the garden, June yelled, "Here, Legs! C'mon, girl! Legs, c'mon!" Before long, she heard the distinct clinking of the cowbell. "C'mon, Legs," she called one more time when she saw the old cow leading the small herd of dairy cows up into the barnyard. June called to Thomas, "Here they come. Open the gate."

Thomas didn't have to be told. He was already waiting at the barn door. Leading Legs into the first stall, both Thomas and June noticed her young calf staying close by her side. "Well, would you look at that," commented Thomas.

June replied, "She sure is getting big, isn't she?" Just then, the little calf started bucking and kicking up a ruckus.

"Watch out!" Thomas yelled, as the calf bucked against June, knocking her on her butt. "Looks like that calf doesn't want you getting any milk."

June picked herself up off the floor, dusting the straw from her overalls. When she got close to the milk cow again, the calf lowered her head and started to charge. Quickly, June jumped on the fence. "How am I gonna milk her if the calf won't let me get close?"

Thomas, offering sound advice, chuckled, "Give the calf two tits, and you milk the other two. That way, she'll leave you alone."

"Sure hope it works," June called out. Using all her strength to keep the little calf at bay, June finally managed to get Legs milked.

After all the cows had been milked, Thomas turned them back out into the woods to graze while June took the milk buckets into the house. Carefully, she poured the milk into a separator. As she poured the milk into the container, she watched milk flow from one spout while thick cream came out another spout. Doing as her mom would have done, June saved some of the cream for baking and for making butter. The rest, she divided into smaller jars and put the jars in the icebox in order to keep them good and cold, until the following Saturday when she went to Macks Creek to do the marketing. While in town, she would sell the thick cream to the merchants.

June and Thomas proudly took on the responsibility of taking care of the family, enabling their mom to recuperate. While June did the laundry in the old washtub, kept the house cleaned, cooked the family's meals, and pulled weeds out of the garden, Thomas helped Lonnie with the fieldwork and hoed the garden.

The apple orchard, growing over the hillside across the road from the Moulder farmhouse, was in full bloom. The beautiful fragrant blossoms, honeybees working among them, made the orchard seem like a fairyland. There was Arkansas black apples, with deep red skins and rich yellow meat, and little green June apples, tart and perfect for making apple pie.

As the apples began ripening on the trees, the thought of the fresh juicy fruit was more than Thomas and June could resists. So sneaking into the orchard, they each picked themselves a tart green apple. The apples weren't ripe yet, but it had been so long since they were able to experience that nice fresh crunch. After wiping the fruit on their pant leg, they bit in. Immediately, their back jaws tightened as their face automatically screwed up. When the initial shock to their taste buds was over, the kids sat on the ground, enjoying the first apples of the season. Devil may care about the stomachache that was bound to follow that evening.

As the days turned into weeks, Myrtle was feeling better and was able to help June in the mornings. However, after dinner, the heat from the summer sun forced her back into the chair under the big oak tree. These past days had been uncomfortable for her, watching young June work so hard. Although with her limited medical knowledge, she knew if she was going to get well, she needed to stay off her feet. While she sat in the cool shade, snapping green beans and shelling peas, Myrtle watched her daughter continue with her chores. *She sure is growing up*, she thought to herself with pride.

The mild month of June passed, leaving hot dry days in its wake. Myrtle knew June loved the apple orchard. So during the hottest part of the day, while she herself was sitting in the shade, Myrtle sent her daughter to gather a bushel basket full of apples. "Be careful of those hogs out there," she always cautioned. "We need to get them apples off the ground before they eat 'em all. They like 'um just as much as you do.'"

That year, the apple orchards yielded several bushels of apples. Inside the dark crevasse of the well-guarded hole in the hillside, some of the apples would be safely preserved while the rest would be canned, dried, and made into sweet apple cider.

A few days later, June and Thomas made another trip to the orchard. When they returned to the house, Myrtle was standing by the stove, claiming to feel well enough to help June with the canning and with the making of applesauce and apple butter.

Before the fruit turned soft, June and Myrtle peeled, seeded, and cored a bushel basket of apples. Relying on years of practice, Myrtle welded the paring knife like a pro while June struggled to leave part of the apple while removing the skin. After peeling a few apples, June finally mastered the art.

In a kettle full of water, June made a syrupy liquid mixing together sugar, salt, nutmeg, cinnamon, and lemon juice. While the syrup was simmering, Myrtle sliced the peeled apples and put them into quart jars. When the jars were filled, June ladled the syrup over the apple slices. Screwing the lids down tight, she then placed the jars into another kettle full of bubbling boiling water. After a twenty-minute hot bath, the jars were removed and placed on the table away from any drafts. By the time there were twenty quarts of apples cooling on the table, the rest of the apples were turning soft, perfect for making applesauce.

Myrtle got out two of her heaviest kettles, set them on the back burners of the stove, and added one inch of water to each one. After peeling, seeding, and coring another bushel basket of Arkansas blacks, along with a few tart green ones, June chopped them into bite-size pieces. Carefully, she added them to the water on the stove, covering the kettles with a lid. Within a few minutes, the water started to boil. Then she removed the lids, turned down the heat, and allowed the apples to simmer.

When the apples were soft, June emptied the contents of the kettle into a metal sieve, allowing the juice to run into a dishpan. Then she returned half of the apples to the kettle and the other half to a large bowl.

While enjoying a glass of warm apple juice, Myrtle sat at the table mashing the apples in the bowl before adding just enough cinnamon and nutmeg to give it a nice spicy taste. Then with a wooden ladle, she spooned the applesauce into sterilized pint jars. After screwing on the lids nice and snug, June submerged the jars into the canner that was sitting on the stove. Twenty minutes passed before June removed the hot jars from the water, setting them on the table.

June's attention was now turned to making apple butter. In the kettle that was holding the rest of the apples, she added cinnamon, cloves, allspice, and sugar. Placing the kettle back on the stove, over a low fire, June kept a close eye on the pot, occasionally stirring the contents to keep it from scorching. The hot apple mixture started to bubble up and pop. Through the rest of the day, as the apple butter simmered on the stove, a sweet spicy aroma filled the kitchen. After supper and before they could retire for the day, June and Myrtle filled the rest of the pint jars with the fresh-made apple butter before cooking them in a hot water bath.

Long after Myrtle and June tired of canning apples, applesauce, and apple butter, there were still more apples! With all the jars filled, mother and daughter turned to drying the fruit. A dried apple took up less storage space and was a sure way of ensuring the family had apples year-round.

Late August, with its soaring temperatures, made this a perfect time for drying apples. After the fruit was peeled, they were cut into thin slices, dipped in salt water to prevent them from turning brown.

The roof over the back porch was in direct sunlight most of the day; so therefore, it was the perfect place to dry the apples. Early in the morning, Thomas climbed onto the roof, carrying a clean white sheet and the sliced apples. After spreading the sheet out on the roof, he laid the apples in a single layer on top of it. To keep the birds, bugs, and dust away, he spread another white sheet over the fruit.

Each evening before the sun went down, Thomas went back to the roof to get the apples. The next morning, if it were going to be a sunny hot day, he would take them back to the roof. For several days, each evening after Thomas brought the apples down, Myrtle inspected them thoroughly. When they had a nice rubbery feel, she would place them in cleaned flour sacks, before storing them in her root cellar. Myrtle had to be careful how she stored the dried fruit because during the rainy fall months of October and November and then again in the spring, the fruit could mold and be ruined.

In order to put up the yearly crops of apples, June and Thomas had to pick a bunch. On the average, out of each bushel of apples, Myrtle was able to preserve approximately eight quarts of sliced apples or fourteen quarts of applesauce or twenty pints of apple butter. And by her calculations, it took about twenty pounds of fresh apples to make two pounds of dried apples.

Lonnie and Myrtle were extremely proud of their young daughter. "She's getting to be quite a young lady," Myrtle remarked.

"Yea, but she's still my little Pug."

By late summer, Myrtle was feeling like her old self and was able to resume doing the domestic work around the house. June was pleased she was able to take charge when her Mom was sick, but she had missed being outside with her dad and brother.

Before the first frost of the year, Lonnie needed his kids to help in making apple cider. He had acquired the reputation that his apple cider was the best in the county. When he heard this, he just chuckled and said, "It's all in the mixture." Thomas and June, once again, crossed the road to the apple orchard, filling every available container with apples that had been left on the trees and were lying on the ground. As instructed by their dad, they left the apples in the barn to soften. About a week later, Lonnie announced, "It's time to make cider."

June enjoyed helping her dad make the apple cider. Having heard the rumors, about him being the best cider maker in the county, the young girl listened as her dad informed her about the fine art of making cider. "You have to make sure you use half as many green ones as you do red ones," Lonnie informed his daughter. "That way, you get a nice sweet taste with just a little bit of tartness." "I'll remember," promised June.

While Lonnie was busy gathering the equipment needed to make his cider, June filled her moms' washtub with clear cold water from the well. One by one, she thoroughly washed the skins of the apples, removing all the dirt and dust before laying them on a wooden plank to dry. After checking to make sure the apples weren't bruised or starting to rot, June chopped them into walnut-sized pieces. Remembering her dad's formula, she put two red apples and one green one through the meat grinder.

After taking the bowl filled with pulp from his daughter, Lonnie started layering the fruit into a slatted wooden bowl, sandwiched between two pieces of cheesecloth. He continued to layer pulp into the bowl until the basket was almost full. Then he placed two wooden discs (squeezers) on top of the fruit. Grabbing a ratchet handle, Lonnie started cranking. The two discs were attached to a threaded rod, resembling the screw on a piano seat. The more he cranked, the lower the disk went inside the basket, squeezing juice from the pulp. The cider was now ready to be bottled in gallon jars. After several days, Lonnie and June had a nice supply of a rich, golden-colored apple cider cooling in the root cellar.

Lonnie had just finished making his cider when it started to snow. "I guess we timed that just right," he chuckled, looking up into the dark gray sky. "It looks like winter is here again."

That evening, Lonnie was sitting in the living room, with his wife and daughter, listening to *Amos and Andy* being broadcast over the radio. The snow had continued to lightly fall, leaving just a white skiff over the ground. Myrtle looked up from her basket of mending. "I don't know if it was a good idea for Thomas to take that car into town," Myrtle told her husband.

"Ah, he'll be all right."

"But what if it starts to snow again?" Myrtle questioned.

Lonnie, trying to easy his wife's concerns, said, "I don't think that's gonna happen." Then looking out the window, he told her, "Besides, the stars are out."

Myrtle remained silent for a few moments, and then she asked, "Lonnie, do you think Thomas is feeling all right?"

"There's nothin' wrong with that boy. He's just been running around till all hours of the night, is all."

Not convinced, Myrtle murmured, "I just don't know."

June, who had been stretched out on the divan, reading a book, piped up, "I'd say the only thing wrong with him is he's getting lazy."

"Why would you say something like that?" scolded her mom.

"Cause I'm having to do most of his chores."

Surprised, Myrtle asked, "Why?"

"Cause he says his back's always hurting. I don't believe him though. I think he's just trying to get out of work."

"Okay, you two," admonished Lonnie, "leave Thomas be. I'm tellin' ya. There's nothing wrong with that boy."

54

The War Ends ♥

The hard, cold winter was finally leaving the Ozarks, and Myrtle was more than ready to welcome bright sunny days and lots of hard work. Shortly after dealing with the death of her mom, Mat Gerhardt, who passed away on February 2, 1945, Thomas received his second letter from the government's induction department in Kansas City. Once again, Myrtle stood in the front yard of her home, tearfully waving goodbye to her son. And once again, after Thomas failed the physical, she joyfully welcomed him home. Dr. Meyer conducted several more blood test and determined Thomas's anemic condition had gotten worse and issued him a prescription for iron tablets. All through this, Lonnie remained steadfast in his belief that "there was nothing wrong with Thomas, that hard work and good cookin' couldn't cure." However, Myrtle's mother's intuition was saying something different.

Saturday morning dawned crisp and cool but had the makings of becoming a beautiful spring day. Determining it would be a good day for an outing, Myrtle called out to June, "Wanna go to town? I've got some good rich cream I need to sell before I do the marketing?"

"Sure do," called back the young girl, rushing into the kitchen. "Can you wait a minute?"

"I'm in no rush, take your time." June hurried over to the cupboard door, swung it open, and started shuffling things around. "Child, what are you looking for?" questioned her mom.

Still searching in the cupboard, June replied, "The Arm & Hammer Baking Soda. I need it to brush my teeth."

"Well, you won't find any. I used all I had on the soda biscuits we had for breakfast."

By midmorning, Myrtle, carrying a basket full of several pint jars filled with cream, and June, carrying a basket full of chicken eggs, were across the yard when Lonnie coming out of the barn called out, "Hold on a minute."

June turned, placed the basket on the ground, before running to her dad. "Yes, sir?" she asked. Feeling the effects of a new spring day, Lonnie was overcome with a rare but generous feeling. As a grin spread across his face, he held out his hand toward her. It looked as if he had something clasped in his fist. "Here you go, Pug. While you and your mom's in town, go ahead and treat yourself." Opening his big thick fist over his daughter's small hand, a shiny new nickel and dime dropped into her palm.

Surprised, June looked up at her dad. This was an extra special delight for her. She couldn't remember a time when she had been rewarded so generously. "Thanks, Dad," she cried, giving him a big hug. Quickly, she turned around and ran back to her mom, who was waiting at the side of the road. Picking up the basket from the ground, she looked at her mom and said, "I'm ready."

The two women, one wise with age, the other giddy with youth, were walking down the road when overhead, a flock of ducks high in the big blue sky flew by. "Quack, quack, quack," they called out to each other. While Myrtle and June stood watching, the duck at the front of the V fell back, allowing the next duck in line to take over as they flew north. "That's a pretty good sign winter's over. Soon the ground will be warm enough to get the rest of the garden planted," Myrtle surmised.

Continuing down the road, June asked, "Do you always plant potatoes on St. Patrick's Day?"

"Well, if you want a crop to dig on July fourth, you do," Myrtle informed her young curious daughter.

"Mom, how do you always remember what needs to be planted when?"

"You rely on the signs of the moon."

"The moon? What does the moon have to do anything?"

"Well, there are certain vegetables you plant in the dark of the moon and others in the light of the moon."

"Wait a minute," June interrupted. "I can understand planting things in the light of the moon, but how do you keep your rows straight in the dark of the moon?"

Myrtle stopped in mid stride, a puzzled look on her face as she turned to look at her daughter. "What are you talking about?"

"Well, you said, some things you plant in the light of the moon. That's easy to understand. If the moon is full, it's bright enough to see the rows. However, if you're planting in the dark of the moon, well, I've seen some pretty black nights when the moon isn't shining. So how do you keep the rows straight if you don't have any light?" Myrtle continued standing in the middle of the road, a funny look on her face. All of a sudden, June burst out laughing. "I swear, child, I thought you was serious," laughed her mom.

"My goodness, no. I've helped you plant gardens for as many years as I can remember. I figured you probably knew when to plant because you always have a beautiful garden."

By now, mother and daughter were coming around the last curve in the road. Directly in front of them, at the bottom of the hill, was Highway 54. When they reached the highway, they had to wait at the side of the road for three cars to pass. Myrtle shook her head as she exclaimed, "With all this traffic nowadays, somebody's gonna get killed."

After safely crossing the highway, Myrtle and June entered Osborn's grocery store. Leaving her mom to visit with Mrs. Osborn, June walked over to the candy counter. Opening up her tightly clinched fist, June saw the two coins lying there. She couldn't remember her dad ever giving her so much money all at one time, so she wanted to spend it wisely. After much thought, June ended up purchasing a stick of gum, a handful of peanuts, and a bottle of Coca-Cola.

June was just finishing with her purchase when she heard her mom call to her, "C'mon. It's time to go." Leaving the store, Myrtle, carrying a brown paper bag filled with salt, soda, baking powder, and a pound of coffee, and June, carrying a smaller brown paper bag in one hand that held her treats and bottle of ice-cold Coca-Cola in the other, walked up the street to the post office. Mailboxes for individual residents were built into a wall, separating the front quarter of the room from the back. The postmaster stepped up to the small teller window. Leaning on the shelf, he inquired, "How you doing today, Ms. Moulder?"

"Just fine, thank you."

"How's that boy of yours?"

"He's fine. Why do you ask?"

"No particular reason. Just wondering why a young strapping boy like Thomas hasn't been called off to the war. And you, young lady," he said looking at June. "Are you gonna graduate from high school this year?"

"No, sir, I have one more year," June replied.

"All your young'uns have grown up so fast. Is this your last one?"

"It sure is," Myrtle replied. "C'mon, June, we need to get our mail and head for home."

Leaving the post office, Myrtle turned and started walking back in the direction they had just come from.

"Why are we going this way?" June asked. "I thought you said we needed to get home."

"Oh, I just said that to get away from him," Myrtle told her daughter, nodding back in the direction of the post office. "He's as bad as some old woman, with all his questions."

"Oh, Mom, he meant no harm."

When the two women reached the end of Main Street, June again asked, "Why are we going this way?"

"It's such a beautiful day. I thought we would go down to the slab and have a picnic." At the bottom of the short hill, mother and daughter sat down at the edge of the old rock slab. Myrtle searched in the bottom of her brown paper bag until she found what she was looking for. "Here they are," she cried.

For the next hour, mother and daughter sat on the banks of Macks Creek enjoying a light dinner of longhorn cheese, soda crackers, a big fat juicy dill pickle, and a bottle of Coca-Cola. After they'd finished eating, June looked down at her reflection in the water of the clear cold creek.

"Mom, do you think I'll be an old maid before this war ends?" she asked.

"I surely hope not."

Still looking in the still water below, June continued, "Do you think the war will end soon?"

"I pray to God it does. Now, come on. We need to get home."

The two women were about halfway home when June once again brought up the subject of the war. "I hope this darn old war will be over before I graduate next spring. What do you think is gonna happen when the war does end?"

Myrtle laid the brown paper bag full of groceries on the ground, grabbed her daughter around the waist, and spun around and around right there in the middle of the road. "Well, child," Myrtle laughed. "There will be dancing in the street. The kinds of dancing like you have never seen before." After a few more fancy steps, Myrtle stopped, brushed her short brown hair back from her forehead, picked up the bag of groceries, and told her daughter, "That's about enough of that kind of nonsense. Let's get on home."

That summer flew by. June was getting ready to enter her senior year at Macks Creek High School, and a flurry of activity invaded Lonnie Moulder's quiet abode. He couldn't understand why his youngest daughter had suddenly gone crazy. There were clothes to make, a new pair of shoes to buy, a class ring to purchase, and senior pictures need to be taken.

"Just let her be," Myrtle lovingly told her husband. "This is her last year in school. She's just excited, is all."

"Well, there's still a lot of time left before she gets out of school. I don't see any need for all this foolishness."

August 6, 1945, one hundred-fifty miles away from the Moulder home, nestled far back in the hills of the Ozarks, Mayme and Onie were living in the big metropolitan city of Kansas City, Missouri. Onie was working at Pratt and Whitney when he heard a rumor running through the plant. The news media had been reporting that on May 8, 1945, Germany had surrendered to the United States. Now, they were hearing that the United States had dropped an atomic bomb on the city of Hiroshima, Japan. People around the world waited with baited breath. Could this news be that the war was moving in a positive direction? Could this mean the devastating war was coming to an end?

August 14, 1945, Macks Creek, Missouri, 7:00 p.m. central standard time.

Lonnie and Myrtle had just retired to their living room, hoping to catch the first part of their favorite evening show broadcast on the radio. But instead they heard, "This radio broadcast is being interrupted to bring you a special bulletin." June who had been stretched out on the divan reading sat up. *This must be something really important*, she thought to herself. Thomas was just coming in to the house. "Why's everyone so quiet?" he questioned. Then he heard it for himself.

"Japan has surrendered! The war is over!"

With unchecked tears, Lonnie and Myrtle started to cry, hugging each other. "Thank God," Myrtle cried. "My kids can now come home."

Her cry was drowned out by Lonnie's boisterous shouting. "Our boys will be coming home. Now, we can all get back to normal." Grabbing his shotgun from behind the kitchen door, he raced out into the yard. Resounding into the night was the sharp *bang, bang, bang*, as Lonnie fired shots into the air. When the rapport of his gun silenced, he heard the distinct sound of his neighbor's guns. They too had heard the news and were also firing their guns in celebration. June jumped up from the divan, grabbing Thomas as she danced around the living room floor. "Yes, the boys will be coming home," she sang. "And just in time for my senior prom!"

A couple of minutes passed before Thomas was able to detach himself from his sister's zealous action. Silently, without uttering a word, he slipped out the back door, intent on his own silent celebration.

August 14, 1945, Kansas City, Missouri, 7:00 p.m. central standard time.

Onie had just returned home from work when he and Mayme heard the news that Japan had surrendered. The war was over. "Come on, Mayme. Put on your best dress. We're going downtown to celebrate!"

"Oh, my gracious. Give me a few minutes to get ready," she cried. Running into the bedroom, Mayme put on her pretty dark blue dress, rounded toed black pump heels with a dainty strap across the instep, and her best Sunday hat. Not overly concerned about the fact that her best silk stockings had worn out several years ago, Mayme took a black ink pen and drew a very narrow straight line up the back of both legs to look as though she wearing stockings. When she came out of the bedroom, Onie was standing in the center of the living room wearing a brand-new zoot suit, black patent leather shoes, and white socks.

Very gallantly, he opened the front door for his lovely wife and their young son. Just before Onie stepped out onto the porch, he placed his favorite pompadour hat on top of his head, tilting it off to one side.

Hand in hand, the Woodalls raced down to the street corner where an overcrowded streetcar was passing by. They quickly climbed up the steps pressing passed the people who were standing in the doorways. Once inside the car, they joined the other's who were hanging out the windows and leaning over the railing of the back stoop. The driver was ringing a bell that hung over his head. The joyous clanking rang out into the night.

It was a good thing Onie had decided not to drive his own car downtown because the streets had erupted with pandemonium. There were parades everywhere, musicians standing on every street corner playing their instruments, cars' horns honking just to make noise, and people running here and there but not going anywhere. They were shouting and laughing, crying, hugging, and kissing all at the same time. As soon as Onie, Mayme and Leslie stepped off the streetcar, a stranger came running up the street, grabbed Mayme, kissing her, before he ran off into another crowd of people. She quickly turned around, searching for Onie. There he was, vigorously shaking the hand of another man.

Everyone was celebrating. Confetti fell from the high-rise buildings onto people, who were dancing in the streets. The whole town had gone crazy with happiness.

It was predawn before the Woodalls, stumbling with fatigue, found their way back to their apartment. It had been quite a night.

The next morning, Onie received his layoff notice at Pratt and Whitney. After a brief visit to Macks Creek to see their parents, the Woodalls moved to Lake City, Missouri, where Onie had been offered a job. A government-funded ammunition plant, that had closed its doors when the war ended, had reopened the facility. Instead of making ammunition, the employees were making caskets to be shipped overseas to bring home the dead.

August 14, 1945, Richland, California, 5:00 p.m. pacific standard time.

Ruby and George were just finishing their shift at the shipyards when an announcement came over the PA system. "Japan has surrendered. Thank God, the war is over!" the announcer cried out. Unable to believe the news being broadcasted, Ruby and George just stood there, looking at each other, until some man came running past them from behind, almost knocking Ruby to the floor. "Hey, watch what you're doin'," George called out to the retreating man. The young man stopped just long enough to yell back over his shoulder, "What's the matter with you, man? You gone deaf. The war's over! It's finally over!" Then turning back around, he sprinted out of the building. Slowly, the news finally sunk in. Ruby looked up at George; George looked down at his wife. They both had tears overflowing, running down their face. George grabbed Ruby, spinning her around and around. Others joined the happy couple, grabbed the closest person to them, and started to dance for joy. It didn't matter there was no music. The announcement being repeated over and over again across the PA system was music enough. Before George and Ruby left the plant, they were called into the boss's office. "Since the war is over, we won't be needing any more ships. You are now relieved of your duties."

That evening, after Ruby and George returned to their apartment at the government—housing complex, the sirens blared one last time. This time, they didn't run to distinguish the lights or turn off the radio. Instead, they turned up the volume, listening to the joyous news time and time again. It was just too good to be true.

Ruby couldn't keep the happy tears away. "We can go home," she told George. "We can go home to Mom and Dad." The next morning, before dawn, Ruby, George, and their two small boys left California in their car headed east.

The Moulder family had survived the years of rationing, the news of neighbors loosing loved ones, and the lean war years. A week after Ruby and George left California, they pulled into Lonnie and Myrtle's front yard.

"My goodness, my goodness," cried Myrtle, running out of the house to join her daughter and family. "I can't believe you're home."

Lonnie, coming out of the barn to see what all the commotion was about, walked up to George, grabbed his hand, and gave him a big bear hug. "Good to see you, son," he laughed.

It didn't take Macks Creek long to get back to normal. The local businesses were booming. And almost daily, there was a reason to celebrate the return of a homeboy.

55

There's a Stranger in Town ♥

My daughter Suzanne who had been sitting in the living room tending to my one-year-old grandson, Corbin, asked, "Mom, if Mema grew up in Missouri and Papa was raised in Kansas, how did they meet?"

As if on cue, Dad came walking into the room looking well rested after his afternoon nap. "What's for dinner?" he asked.

"There's lots of food in here," Phyllis remarked from the kitchen. "Do you want anything in particular?"

"No. Whatever you fix will be fine."

While Phyllis was fixing something for Dad to eat, I told him that Suzanne was just asking about how he and Mom met. "Would you like to tell her?"

"Oh, I don't remember," he said with a grin.

"Come on, Papa," Suzanne pleaded.

"Yeah, tell us your story," chimed in the rest of his children and grandchildren.

"Well, after World War II ended and I returned to Cheney, I found out that in October 1945, my dad, Lewis L. Slusser, had accidentally been killed while working on a job for the railroad. A few weeks later, my mom, Dorothy J. Slusser, received a fair amount of money from the railroad as a settlement for his death. I also found out she had used the money to purchase a small farm in south central Missouri."

"Why would she want to move to Missouri?" Suzanne inquired.

"When your grandma Slusser was a little girl, she used to live in El Dorado Spring, Missouri. That's where her parents are buried."

"Oh yeah, I forgot. Sorry I interrupted you."

"That's all right. Anyway, sight unseen, she had bought a farmhouse and a few acres of land on Coffey Holler Road, about six miles north of Macks Creek."

As Dad talked, we all settled deeper into our chairs, anxious to hear about Mom and Dad's courtship.

After Lewis Slusser had died, his wife, Dorothy J. Slusser, and their two minor children, Charles and Lloyd, moved from Cheney, Kansas, to a small farm outside of Macks Creek, Missouri. Max Slusser, who in December of 1945 had been honorably discharged from the United States Marine Corps, and one other son, Guy, helped their mom move to Macks Creek.

Early one morning in March of 1946, the two brothers packed up Max's 1934 Chevy coupe with the rest of their mom's belongings. Max had just purchased six baby shoats (pigs) that he put in the trunk. A horse trailer, carrying a horse, was hitched up to the back of the car, a crate of chickens was wired to the tongue of the trailer, and two dogs rode inside with the men. The look had the similarity of John Steinbeck's novel *The Grapes of Wrath*.

One late afternoon, a few weeks later, some of the local boys from Macks Creek were shooting hoops in the high school gymnasium. Max, a stranger in the Macks Creek community, was eager to meet some new friends, so he joined them.

Max loved the game of basketball. With his ball-handling skills, he had gained quite a reputation during his high school days in Cheney and after graduation in neighboring towns. His reputation preceded him because shortly after he returned home from the war, he was asked to join Cheney's city league basketball team.

A few days before Max left for Missouri, he was playing ball when, trying to capture a rebound, his feet became tangled up with those of another player. Using his arms to protect the ball that was tucked tightly into his chest, Max fell head first into the backdrop. Blood started gushing out of his forehead. He was quickly rushed to the hospital where the doctor put in twenty-seven stitches before wrapping his head in a turban-style bandage.

He was still wearing the bandage when he joined the men in the gymnasium that March afternoon for a game of basketball. Soon after the friendly competition began, a group of giggling high school girls entered the gym. Max was used to being singled out because of his easy good looks and quick and fluid ball-handling skills. Furthermore, on this particular day, the bandage he wore gave him an added air of mystic. At first, he just ignored the girls. They were, after all, several years younger than he was.

Max soon became aware of a calm presence among the gaggle of giggling girls. He was struck by the quiet composure of a small dark-eyed, dark-haired beauty. She was different somehow from the others. Hoping to catch her eye, he began to show off. It worked. It wasn't long before the pretty girl, Martha June Moulder, pretending to ignore him, whispered to her best friend Joy, "See that man over there, the one with the turban on his head? I'm going to marry him."

Max continued to notice June around town. He wanted to strike up a conversation with her but kept his distance because she was always in the company of a young man who had recently been discharged from the army.

A couple of weeks passed, and it was Saturday morning. June asked her dad if she could go into town with Joy. "There's a medicine man in town, and we want to see him."

"Did you get the tobacco patch weeded yet?" Lonnie asked.

"Yes, sir, I did."

"Did you check for worms?"

"No, sir, I didn't," June replied, looking down at the floor.

"Well, don't you think you ought to finish your chores before traipsing off to town?"

Racing out of the house toward the tobacco patch, June called back over her shoulder, "Yes, sir, I will!"

Later that afternoon, June joined Joy in the café sharing a Coca-Cola. They were sitting at the counter discussing their upcoming graduation when in walked the tall handsome stranger the girls had seen in the gym. "Look," June whispered. "There's that guy we saw playing ball."

"I wonder who he is," replied Joy.

"Shhh! Quick, turn around. He's coming this way," June giggled.

June felt Max's presence behind her before she heard him say, "Hi, girls." Turning around on the stool, June looked up into the handsome face of the stranger. He was looking directly at her. "Didn't I see you in the gym last week? It seems as though you were practicing cheerleading, weren't you?"

"Yes," June stuttered. "Yes, we were."

"So you must be in high school?"

"I'm a senior," June proudly said.

Max looked at her as if she were joking. "A senior? How old are you, anyway?"

Becoming slightly annoyed, June told him she was seventeen and a half. Max let his eyes wander down, from the top of her head to her feet, as if summing up this little person. "What, you don't believe me?" June asked slightly perturbed.

"It's not that, it's just, you're so little. How tall are you anyway?"

"If it's any of your business, I'm four foot eleven and three-fourths," June said, standing up to prove it.

"Okay, okay, I believe you," the young man laughed. "Well, Ms. Senior, what's your name?"

"June Moulder."

"Do you have a boyfriend, June?"

"Not really," was her short reply.

"In that case, would you like to go out to supper with me some night?"

"I don't even know you," June said, turning back around to her friend Joy.

Persistently, the young man continued, "I'm Max Slusser. I fought in the South Pacific during the war. After being discharged from the marines, I moved here from Cheney, Kansas. I live with my mom and brothers up on Coffey Holler road. And I want you to go to supper with me."

Turning back around to face this tall good-looking man, June whispered, "I don't know if I can. Dad doesn't like me dating service boys."

Max thought a moment and then said, "How about if you ask him. If he says yes, we can make plans."

"Okay, I'll do it," June promised.

"I'll meet you right here next Saturday afternoon," Max told the young girl before turning to leave.

The girls, unsure of what had just happened, finished their Coca-Cola. Leaving the café, June found her dad sitting on the liar's bench.

"There's your dad. Go on, ask him," Joy whispered, nudging June closer.

"Not yet. I'll wait until I'm sure he's in a good mood."

Just then, Lonnie noticed his daughter coming out of the café. "Hey there, Pug. What are you girls doing?"

"We're going up the street to watch the show," explained June.

"I was just thinkin' of headin' up that way myself."

By the time Lonnie, June, and Joy arrived at the end of Main Street, the medicine man had already drawn a crowd. The young girls, pushing their way through the throng of people, stood wide-eyed looking up at the brightly colored wagon. There was bold colorful writing on all four sides advertising cold remedies, cough syrup, and '*rheumatiz*' oil. Their attention was then drawn to a man standing on the ground, holding a brown bottle high in the air. He was shouting something that was lost on the girls. They were too amused with what he was wearing to comprehend what he was shouting. The hem of his brown jacket came down to the tops of his knees and was open in the front. Underneath his jacket was a bright red shirt; his brown-and-orange-striped trousers were tucked into his short topped, pointy toe black boots. For several minutes, June and Joy stood in the middle of the street, unsuccessfully trying to hide giggles, escaping from behind their hands. He was quite a sight.

When the show was over and the medicine man was packing up to leave town, June looked around for her dad. She found him on the outskirts of the linger crowd, visiting with a group of his friends.

"Dad, can Joy and I stay in town a little while longer?" she asked.

"What for?"

"We just want to go to Millers and get a Coke. Can I?"

"I suppose I don't care. But then you come right home."

"Thanks, Dad, we will. C'mon Joy, let's go." After purchasing their bottles of soft drinks, June suggested they had better head on home. After all, she reminded her friend, "I need to keep Dad in a good mood this week."

When June walked into the front yard, she saw her dad, sitting in his rocking chair looking out the big bay window. Even from several feet away, she noticed a long, deep furrow creasing his forehead. She knew he was mad about something, but what? June softly closed the front door behind her.

"Where have you been?" Lonnie yelled.

"In town," June said, walking into the living room. "You said Joy and I could go get a Coke."

"It didn't take that long. Now, where have you been?"

June tried to explain, her tears on the verge of overflowing. "I haven't been anywhere. Honest. After you left, Joy and I went straight to Millers, bought a bottle of Coke, and came straight home."

Turning to glare out the bay window, Lonnie said, in a stern voice, "Git on up to bed. We'll deal with this tomorrow." June, not knowing what she had done, knew better than to say anything else. Like her dad said, "We'll deal with this tomorrow."

The next morning, when June came downstairs for breakfast, she stopped at the foot of the staircase. Looking down the long hallway toward the kitchen, she saw her dad, sitting in his usual chair, sipping coffee from his saucer. The crease in his forehead had softened some, but it was still there. Tiptoeing down the hall, June joined her family at the table. She was seated in her chair beside Thomas when her dad spoke.

"Young lady," he said.

Just then, June heard her mom softly sniffle. Glancing up, she noticed Myrtle's eyes were red and puffy. *She has been crying*, thought June.

Lonnie cleared his throat, bringing June's attention back around to him. "Young lady," he repeated. "I'm sorry I was hard on you last night. Now eat your breakfast before it gets cold."

"Why was Grandma crying?" asked my own young granddaughter Chelsea.

"I imagine, after they had gone to bed that night, Grandma had a talk with Grandpa about being so hard on Mema. Mom and her sisters felt Grandma had come to their rescue on more than one occasion during their young lives."

The following Saturday morning arrived. All week long, June had been thinking about the ex-marine she had met in the café. She didn't know what to expect from him. During the past couple of years, because of her dad's strict rules, she had often felt like a hermit. Even though she had met a number of service men coming to town for various reasons, her dad didn't like the idea of her dating them. "You're too young," was always his reply. Now she was a senior in high school with graduation just a few weeks away. June felt it was time she proved to her dad that she was old enough to take care of herself. And besides, she was tired of having to sneak out the upstairs window to join Thomas and their friends in town. She was interested in this tall good-looking stranger but knew better than to get her hopes up about being able to go out with him. However, she reasoned, she would never be able to go on a date with him if she didn't ask her dad.

June waited until Lonnie had finished breakfast and was slurping the remainder of his coffee from a saucer before she approached the subject. "Dad, there's a new family in town. They're living up on Coffey Holler road."

Lonnie sat back in his chair, belched long and slow before he spoke. "I've heard about that bunch. What about them?"

"Last Saturday, when Joy and I were in town, one of the boys came into the café. He ask if I would go out with him sometime."

Lonnie hesitated before questioning his daughter. "What do you know about this boy?"

June sat up straight in her chair, looking directly at her dad. "He told me his family was from Kansas. After he got out of the marines, he moved down here with his mom. She bought that old farm up on Coffey Holler. Can I go?"

"Before you go anywhere with that young man, there's three things I want to know," instructed Lonnie.

That afternoon, June joined her mom on the weekly trip to town. The young girl was deep in thought as they walked down the road. *I don't even know this man*, she said to herself. *How can I ask him such personal questions?* Then she reasoned with herself, *If I don't ask, I'll never get to go out with him.*

"Are you all right?" Myrtle asked, startling June out of her thoughts.

"I'm fine. Mom, there's something I need to do. Can I meet you at the store?"

"Okay, but don't be long."

June entered the café, halfway hoping Max wouldn't be there. When her eyes became accustomed to the dim interior, she saw him sitting in the corner booth. Her heart was beating so hard in her chest she just knew he could hear it. Max had evidently been watching because when she neared the booth, he slid off the bench seat and stood up. "I'm glad you came. Here, slide on in. Would you like something to drink?" he asked.

"Yeah sure, that would be good," she said in a low whisper.

"Another Coke, please," Max called to the waitress. Then to June, he asked, "What did your dad say?"

Nervously, June cleared her throat a couple of times. "Before I can go out with you, my dad wants to know something first."

"Okay, fair enough. Shoot."

"Where's your dad?" June asked.

"He was accidentally killed last October while he was at work. That's why we're here. With the little bit of money Mom got from the railroad, she bought that farm up on Coffey Holler."

Looking down at her hands laying in her lap, June said, barely loud enough for him to hear, "I'm sorry about your dad."

"Thanks. Anything else?"

"Yes." Still feeling uncomfortable, she blurted out, "Is your family Catholic?"

Shocked, Max replied, "What difference does that make?"

Embarrassed, June looked back down at her hands, lying in her lap. "I don't know. Dad just wanted me to ask."

"Okay then. No, we're not Catholic. We're Baptist."

"That's good." Now comes the hard one. June thought. *How can I ask this one?* After several moments of silence, Max reached across the booth, crooked his finger underneath her chin, and gently lifted her head until he was able to look directly into her brown eyes. Slowly she met his gaze, staring back into the eyes of this tall stranger.

"There's more, isn't there?"

"Yes." June hesitated.

"Well, what is it?"

"I don't know how to ask this," the young girl replied softly.

"Just ask. I'm not going to get mad."

Embarrassed, June blundered, "What's wrong with your brother?"

"You must be talking about my brother Lloyd," Max said softly. Wanting to put this young woman at ease, Max continued talking softly. "June, I really don't know. He was born little retarded. If there's a name for what's the matter with him, I have never heard it."

"Is anyone else in your family like him?"

"Don't you mean, is his condition hereditary? I don't think so. As far as I know, he's the only one."

"Good. Okay, good," June replied.

With a wink, Max said, "If you're finish with your questions, why don't we drink our Cokes before the ice melts." June, her lips already tight around the straw, just nodded. Before they left the corner booth at the Macks Creek café, June had asked him to supper that evening.

"You sure it's okay with your folks?"

"Well, if you ever have any hope of taking me out, you're gonna have to come up to the house and meet them," June laughed, obviously much more relaxed than she had been when she had entered the café.

Evidently, Lonnie had been satisfied with Max's answers because the young couple was soon caught up in a whirlwind romance. That spring Max proudly accompanied June to her senior play and the school's baseball games. June stayed in town after school on several occasions to watch Max and his friends shoot hoops in the gym before racing home in time to do her chores. Then graduation day arrived. Having to be at the school an hour before the ceremony was scheduled to start, June was unaware Max was in the auditorium. She was pleasantly surprised when, gazing around the gym, she spotted him sitting on the bleachers beside her parents. "Martha June Moulder," the school superintendent's voice blared over the loud speaker. June rose from her seat and, with pride, gracefully walked up on stage to receive her well-earned high school diploma.

The night following June's graduation, Max made plans to take her out for a celebration supper.

"I still owe you a meal," he told her after helping her into his car.

"What are you talking about?" she asked, looking a little confused.

"Remember, the first time we met in Macks Creek's café? I told you I wanted to take you out for supper."

Laughing, June answered, "Oh, now I remember."

The young couple headed to the Night Hawk restaurant in Camdenton, Missouri. They located a corner booth and sat down. The waitress came right over, bringing them the menus. "Boy, am I ever hungry," Max stated, opening his menu. As he started to read what choices the café had to offer, he noticed June was just sitting there, staring at the cover of her menu. "Aren't you hungry?"

"Yes," she replied.

"Well, what would you like?" Unsure of herself, June replied, "I don't know what they have."

Realizing his date was embarrassed about something, he gently asked, "Haven't you been here before?"

"No, I've never eaten in a café," she whispered.

"Oh, that's okay. How about if I chose?"

Memorial Day arrived a week after June's graduation. There had been a constant buzz going around town about how this Decoration Day would be different. In addition to the usual potluck dinner at Parrack Grove Cemetery, there would be special speeches given to honor those soldiers who had fallen in war. Plans had been made to hold a horseshoe tournament for the men and organized games for the children. June explained to Max that Decoration Day would be spent at Parrack Grove Cemetery and wanted to know if he would like to join her family at the festivities. To her delight, Max said yes.

Early that morning, June was out of bed and in the kitchen, helping her mom with the dinner preparations. Together they baked a ham, made a sweet-tasting potato salad, and baked a chocolate cake. June placed a red-and-white-checked tablecloth in the bottom of a sturdy cardboard box, carefully layering in the food before glancing at the mantle clock. "Oh my goodness," she exclaimed. "It's already ten o'clock. Max is going to be here in a little over an hour, and I'm not near ready. Mom, is there any water in the rain barrel outside? I need to wash my hair."

"There should be. It rained just a couple of nights ago," Myrtle remarked.

"Good. I'll go get it," June said, rushing outside.

Using the warm rainwater that had been heated up in a kettle, June leaned over the dishpan, washing her hair with lye soap. When she was certain all the soap had been rinsed out, she wrapped her wet head in a large soft cotton towel before leaving the kitchen to go sit on her dad's wooden toolbox.

It was the beginning of summer. A gentle warm breeze was blowing in from the south, shaping soft white clouds floating in the sky into forms resembling old men with long white beards. June sat on the old wooden toolbox, drying her hair, smiling a smile of contentment. She thought, *My whole world is in front of me.* But then, a frown replaced her small smile. She was thinking about when her dad said no to her plans for getting a job in Camdenton. "Thomas isn't up to helping much lately. I'm gonna need you to help out around here." Then he refused to let Fern and her brother-in-law Eldon pay for her schooling so she could get a teaching degree. "No," her dad had said once again. "I need you here on the farm." All of a sudden, she reasoned with herself, *Dad's gonna have to realize I'm a big girl. He can't keep me reined in forever.* June's thoughts turned to the handsome young man who was going to escort her to the Decoration Day picnic. Just then, the mantle clock struck eleven. Jumping up from her seat on the toolbox, June exclaimed, "Oh no! I have to hurry."

June ran upstairs to her room. Striking a matchstick against the doorframe, she watched the wick of the coal oil lamp flutter before it became engulfed in a small dancing flame. She then slid the barrel of her curling iron into the glass globe, in order to get it hot. After changing into her new blue and gray plaid skirt and short-sleeved white blouse, the young woman slipped her small stocking-clad feet into her brown oxford shoes. By now, the curling iron was hot enough to curl her hair into soft bouncy ringlets. When she heard the familiar rumble of Max's car pull into the yard, she quickly ran her brush through her hair, glanced at her reflection in the full-length mirror, and dashed down the stairs. Thomas was standing there holding open the front door.

"Are you ready?" Max asked when he saw June racing down the stairs.

"I will be as soon as I get the box of food."

"I'll get it, if you tell me where it is. Thomas, want to come with us?" Max asked, as he joined June's brother, walking down the hall toward the kitchen.

"No, I'm gonna drive Ma and Dad. I'll see you there."

When Max and June arrived at Parrack Grove Cemetery, Max's first comment when they got out of the car was about the little church in the clearing. June proudly explained to him that this was the church where her parents were supposed to have gotten married. Max was almost overcome with laughter when he heard about Lonnie almost chickening out of his own wedding. He couldn't envision the big robust Lonnie Moulder being afraid of anything.

Following June's instructions, Max placed their box dinner on the makeshift table that was nothing more than plank boards lying across wooden sawhorses. By this time, Lonnie, Myrtle, and Thomas had arrived at the cemetery. "Let's go join them," June said, pulling on Max's arm.

When they reached the grave of June's grandparents, Martha and T. H. Moulder, Myrtle was gently placing some wildflowers on their tombstones. Looking back over her shoulder, toward the little church up on the hill, Myrtle stated, "It looks like everyone's starting to gather. We better git on up there and set out our food."

When they returned to the churchyard, the tables were already heavily laden with food. There was crispy fried chicken, baked hams, pork ribs with sauerkraut, corn bread, homemade white bread, freshly churned butter, steamed turnips, creamed peas, fresh green beans seasoned with bacon grease, long-stemmed green onions, radishes, home-canned sweet pickles and bread and butter pickles, fresh fruit pies, angle food cakes, chocolate cake, and cookies galore. It was a feast of all feasts.

Max and June filled their plates and wondered off to sit beneath the wide branches of a great oak tree. Looking up, June teased, "I wouldn't think you would be much interested in potluck dinners."

Max hurriedly swallowed a bite of fried chicken before he spoke. "Well," he chuckled, "I can't say I've ever eaten at a graveyard before. However, as for box suppers, if there's always this much food, I'm game."

"What I meant was you have all that worldly experiences and all," June explained.

Looking deep into her eyes, he just nodded. He did have a lot more of life's experiences than this cute little bit of a girl sitting beside him, but that didn't really matter. He was already smitten.

The following Saturday, several of June's friends had made plans to go the Whistle. "What's the Whistle?" Max asked.

"It's a swimming hole," she explained. "C'mon, let's go."

When Max and June arrived at the Whistle, Max realized it wasn't a hole at all. It was a small swift-flowing creek that, for the most part, was about waist deep. Stopping alongside the other cars that were already there, Max heard a low-whistling noise. "Where's that whistling coming from?" he asked.

"Over there," June said, pointing in the direction of a cement slab that had been built over the low part of the road. After they left the car and were standing on the rock beach, Max noticed water running through eight large metal pipes underneath the slab. When a gust of wind blew down the holler through the pipes, it caused a low-whistling noise.

Swift-flowing water was running through the pipes into the creek, creating a deep hole downstream. Max's attention was drawn to a young man swinging from a rope wrapped around a sturdy tree limb. "Geronimo!" the young man yelled, just before he landed with a splash in the cold clear water.

"That looked liked fun. C'mon, let's get in," he said, trying to persuade June into getting in the cold water.

"No, thanks. I'll just sit here and watch."

"What! Not go swimming on this beautiful day? Why not?"

Shrugging, she replied, "I can't swim."

"Oh then, I'll just sit here by you and watch."

"I wouldn't want you to miss out on the fun. Go on, get in."

Not needing any more coaxing from this pretty little woman, Max soon had his shirt stripped off and was splashing around with her friends in the Whistle.

June certainly had not expected to be enchanted by this young stranger who came, bouncing a ball, into her life a couple of months ago. As she sat there on the bank of the little creek, she admired his lean muscular body and his dark wavy hair but also his quick wit, his easy laughter, and his never-ending concern over her well-being. The simple fact was June was falling in love.

A couple of weeks passed with June spending every available moment she could with Max. When he wasn't playing basketball at the high school gym, he was a supper guest at her home. Lonnie and Myrtle couldn't help but like this young man who made their young daughter's eyes dance with joy every time he came driving into the yard. Lonnie felt Max was wise beyond his years, and Myrtle made him feel welcome in their home. Max's feeling of being a stranger in town quickly faded.

All of a sudden, Dad quit talking. "Are you okay?" I asked. He seemed to be looking at something far off in his mind. "Dad," I said a little louder, "are you all right?"

"What? Oh yeah, I'm okay. I was just thinking about something," he said.

Leaving him to his own private thoughts, I continued with Mom and Dad's story.

56

June Marries the Marine ♥

"My eighteenth birthday's next week," June informed Max, while they were sitting on the old toolbox.

"Really," he replied. "What day?"

"The twenty-second."

"Well, I suppose we need to do something special."

"What? C'mon. Tell me, please," June pleaded.

"Nope, you're just gonna have to wait and see," teased Max. The week slowly passed. Each time June asked what he had planned, Max would just grin and tell her to be patient. She would find out soon enough.

June 22, 1946, June's eighteenth birthday finally arrived. With great anticipation, June was up at dawn and had the cows milked, chickens fed, and eggs gathered before breakfast. After she joined her family for their morning meal, she dashed out to the field to help her dad put up some hay. When her mom rang the bell, summoning them to the house for dinner, June ran inside, quickly washed the dust from her hands and face before sitting down at her usual place at the table. She was famished.

"What are you so excited about?" Myrtle laughed.

"Max is coming over this evening," she explained to her Mom. "He has a surprise for me."

"Well, you just need to slow down a might. It's a long time before that clodhopper gets here," Lonnie scolded his daughter.

"Yes, sir. I will," she mumbled, turning to the food on her plate.

While June hurried through her daily chores, trying to make the hands on the mantle clock move faster, Max had chores of his own he needed to take care of. Shortly after dinner, he made a fast trip to Buffalo, Missouri, a small town twenty miles southwest of Macks Creek.

The afternoon dragged on. June had finished helping her dad in the fields, and it was too early to start supper. Myrtle, who was sitting in her rocking chair doing some mending, grinned when the sound of a vehicle coming up the road sent her young daughter racing toward the big bay window. "It's just the neighbor's old truck," she mumbled. Disheartened,

June picked up a book and started to read. Before she had the chance to turn a page, she heard another vehicle come driving up the road. Again, she was disappointed when the car drove on down the road, passing the house. "June," her mother spoke, "leave that window. Max will get here when he gets here. Your constant looking out the window isn't going to hurry him up none."

Supper was over, and the dishes were washed and put away when June heard the familiar rattle of Max's old 1934 coupe pulling into the yard. Throwing down the dishtowel she had been using to wipe down the cupboards, June ran to the front door. There, standing in the middle of the yard was Max and her dad. June came to an abrupt halt. *That's odd*, she thought. *I wonder what they're talking about.* Just as June came walking down the back steps, Max and her dad shook hands.

"What was that about?" June asked.

"What?"

"What were you and dad talking about just now?" she persisted.

"Oh, that. Nothing. Are you ready to go?" Max asked, helping June in to the front seat of the car.

"I've been ready to go all day."

It was a beautiful summer evening with just a slight breeze blowing from the south. The windows of the car were down, allowing a warm summer wind to blow through. Max turned east onto Highway 54. A few miles down the road, he turned off the highway onto a gravel road. June knew exactly where they were heading. It was a favorite parking place of the young people. *Good, we are the only ones here,* Max thought to himself, as he pulled the car to a stop overlooking Chapel Bluff.

Soon after they arrived, Max reached into his pant's pocket and pulled out a small red velvet-covered box. "I have something for you," he whispered. "I hope you'll accept it."

With shaking hands, June flipped open the top of the box. There, nestled in folds of red satin, was an engagement ring. With tears swimming in her brown eyes, she quietly said, "It's so pretty. Where did you get it?"

Surprised by the bluntness of her question, and being quick witted, Max told her he had found the ring in the bottom of a Cracker Jacks box. He had to buy five more boxes of Cracker Jacks before he found a wedding ring to match. That's what had taken him so long today. June giggled. "After going through all that trouble, how can I say no!" Max slipped the beautiful little ring on June's ring finger. Tucking her safely in the crook of his arm, her head lying on his shoulder, the young lovers sat silently, watching the sun slip down behind the Ozark Hills.

Max had seen the sun sink gloriously into the sea and had been awed by the colors and brilliance of sunsets in the snow-covered mountains of

New Zealand. He had seen the deserts of Guam vibrate with color at dusk and cities glow with twilight. Somehow, watching the caramel color of gold and mauve and pink layer over what were hardly more than foothills of a great range, he was much more deeply affected. Perhaps it was foolish, perhaps it was fanciful, but he felt more a part of this place than in all the other places he had been. He looked down at the brown-eyed beauty sitting close to him in the front seat of his car. On impulse, he leaned over and kissed her. She returned his kiss.

A few days after becoming engaged, June was looking through the Montgomery Ward catalog when she saw a beautiful blue dress. "Mom," she said. "This is the dress I want to be married in. Can you make it for me?"

Looking at the dress her daughter was pointing to, Myrtle replied, "I think so."

During the next month, Myrtle lovingly hand stitched her youngest daughter a light blue linen wedding dress. The sleeveless dress had a scooped neckline with tiny pleats defining the shoulders. A tie belt accented a dropped waistline. June planned to wear a pair of dainty white slippers on her small feet. Her sister Mayme made the loan of a pair of pearl drop earrings. June's wedding ensemble was complete when her mom fastened a single strand of pearls around her daughter's delicate neck. "You're gonna be a beautiful bride," Myrtle whispered in her daughter's ear.

A month later, on July 20, Max unexpectedly drove over to the Moulder farm looking for June. She had just come in from milking the cows. Wiping her hands on her overalls, and tucking a loose strand of brown hair behind her ear and away from her face, the young woman was obviously embarrassed by the way she looked. In her mind, she resembled a farmhand. But to Max, he thought this young woman was just about the prettiest thing he had ever seen.

Max took June by the arm, guiding her to the porch. "Can we talk?" he asked.

Fear gripped June's heart as she sat down on the toolbox. "Of course. What's wrong?"

Max, leaning on the corner post, replied, "Nothing's wrong. At least I don't think so. I've been offered a job back in Cheney, at the dry cleaners. I start Monday. Would you go with me?"

"When would we have to leave?" June asked as her forehead furrowed with concern.

"Day after tomorrow."

"Dad won't let me go if we're not married," June cried.

"Well then, let's get married."

"There's not enough time if you're leaving in two days."

"Why not?"

"Because we have to wait three days after you get the marriage license."

"Oh well, let me think. I know there's something we can do." Then all of a sudden, he remembered there was no waiting time in Kansas. "Do you think your parents will let you go with me if we promise to get married as soon as we get back to Kansas?"

"I think it'll be okay with Mom. But I'm not so sure about Dad."

"We can surely persuade him. Get your things ready, and I'll be back day after tomorrow." After a quick kiss on her cheek, Max ran back to his car, jumped in, and sped off.

That evening after supper, Lonnie retired to his favorite chair in front of the picture window, while June and her mom finished washing the supper dishes. "Mom," June said. "Max has accepted a job back in Kansas. He's leaving the day after tomorrow, and he wants me to go with him."

"June," Myrtle said, "you aren't married yet."

"I know. But he said we could get married as soon as we get to Kansas. They don't have a three-day waiting period like Missouri does."

A long pause followed while Myrtle poured herself a cup of coffee and sat down at the kitchen table. "Kansas is so far away. Are you sure that's what you want?" she asked.

"I love him, Mom. I'm afraid if he leaves, he won't come back for me."

"If he loves you, he will," Myrtle tried to explain.

"I just don't want to take that chance," whispered young June. Myrtle finished with her cup of coffee, rose from the table, and left the room.

July 22 dawned hot and dry. The early morning sun was boring down on the parched ground. Summer was only half over, but already the heat of the day was playing havoc with the crops in the fields, Myrtle's garden, and the livestock.

That morning, after breakfast, Lonnie told June to stop daydreaming and get busy. "We need to get that hay up today," he said without looking up from his coffee. Since there was no mention of her going to Kansas, June figured her dad didn't know she was planning to leave with Max. Afraid to say anything, June rose from the table, helped her mom clear the breakfast things, put on her work clothes, and went out into the barn. Later that morning, when she came in to the kitchen to help her mom fix dinner, Myrtle looked up over a plate of sliced ham. "June," she said. "After you finished eating, go on upstairs and pack. Max will be here soon."

June spent the next hour up in her room getting ready for her trip. *It's really happening*, she thought to herself. *I'm really going to Kansas with the man I love. I'm getting married!* Twirling around her room, June could hardly contain the excitement she was feeling. Holding out her small hand to gaze at the beautiful engagement ring Max had given her, she couldn't help but think, *I have dated a sailor and a soldier, but I'm marrying a marine!*

It didn't take long for June to pack everything she owned in a small leather-bound suitcase. On top of her everyday dresses and extra pair of shoes, she gently laid her beautiful linen wedding dress, white slippers, and the strand of pearls her mom had given her.

Sitting on the side of her bed, waiting for Max to come and pick her up, June barely noticed her stomach had started doing flip-flops. At first, it was only light and sort of tickled. Then her heart began to race and the flip-flops turned into thuds. She looked once again at the shiny little ring on her finger. *I'm really going. This is really happening. I wonder how far away Kansas is?* she wondered.

All of a sudden, Samantha interrupted me, "That's silly. Kansas is just the next state over. Why would she wonder that?"

Dad quickly explained, "According to what June told me, the farthest she had ever been away from home was the time she went to Missouri's State Fair up in Sedalia. That's only about seventy miles away from Macks Creek."

While June sat on the edge of the bed, waiting for Max, her feelings turned from excitement to nervousness, from being giddily happy to terrified. Those feelings were quickly squelched when she heard Max's car come rumbling into the yard. Jumping up from the bed, June grabbed her packed suitcase and chased out the bedroom door. Her mom was standing in the kitchen, fixing dinner when June came running through. "Hold on there, child." Handing her daughter a faded hanky, Myrtle continued, "Here, take this."

"What's this?"

"My egg money."

"Mom, I can't take that. You guys need it."

"Go on. I said take it." Taking hold of her daughter's hand, Myrtle laid a hanky that was knotted in one end to hold seventy-five cents in the center of June's open palm. Brushing her little girl's cheek with a soft kiss, Myrtle turned back to the stove.

Hugging her mom from behind, June whispered in her ear, "I love you."

"Hurry up now before that young man leaves you standing here," scolded Myrtle, not wanting June to see she was crying.

June picked up her suitcase and continued to hurry out the back door. Max was just walking up the steps.

"I'm ready to go," she stated.

"Not yet," Max replied with a wink. "I need to talk with your dad first." June's face fell. She still wasn't certain her dad was going to let her go.

Once Max had disappeared through the kitchen door, June grabbed her suitcase and ran back through the kitchen, throwing the hanky on the table, ran down the hall and up the stairs to her room. Throwing herself on her bed, she broke out in uncontrollable sobs. "Dad's not gonna let me go," she cried. "He's gonna say he needs me here. My life's ruined." The distraught young girl raved, striking the mattress with her balled-up fist.

After a few minutes, a familiar voice came calling up the stairs. "Hey, you up there? If you're going to Kansas with me, you better get on down here."

Startled by what she was hearing, June jumped up from the bed, straightened out her skirt, smoothed down her hair, and dried her tears before grabbing her suitcase. Standing at the top of the stairs, she looked down into the face of the man she was about to be married to. This time, she slowly descended the stairs into the arms of her future husband.

Max's old car had just turned onto Highway 54 when he started singing, "Wildcat Kelly, lookin' kind of pale." When he finished with the last verse, June was laughing so hard her eyes were tearing. "What's so funny? Don't you like my singing?" he asked.

"It's not that. It's the song. Where did you hear it?"

"It's one of Roy Rogers's songs. You've heard of Roy Rogers, haven't you?" he teased.

"Of course, I have. Just not that song." Riding in the car, heading to Kansas, the young couple was in their own happy little world.

The next day, July 23, 1946, was one of the hottest days of the year. Early that evening, Max and June met one of Max's old marine buddies Chuck Johnson and his wife Betty at a small church in Wichita, Kansas. While the foursome waited for the minister to arrive, Max looked around the chapel for a fan, hoping to circulate the sultry hot air. Not being successful in his search, he returned to June's side just as the minister walked in. The foursome was shocked by his appearance. It looked as though the man had just stepped out of the shower and had forgotten to dry off. The young couple could hardly remain solemn, as they stood there repeating their wedding vows before this man, who's hair was sopping wet and a drop of sweat hanging from the end of his nose. Between giggles, Max and June managed to get through their wedding vows, making Martha June Moulder the wife of Max Slusser.

With only $170.00 to his name, Max couldn't afford an extravagant honeymoon. So instead, he took June to a carnival at Matthewson's pasture that evening. Then on the second evening of their marriage, he took June to her first semiprofessional baseball game at Lawrence Athletic Stadium, on the corner of Maple Street and McLean Boulevard. During the seventh inning stretch, Max handed his young bride a shiny brand-new 1946-dime. "Keep this forever," he told her. "That way we will never be broke."

Within ten years, Max bought a home on the east side of Cheney, Kansas, where they lived, raising their family.

"What did Grandpa say to you that day?" Suzanne asked Dad.

"When I told him I was taking June to Kansas to get married, all he said was, 'Take care of her and bring her home once in a while.'"

57

Thomas ♥

A few weeks after Max and June left Missouri to get married, Lonnie and Myrtle were summoned to Dr. Meyer's office. "I have ran some more blood test on Thomas. His condition is getting worse. I have taken the liberty of setting up an appointment for him with a doctor in Columbia, Missouri. I suggest you leave right away."

The next morning, Eldon and Fern drove Lonnie, Myrtle, and Thomas to Columbia. Thomas had orders from Dr. Meyer to go directly to Ellis Fischel Cancer Hospital where the doctor's staff was expecting him. After a day of extensive blood test and X-rays, the Moulders were called into the doctor's office. A dark mass had shown up on Thomas's bowel. The prognosis was grave. He was going to need an operation.

The next morning, while Thomas was being prepared for surgery, Ethridge and Beryl arrived at the hospital. While Thomas was in surgery, the family huddled together in a little waiting room. Several hours passed before the doctor came walking into the room. Before speaking, he sat down in a chair beside Myrtle. In a strong, sure voice, he informed them that what he had suspected was confirmed. Thomas had cancer. He then informed them that during surgery, several feet of their son's lower bowel had to be removed and a short plastic tube had been inserted into his abdomen. This was so the infection could drain out. Then with a more gentle tone to his gruff voice he cautioned, "Just make sure he keeps the opening clean and dry."

Lonnie was speechless with shock. Sure, he had noticed Thomas was a little sluggish lately, and he was having nosebleed more often, but never had he suspected there was anything this seriously wrong with his boy. Myrtle, sitting in a hardback chair, wept silently. She didn't fully understand what was happening to her son or what cancer really was. However, for several years, her motherly instinct had been trying to forewarn her that something was dreadfully wrong with Thomas. Now she knew. Eldon, seeing the need to take control of the situation, approached the doctor. "How much time does Thomas have?" he asked. "Less than a year." Before the doctor left the waiting room, he told the family that Thomas may need a blood transfusion and would they consider donating some of theirs. Fern and Beryl immediately consented.

A few minutes after the doctor left the room, a nurse came to summon Fern and Beryl. The two women followed her down the hall to an elevator. Lower and lower they went, until they reached the basement. "Go through that door," she instructed. Beryl looked down the long dim hall in the direction the nurse had been pointing. A sign reading Laboratory hung over a double door. "That must be the place," Beryl whispered to her sister.

A small area, sectioned off by curtains, was inside the laboratory. A lab assistant appeared out of nowhere. Briskly, she instructed Fern and Beryl to lie down on those gurneys behind the curtains and that she would be with them shortly. Fern had given blood at the blood bank in Macks Creek before, so she knew what to expect. However, this was a new experience for Beryl. After their blood had been drawn, the lab assistant gave them a glass of orange juice and a couple of cookies. Fern took her time eating the snack. Beryl, on the other hand, gulped hers down before saying, "We best be getting back upstairs. Mom and Dad are going to be needing us."

Fern sat up. Grabbing her head between her hands, she murmured, "Oh my, I feel as weak as a kitten. I'm so woozy."

Beryl, being the younger of the two women and feeling normal, jumped up, intending to race to the aid of her sister. Her feet had just hit the floor when the room started spinning out of control. Down she went like a limp rag doll. The next thing Beryl knew, she was back on the gurney, a wet cloth across her forehead and feeling extremely nauseated.

Early that evening, after they had made sure Thomas was resting comfortably, Eldon drove Lonnie and Myrtle back to Macks Creek while Ethridge drove Fern and Beryl in Lonnie's old Ford. Realizing that the rest of their family had been anxiously waiting for any news of their brother, Lonnie and Myrtle called them over to their home. "Something is dreadfully wrong with Thomas," Eldon told the family. "He has a disease called cancer. There is no cure. Thomas is dying."

A couple of weeks later, Thomas returned home. For the next few months, the young man never lost his sense of humor or his zest for life. Maintaining a positive outlook, Thomas continued chasing through the hills, in his dad's 1929 Ford sedan, wooing the young women in Camden County. He loved to laugh and to socialize with his friends. On several occasion, however, he would seek refuge in the woods surrounding his home or the solace of the corncrib. Thomas wasn't afraid of drying. In accepting Christ as his Savior, he knew there would be life after death. What he didn't know was, in heaven, would there be the sounds he so loved—the calling of the whip-poor-will just as the setting sun disappeared over the hills, the croaking frogs down at the pond, or the baying sound of his little foxhound in hot pursuit of red fox. When he got to heaven, would he be able to recall the smell of freshly mowed hay or bacon frying in his mom's cast-iron skillet. Or the soft touch of his mother's hand, comforting him on sleepless nights when he laid awake in his bed, watching the big round moon ascending into the inky black sky; or the feel of an early Easter-morning swim in a frozen pond. But most of all, Thomas knew he was going to miss the loud robust voice of his dad calling up the stairs, ordering him to get his butt out of bed, the soft footsteps of his mom as she moved around the kitchen, and the happy noises that penetrated throughout the house when his little sister June and her husband came home for weekend visits. These things Thomas pondered as the cancer slowly crept throughout his young body.

Before the spring of 1947 made its yearly appearance, the cancer in Thomas body had taken its toll. He had become extremely weak and had to be hospitalized. At the end, Lonnie Myrtle, Florence, Ralph, Eldon, and Fern were by Thomas's bedside. June and Ruby, both pregnant at this time, held their own vigil, together, in the living room of their parent's home. Myrtle had told her daughters not to come to the hospital because watching their brother die could traumatize them, "marking the baby."

The day dragged on for the Moulder family. Lonnie and Myrtle never left their son's side. Eldon was keeping the rest of the family, back home in Macks Creek, informed as to what was happening. Night descended on the grieving family. Thomas, resting peacefully in his hospital bed, suddenly opened his eyes. With a weak smile, he told his family, "I hear beautiful singing." Then he gently closed his eyes for the last time. On March 10, 1947, Thomas Fredrick Moulder was dead before dawn.

Lonnie was insistent that his son be brought home for burial at Parrack Grove Cemetery. He hired his good friend L. B. Jones, a funeral director from Buffalo, Missouri, to bring his son's body back home to Dry Ridge.

The bedroom window had to be removed in order to get Thomas's casket into the house, where it would lay across two wooden sawhorses until the day of the funeral. Wooden folding chairs, borrowed from the First Baptist Church in Macks Creek, had been set up around the interior of the room. A black shroud was hung over the open window, keeping out the bright sunlight. The hands on the mantle clock were set to show the exact time of Thomas death before the batteries were removed. Time was standing still for the Moulders.

A custom that was being practiced in the hills was that a few neighbor women would arrive at the home of the deceased to prepare the body for burial. Myrtle, in her gentle, insistent way begged off the offer. She needed to do this one last thing for her son. Mayme's husband, Onie, and their young son, Leslie Lee, offered to stay over and sit with Thomas' body while everyone else slept.

Funeral services were held Wednesday, March 12, at the Macks Creek Baptist Church with Reverend Robert L. Shank officiating. Thomas was laid to rest in Parrack Grove Cemetery.

58

Time to Retire ♥

Over the past fifty years, Lonnie and Myrtle had worked hard trapping, fishing, and farming. They grew gardens large enough to feed a small army, raised mules, chickens, and pigs. During that time, ten of their children found lifelong mates, and they lost one child to a devastating illness. Now, with an empty nest, Lonnie decided it was high time he retired. In 1953, he sold the farm up on Dry Ridge and bought a stucco bungalow house on the west side of Macks Creek, Missouri. The house had only three rooms—a front room, one bedroom, and a kitchen. A narrow enclosed porch had previously been added to the back of the house where another small room, serving as a second bedroom, had been sectioned off.

The long narrow living room took up the entire front part of the house. A daybed and a divan, which when folded down made into a full-sized bed, two oak rocking chairs, an oak buffet, and two floor lamps were the only pieces of furniture in the room. The wood-burning potbellied stove sat on the north wall, next to the front door. A single doorway, on the west side of the room, led to a small bedroom just big enough for a full-sized bed, small dresser, and wardrobe, where Lonnie and Myrtle hung their clothes. Another single doorway, on the east side of the room, led into the kitchen. Just inside the doorway, along the east wall, set Myrtle's brand-new Westinghouse Frigidaire. Next to the electric refrigerator sat a drop-leaf table and four chairs. A gas-burning stove and baker's cabinet stood along the west wall. Right beside a single door leading to the enclosed back porch was a small table, holding a wash pan, water bucket, and dipper. A few feet from the back door was a pump jack. The chicken coop and outhouse stood toward the back of the property. Standing in the southeast corner was an old weatherworn barn. A small woodshed, with a root cellar underneath, sat just off the east corner of the house.

It didn't take long for Lonnie and Myrtle to become accustom to retirement life. One of their favorite pastimes was sitting in their metal lawn chairs on a big cement porch that stretched across the entire front of the house. They hadn't been living in town long when, one day, while passing the afternoon watching traffic move along Highway 54, Lonnie commented, "This house is just my size."

Another of Lonnie's favorite pastimes was walking a couple of hundred yards to the liar's bench sitting in front of the café on Main Street. One particular morning, a friend of his called out, "Hey LB." Pointing to Lonnie's big round stomach, Frances teased, "Your breadbasket just keeps getting bigger and bigger. How much longer do you think you can push that around anyway?" Laughing, Lonnie called back, "Well, I suppose when the day comes that I can't push it any longer, I have a tongue to pull it with."

Myrtle, on the other hand, constantly remained busy, puttering around in her little kitchen or watching out her east living room window at the comings and goings of her neighbors. She looked forward to visits from her family and friends who would stop by just to chat. There was always a piece of homemade cherry pie, chocolate cake, or fresh-made cookies to offer them.

Two years after Lonnie and Myrtle left the farm, they celebrated their fiftieth wedding anniversary at the Masonic Lodge in Macks Creek—an open house complete with a three-tiered cake, punch, and coffee—held in their honor, given by their children.

During the summer of 1964, Lonnie was bedridden as a result of suffering from having a stroke. Myrtle insisted a hospital bed be set up in the living room of their home, where she could continue caring for her husband. On September 26, 1964, Lonnie Moulder passed away at his home with his wife by his side.

Myrtle's eighty-seventh birthday was celebrated at her home, where she enjoyed reminiscing for her children of her life as a child and throughout her fifty-nine years of marriage. With her failing health, she realized she could no longer live alone. She told her family she would like to live at Windsor Estates Home in Camdenton, Missouri. On October 4, 1983, one week shy of turning ninety-nine years old, Myrtle Gerhardt Moulder passed away.

"My mother-in-law was the best of all mother-in-laws," Dad shared with his family. "I don't remember, in all the years that June and I were married, Myrtle ever saying a cross word to me. She was a soft-spoken woman and would always go out of her way to make me feel welcome in her home."

"Dad," I said, "I think a lot of people experienced the goodness in this little woman. By the time Lonnie and Myrtle retired, several of their grandchildren were in high school. It wasn't uncommon for one, two, or sometimes even three of the teenagers to stay in town on a Friday to attend a school or sporting event. After Grandma fed them supper, she would send them on their way, knowing they would be returning to spend the night. No matter what time they arrived, the divan and daybed in the living room were turned down with clean bedding."

"Like the times we would go visit," Phyllis said. "Remember how Dad would drive all the way from Kansas, getting us there late at night. Then shortly after Mom knocked on the door, a light would come on inside the house. We would stand on that big cement porch, waiting for Grandma's face to appear in the little window before opening the door to welcome us in."

"I remember as soon as we got in the house, we would head to the kitchen," Tom laughed. "We would go immediately to the table, raise the red-checkered tablecloth looking for a feast of leftovers. We never knew if we would find crisp fried bacon or pork chops left over from breakfast. But there were always homemade soda biscuits and a jar of Grandpa's homemade molasses."

While I set there, listening to my family sharing their memories of Grandma and Grandpa, I looked outside and noticed the sun had set. The hot August day, the day we had buried Mom, was coming to an end. Letting my eyes wander across the dining room and into the living room, I realized that my whole family was still there. They were taking up every available chair, spread out lying on the floor, and babies were even sleeping soundly in their mom's arms. Suddenly, I remembered the words Mom had told us many times over, "Family is the most important possession you will ever have. Love them, lean on them, and comfort them."

That's exactly what we had been doing over the past several days. We are so blessed by the fact that we do have family. Standing up, I spoke, "It's getting late. Before we leave tonight, there is one last request I would like to ask of you. Now that you know why you are, who you are, please take these colorful stories with you to share with your children and grandchildren. In doing so, you will be helping to keep our heritage alive. And who knows, someday, when visiting the Missouri Ozarks, you may hear the loud booming voice of Lonnie Moulder or the gentle sweetness of his wife, Myrtle, calling you to supper, or you might even hear the laughter of children as it echo's through *These Kaleidoscope Hills*."

Epilogue

Alonzo Belfred Moulder (Lonnie)   March 15, 1884-September 26, 1964
His wife, Myrtle Gerhardt Moulder   October 11, 1885-October 4, 1983

Taken in part from the writings of Mayme Woodall: Lonnie and Myrtle lived a kind of life that erects monuments to their memory, more lasting than marble or bronze, a life that put an all-time trust in their Savior and through the years held on to God's unchanging hand.

Lonnie and Myrtle Moulder were married March 5, 1905, and lived their entire lives within fifteen miles of their birthplace. After raising eleven children, they retired to a small home in Macks Creek, Missouri. A few years after Lonnie's death, Myrtle requested that her family move her into Windsor Estates in Camdenton, Missouri, where she remained until she peacefully passed away in her sleep.

Howard Valentine Moulder   April 3, 1906-January 1, 1985
His wife, Lillie Degraffenreid   January 10, 1906-December 21, 1957

Howard and Lillie were married on August 18, 1928, and lived most of their married life on a farm south of Macks Creek, Missouri. Together they raised six children. Several years after Lillie's death, Howard sold his farm and bought a small house a couple of miles west of Macks Creek. He then married Oma Cowen. Shortly after Howard's death, Oma returned to her family in Arizona.

After his dad's death in 1964, Howard resumed his role as big brother. Every evening after supper, he would take a few minutes to call his ma and each of his sisters just to say goodnight. This loving call that assured him they were all home and safe continued until his sudden death in 1985.

Nera Pearl Moulder Ricker   September 14, 1907-January 1, 1998
Her husband, Henry "Sug" Ricker   October 4, 1907-October 30, 1976

Nera and her husband, Sug, were married on March 31, 1921. During their life together, they made their living farming until the early 1950s when they purchased a small grocery store and gas station at the Y, the intersection of Highway 54 and 73, three miles west of Macks Creek. Four children were born to this union.

Throughout Nera's life, she drew immense strength through her faith in Christ. This was very evident to her family and friends who were fortunate enough to witness her soft-spoken words and gentle kindness. She loved spreading the word of Christ through many years of teaching Sunday school at the First Baptist Church in Macks Creek, Missouri.

Ray Earl Moulder January 5, 1909-September 10, 1970
His wife, Florence E. Ricker February 24, 1910-March 29, 1979

Ray and his wife were married November 25, 1933. Throughout Ray's life, he was able to travel around Missouri and as far away as California to gain employment at several different types of different jobs. He and Florence finally settled in Warsaw, Missouri, to live out their retirement. Florence bore two sons, one of which preceded his parents in death.

Florence Irene Moulder Morgan September 2, 1910
Her husband, Ralph Morgan November 4, 1911-September 18, 1991

Florence and her husband, Ralph, were married March 7, 1931. Ralph, a successful businessman, owned and operated several gas stations in the surrounding areas of Camdenton, Missouri.

At the time of this writing, Florence is still living in the home she shared with her husband during their sixty years of marriage. Florence, a respected member of the community, spent her life working beside her husband in the family business. She is a member of the Eastern Star and an active participant in her church. With the help of her husband, they raised one son.

Zilpha May "Dick" Moulder Ricker November 6, 1912
Her husband, Leon E. Ricker July 22, 1906-October 22, 1974

Zilpha (Dick) and her husband, Leon, were married March 6, 1932. Leon spent his life employed in the field of education while Zilpha raised their three children. For several consecutive summers, after school had been dismissed for the year, he and Zilpha traveled to Washington, helping with the harvest of apples before working their way down the West Coast picking cherries. In 1959, Leon and Zilpha moved to Appleton City, Missouri, where Leon continued teaching until he retired.

Zilpha May raised, and then buried, all three of their children. She is now living in the Appleton City Manor where she has a loving son-in-law who sees that her every need is met.

Ila Mayme Moulder Woodall   *December 12, 1914*
Her husband, Onie L. Woodall   *August 21, 1910-September 17, 1977*

Mayme and her husband, Onie, were married March 12, 1932. Onie was Mayme's soul mate. They traveled through life together enjoying each new experience. Nothing ever seemed to get this couple down. Even after Onie got sick, he was the model patient while Mayme tended to his care.

Mayme is still living in the little house west of Macks Creek where she helped her husband on their farm making a living for their two boys. After Onie's death, Mayme remained busy working at the Macks Creek School where she was a cook in the cafeteria. Her fun and loving ways had the schoolchildren eating out of her hand. She is still an active member of the Branch Homemakers Club and regularly attends the First Baptist Church in Macks Creek.

Ruby Edith Moulder Kincaid   *March 31, 1917-November 11, 2007*
Her husband, George V. Kincaid   *September 20, 1914-November 24, 1974*

Ruby and her husband, George, were married July 20, 1935. During their marriage, they were never afraid of tackling hard physical work. George worked in sawmills, meatpacking companies, built warships and highways, and farmed. With Ruby by his side, he followed the harvest up the West Coast picking apples and cherries. After an unfortunate accident that broke his neck, George wasn't about to stop. He sold the farm south of town, moving into Macks Creek, and hired on as a janitor and school bus driver for the school system. As hard as George worked, he never gave up the chance to go fishing on a good day.

Ruby was no stranger to hard work herself. She loved the summer trips she would take with George to the West Coast helping with the harvest. Looking forward to retuning to the Ozarks in the winter, it never took her long to find employment. She worked at waiting tables in the local café, made candy at a candy factory, made furniture, did light housekeeping work, and was a welder in the shipyards during World War II. After moving into town, Ruby was a cook at the Macks Creek School until she retired.

Before Ruby and George retired, they raised three children, had moved thirty-six times, been in forty states, Mexico, and Canada. Until Ruby had been admitted into Windsor Estates Care facility, all you would have to say is, "Ruby, would you like to go with me?" "Let me get my hat," would be her reply as she headed out the door.

Ethel Fern Moulder Clemmons   *July 20, 1919*
Her husband, Eldon Clemmons   *April 8, 1914-October 18, 1990*

Fern and her husband, Eldon, were married January 16, 1937. Eldon served in the financial section of United States Air Corp while stationed in the Philippines. After World War II ended, he resumed his job as an auditor for the Missouri Farmers Association (MFA) while involved in the banking business. After his retirement, Eldon became the major stockholder in the Bank of Macks Creek.

Fern stayed busy working as a full-time mother of their three children while working at a novelty factory making Ozark souvenirs from cedar wood. After Eldon became ill and was unable to continue working, Fern became involved in the banking business.

Fern is now residing at Windsor Estates in Camdenton where she enjoys the many visits she gets from family, friends, and neighbors.

Letha Beryl Moulder Rash   *July 1, 1922-March 13, 2004*
Her husband, Ethridge L. Rash   *July 16, 1916-December 14, 1977*

Beryl and her husband, Ethridge, were married August 12, 1938. Along with farming, Ethridge was involved in the cattle business. He raised and sold Hereford cattle while milking fifteen cows, selling their milk in Lebonan, Missouri. When their oldest daughter started attending Macks Creek grade school, Ethridge accepted a job driving the school bus. After Beryl married Ethridge, it didn't take her long to realize just how hard married life could be. However, throughout their thirty-nine years of marriage, and with her zest for fun, she never regretted it. While raising two daughters, Beryl worked hard as her husband's partner on the farm. She started working as a cook at the Macks Creek School where she was later joined by her two sisters Mayme and Ruby. On special occasions around town or at school, Beryl would show up dressed as Minnie Pearl. With a resounding "Howwdyyy!" she would make sure everyone was having a good time. After Ethridge retired from farming, the two of them would travel to Osage Beach, Missouri, where they enjoyed working for the Ozark Opry.

Thomas Fredrick Moulder   *April 24, 1925-March 10, 1947*

During Thomas's twenty-one years of life, there were very few days that got him down. While helping his dad on the farm, Thomas was always looking for the next adventure in his life. Everyone who knew him loved him. Until he was admitted into the hospital the last time, Thomas never lost his easy laugh of his good-natured personality.

Martha June Moulder Slusser   *June 22, 1928-August 5, 2001*
Her husband, Max E. Slusser   *November 7, 1922*

June and her husband, Max, were married July 23, 1946. Max served as a sergeant in the United States Marine Corp, fighting in the South Pacific during World War II. After the war ended and Max and June were married, Max worked at Boeing aircraft in Wichita, Kansas, for thirty-six and a half years before retiring. After his retirement, he and June enjoyed traveling by car, seeing the United States.

June was a stay-at-home mom, raising their six children. When their last son entered high school, June went to work in the aircraft industry. When June left Missouri to marry Max, the farthest she had been away from her home was seventy miles. After fifty-five years of marriage, she and Max had traveled to forty-six states, Mexico, and Canada.

On the first visit Lonnie and Myrtle made to Kansas to see their daughter June, they had traveled approximately one hundred twenty miles when Lonnie commented, "If there's as much land on the east side of Macks Creek as there is on the west side, this is a big country."

Excerpt from Ruby Moulder Kincaid's Journal, written in 1989:

"We may not have everything like some people, but we have LOVE for one anther and try to be kind to everyone else. Dad always said, "Respect them all as the old saying goes, 'If you get slapped in the face, ignore it.' Be kind to your neighbor. Help them and they will help you."

Note from the Authors

In this documentation, we have written our memories of the stories mom, Martha June Moulder Slusser, and her sisters have told us through the years. For each chapter, there are more ideas and opinions we wanted to share than space and time allowed, more people to include than could be named, more places visited than could be described. Although we have had to be selective, we hope we have conveyed the push and pull of events and relationships that affected our mother and her family and that even today continue to affect our lives. We hope you enjoy reading these remembrances as much as we have enjoyed documenting them.

Lonetta and Donnis

Reference material from the following:

Ruby Moulder Kincaid's journal
Writings from Mayme Moulder Woodall
Writings from Fern Moulder Clemmons
Excerpts from Myrtle Moulder's diary
Family Genealogy Tree by George Moulder
The Builders: A History of Macks Creek
Authored by the Macks Creek Lions Club

Missouri Becomes a State
    http://members.aol.com/micron612/statehood2.html

Missouri: Facts, Maps and State Symbol
    http://www.enchantedlearning.com/usa/states/missouri

The Story of Bagnell Dam; A Keepsake Book
Authored by Carole Tellman Pilkington

Welcome to the Jefferson City Convention and Visitor Bureau
    http://www.visitjeffersoncity.com/attractions_capitol_grounds.html

Camden County Missouri
Camden County e-books